Revitalizing Christianity

The Exciting Message of Christianity

First Edition – April 2011

ISBN
978-1-77067-414-1 (Hardcover)
978-1-77067-415-8 (Paperback)
978-1-77067-416-5 (eBook)

Catalog as Religion - Practical Theology - Practical Religion - The Christian Life or as Religion - Christian Experience, Practice, and Life (Dewey Decimal 248).

Published by:

FriesenPress
Suite 300 – 852 Fort Street
Victoria, BC, Canada V8W 1H8

www.friesenpress.com

Distributed to the trade by The Ingram Book Company

For further information on this book or the author, visit www.NewCenturyMinistries.com

TABLE OF CONTENTS

ACKNOWLEDGEMENT

I am deeply indebted to college professors, ministers, church leaders, and various individuals among my family and friends who have contributed to my understanding of the Bible and my ability to write this book. I especially thank those who offered me the one thing I value most—good criticism that forced me to think through what I was saying from different perspectives. And I cannot overstate how important the advice and support of Karen, my wife, has been in this process. It is to her that I dedicate this effort.

INTRODUCTION: THE ROAD MAP

This is not the Great American Novel, and I have no desire to keep the reader in suspense as to what is coming. Therefore, the following paragraphs summarize the chapters to provide the reader with a roadmap of the motivational factors we will be addressing:

The world would tell us that there is no god or else that there are many gods who are all equally likely to be the real God. These two messages affect Christian motivation, because Christians who hear highly educated people making these arguments often begin to wonder if there is any reason to live as a Christian. And too often when Christians do try to answer such challenges the answers get into detailed arguments that cause people's eyes to glaze over before the conclusion. To make matters worse, in the name of Christianity some people have even used falsehoods and hoaxes to try to "prove" that the Bible is right. In Chapter 2 we will consider only a few key, easily understood points to make the case that believing in God is more reasonable than not believing in God (though no one can prove that God is) and that the claims of Christianity fit the evidence far better than the claims of any other religion.

The world would also tell us that our God is a terrible God who has encouraged every sort of evil. George Bernard Shaw called the Bible "the most dangerous book on earth," and many others have echoed that opinion. Indeed, while the Bible properly claims to be God's own word, it has been and continues to be misused to justify just about every form of evil in the world. No one is likely to be motivated to live for a God who is perceived as evil. Chapter 3 looks at some of the key charges made against God to show that, while God may indeed give an appearance of evil from a human and worldly perspective, when we take the time to give God's perspective a fair hearing, he consistently acts out of love for humanity.

The world would persuade us that we are not really bad and that if there is a loving God, he certainly would never condemn good people such as ourselves to eternal agony. So the Christian message that all people are lost and need God's salvation is viewed as turning God into some kind of monster. And when Christians are influenced by such arguments, the motivation to serve God is minimized. We may be motivated enough to try to get his salvation, but we would not be motivated to live daily for him or to love him. In Chapter 4 we look at the truth about ourselves—how we rebel daily against God's authority, selfishly refusing to do what we ourselves know to be good and right, and how from God's perspective this makes us accessories to every imaginable kind of evil.

If we do come to accept that we are traitors to God's kingdom and that we do need to be saved, Satan would have us believe that all we need to do is believe that God is willing to save us and we are then guaranteed to be safe for all eternity. In fact, there are many passages in the Bible that could be understood this way if we do not pay attention to what the Bible itself says about saving faith. If we misunderstand the message in this way, we have no motivation to live a Christian life once we agree to believe in God and accept his salvation. Chapter 5 addresses the biblical definition of saving faith and how that definition reinforces the need to live a Christian life. Chapter 5 also shows why the biblical idea of saving faith is important in light of eternity.

But if the errors that hurt our motivation were all resolved properly up to this point, our motivation would be primarily to do the minimum required to gain salvation. The words, "What must I do to be saved?" would come to mean "What is the least I can get by with and still get into heaven?" And the world has convinced most of us that heaven is to be desired only as an alternative to hell, with earth being much better than heaven. Chapter 6 presents a concept of heaven that is both consistent with biblical teaching and far more motivating than the concepts generally held by most people including most Christians.

Yet if we accept that there is a God, that he is the Christian God, that we have committed treason against his kingdom and deserve his condemnation, and that the reward he offers to those who turn back to him is indeed wonderful beyond description, we are still left with a dilemma. There are literally hundreds of different Christian organizations that all claim to have God's true plan of salvation, so how are we to know which one is right and which ones are wrong? It's hard to be motivated to follow the claims of one group over another if we can't tell which one is right, and we may well suspect (correctly) that all of them are wrong in at least some aspect of what they teach. Chapter 7 addresses the overwhelming biblical evidence for God's plan and shows how this plan is consistent with what has been addressed in the preceding chapters and how people in practically all of these different groups do manage to find this one plan.

So once we get on board with God's plan to bring us into his kingdom, everything should be wonderful, shouldn't it? In fact, that is not the case. All Christians suffer in this world, and many of the most faithful suffer terribly. Disease, disaster, and death are as much a part of the lives of Christians as they are part of the lives of non-Christians. Satan wants to rob us of our motivation by convincing us that this experience of suffering is evidence that God really does not care about us or that we should turn against God as our way of getting back at him. Chapter 8 deals with suffering and its true and positive role in our earthly lives as Christians.

Some believe that the solution to all the ills and suffering of this world should be prayer. After all, the Bible promises that God will do whatever we ask in Jesus' name. So when we as Christians pray and do not receive what we ask for, Satan tries to rob us of our motivation either by convincing us that we were wrong and that God really does not exist or by convincing us that God does not really care about us enough to solve these problems. Chapter 9 looks at what the Bible actually teaches about prayer, how our experiences are reasonable in light of that teaching, and how we can adjust our prayer lives and see the miracles that result. Seeing these miracles then becomes highly motivating. (This chapter begins a set of four chapters that look at things we can do as Christians that will bring strong motivation for ourselves and for others around us.)

One of the most difficult challenges of a Christian's life is forgiveness—we just do not want to do it. Satan knows how Christians who practice forgiving are motivated by the sense of freedom forgiveness brings and the presence of God's Holy Spirit approving the practice of forgiving, and he will throw up every barrier he can to prevent these benefits. Chapter 10 goes into the reasons we give for not wanting to forgive others and God's answers to those reasons as well as the blessings that come from practicing this grace.

Up to this point we've looked at motivational factors for Christians as individuals, but Christians are (whether they like it or not) part of a much larger organism known as the church. One of Satan's greatest victories is how many church programs he has turned into dull, boring, tedious meetings. Chapter 11 considers God's plan for what the church meetings should be and how that is a key aspect of what should motivate Christians.

One aspect of church meetings needs special attention, and that is the training of Christians as disciples of the Lord. The way that such training is conducted now is another major victory for Satan. Chapter 12 examines what we are doing to train Christians and what we should be doing that would better motivate both the teachers and the learners.

CHAPTER ONE: THE KEY IS MOTIVATION

This book is for Christians who want a better understanding of what Christianity is all about, or a stronger faith in and relationship with God, or a better hope for now and for eternity. If you are not a Christian, you may find this book helpful in considering the claims of Christianity, but this book is primarily meant to encourage and inspire Christians.

Off Course

The pilot's voice said, "Do you see anything you recognize?"

I was flying from Little Rock to Memphis in a small commuter airplane. I was sitting in the first seat behind the cockpit, and there was only a curtain between my seat and the cockpit. What I was hearing was a discussion between the pilot and the co-pilot. This was before GPS navigation, and the conversation made me more conscious than ever of some of the difficulties of flying (as well as making me a little nervous).

Without modern systems, air navigation can be tricky. When a pilot plans his flight, he knows that he cannot aim his aircraft directly at his destination because he will be flying through winds that will blow his aircraft off course. To get close to his destination, he gets a weather briefing and adjusts his aim based on the reported winds he'll be flying through. However, once the aircraft takes off, the winds will not be exactly as predicted, and the aircraft will still be blown off the planned course—just not as much. Pilots know that they need to have either some electronic means to check their actual flight path or some way to visually spot things along the flight path that will allow them to make corrections.

Christianity can be like this. Satan applies constantly changing pressures to cause Christians to deviate from God's will as revealed in the Bible. And as humans, we can become so wrapped up in what we are doing that we fail to honestly check our bearings. We don't have to get far off course to be heading the wrong way. As soon as we are off course, we are off course—close is often far enough off to serve Satan's interests.

One of the problems we face as humans is that when we get off course, we tend to get into a rut and like it. Once someone gives us a way of looking at life and this world and we buy into it, we are very resistant to anyone's call to get back on course—we keep telling ourselves that we are on course.

"Back on Right"

So, what do I see as factors that get us off course in ways that hurt Christian motivation? In this book we'll address some situations I have personally experienced where a large number of Christians have gotten off course—never intentionally, but as a result of some persistent seemingly gentle outside influence.

I recall from my college days seeing the president's wife come out of the White House with a very irritated look on her face because one of the staff working the landscaping was not doing his or her job properly. Often she would start by saying, "I'm going to pinch your head off and put it back on right[1]." Sometimes I'm sure God wants to say something just like that to us—and we need to listen. This book is about eleven areas where this is too often true.

Head-Smacking Experiences

Much of this book deals with the "why" aspects of Christianity: "Why should I be a Christian?" "Why should I change my way of life just to be a Christian?" "Why should I be excited about being a

1 This was the wife of the college president, not the President of the United States, and the White House was the name of the official residence of the college president.

Christian? "Why does God sometimes seem cruel?" "Why does God sometimes seem uncaring?" "Why should I go to church?"

Emerson wrote, "The man who grasps principles can successfully select his own methods. The man who tries methods, ignoring principles, is sure to have trouble." This book is about understanding the principles of Christianity in such a way that a person can successfully select methods. This is really what God wants, and if you comprehend the concepts, principles, and ideas in this book, you will also understand why God wants us to learn Christianity this way. As a Christian, if you don't understand the principles behind what you do, you are sure to have trouble getting the methods right.

The information in this book is meant to be what I call head-smacking information. Much of what is contained here I learned by looking at what is going on in churches and among Christians, seeing things that just could not be right if God is real, and going back to the Bible to understand how things went so wrong. Over and over in this pilgrimage, as I would turn to the Bible for answers, I would find some truth that should have been obvious. Sometimes actually and always figuratively, I would smack my forehead and say, "Of course, that has to be right!" (That may be why my hairline has receded so far.) In fact, I believe that anyone really open to understanding more about what God is doing will find many of these items to be head-smacking in a very good sense.

Now, I certainly don't claim to have all of the answers to all of the questions, but I have found what I believe to be some very important answers to some very important questions. Some of these I found through studying what others had said or written—often learning from giants in the faith. Others I found through self-study as I dug deep into the Bible and tried to let God's Holy Spirit guide me. In every case I owe the results to God who provided both the spiritual giants and his Holy Spirit and, in many cases, to others among my family and friends who have helped me in my search for God's truth.

This book is meant to help Christians see how Christianity as taught in the Bible overcomes Satan's attacks. It is meant in many cases to open our eyes to areas where Satan has been very successful while hiding his success from our view.

About Motivation

There is an old story about a man (we'll call him John) walking through a cemetery at night and falling into an open gravesite. The gravesite had been opened that day in preparation for a funeral the next day. John often walked through the cemetery, but had not known about the preparations for the coming funeral. Since the opening was six feet deep and John was not that tall, though he tried and tried, he was unable to pull himself out of the opening. After many futile attempts, John decided to sit in a corner and wait for daylight; certain that he would be able to get help the next day. Sitting in the corner exhausted from his efforts, John quickly fell asleep. Not long after that Sam fell into the same opening. Like John, he tried and tried with no success to get himself out. The noise of his efforts woke John, who quickly figured out what had happened. In a voice deep from sleep John said, "It's no use, you can't get out." But Sam did. When he heard that voice, Sam was suddenly motivated.

Let's start by noting that no one does anything serious without some motivation, and with the proper motivation, there is no way to predict how much a person can accomplish. The motivation may be a thrill, an economic advantage, love, power, pleasure, or even terror. But when we invest time or resources in something, we always have some reason for doing so—whether our reason is reasonable or not.

Satan has always attacked God's people, and he does so in many ways. One of his most effective tools is that gentle nudge in a wrong direction applied over a long period of time to blow us off course. It's like the old story of the frog in a frying pan. I've never tried this, but the story goes that if you put a frog in a hot frying pan he will immediately jump out, but if you put him in a cold pan and gently raise the heat, he will sit there until he cooks. Satan is gently raising the heat. In many cases, the point Satan chooses to attack is in the form of something that seems very good and right—but that eventually leads to seriously wrong ends. Whenever the church experiences a major new sense of dedication to serving God as God intended, Satan's gentle nudges soon have us drifting from our intended path like an airplane gently blown off course.

The Bible or Tradition?

Most of us as Christians claim the Bible as our guide. We advertise that we are all about implementing the pattern of Christianity approved in the New Testament, modified only to make exactly the same message communicate well to this generation. Christianity as taught in the Bible is highly motivating—just look at what those early Christians accomplished. If we renew that kind of Christianity, a Christianity in which God's Holy Spirit is really turned loose in people's lives, I am convinced that we will see similar results. This kind of motivated Christianity is actually going on in many isolated areas, but it needs to be far more prevalent.

Too often we prefer our comfortable traditions to serious Christianity, but that is a very dangerous path. During his earthly ministry, there was no one Jesus condemned more soundly than the Pharisees, and he condemned them for exactly this problem of clinging to tradition instead of listening for God's voice. Often our traditions are the result of Satan's gentle pressure to send us in a wrong direction.

For much of my life I have said that if a Christian does not wake up excited to be a Christian and full of joy, that Christian does not really understand Christianity. I learned this truth even before I knew some of the most powerful motivating factors God provides for us, and learning those motivating factors has simply reinforced my awareness of this truth. If the gospel as you understand it is not the best news ever, then you need to understand it better. This book is an attempt to help Christians understand the gospel as they were meant to understand it.

CHAPTER TWO: CHRISTIANITY—THE ULTIMATE RELIGION

The Lord our God is the one and only Lord – Mark 12:29

This chapter may be summarized by saying that there is a God, and that this one and only God is the God of Christianity. If you are a Christian who is already fully convinced that this is true, you may want to just skim through this chapter. But if you are not a Christian or if you are a Christian but the questions raised by the doubters and skeptics of this world or by other religions have caused you to wonder, I encourage you to read this chapter carefully. (If you are a teacher or minister or leader, you can be sure that some in your flock struggle with these issues, so I encourage you also to read this carefully.) This chapter is important for the reader, not because you will find proof, but because you will find very strong affirmation of these truths if you are a Christian and very powerful arguments needed as a background for the rest of this book.

Do you know the difference between a man-made diamond and a natural diamond? Any good jeweler can tell the difference, but only with careful examination under a powerful magnifier of some sort. Any natural diamond will necessarily have at least some minor flaws—a man-made diamond will not. Strangely, a perfect diamond (man-made) is much less valuable than an imperfect (natural) diamond. A jeweler will examine diamonds carefully to be sure the price he pays is appropriate for the diamonds he is receiving. How much more important is it to know that you have found the "pearl of great price" that is the gospel message as God intended?

As mentioned above, it would be hard to get seriously motivated about something we are not convinced is true. (Far too many nominal Christians are not at all sure about God, even including some ministers and church leaders.) The purpose of this chapter is to provide powerful evidence that should convince Christians that there is no reason to doubt that their God is real and that Christianity is the one true religion. But please do not get the wrong idea here. I do not intend to prove that God exists or that Christianity is the one true religion with some sort of scientific proof. That is not possible. And I do not intend this to function as a tool to convert those who hold to atheism. All I plan to do is present what I believe any reasonable person will view as convincing evidence—evidence the average Christian should be able to understand. Given this evidence, any person should be able to stand tall as a Christian and tell those who would deny Christianity that the things that they teach do not pass the sniff test of common sense while Christianity does. We do not have to be embarrassed to say, "I am a Christian!"

In my experience, I have never met anyone I believed to be a true atheist. I'm not even sure there is a true atheist. What I have found is that those who claim to be atheists generally fall into one of four categories: 1) people who are so angry with God that they choose to deny his existence as the only means they have to try to get back at him; 2) people who (often quite correctly) absolutely reject the concepts of God presented by the various individuals or groups with whom they have come in contact; 3) people who are so preoccupied with their lives that they refuse to consider God at all; and 4) people who just don't want God or anyone else telling them what to do or how to live. And I have often said that if all I knew about Christianity were what many churches present, I would not be a Christian. That is sad, but it is true.

Point One—There Is a God

A parable—Part 1: Let's say you received a message that you had inherited a fortune in diamonds from an uncle living in South Africa. Let's say that the message comes from someone claiming to be the executor for this uncle's estate, and that he only wants you to send him a few thousand dollars to cover his costs in closing out the estate and forwarding the ownership documents to you because the will specifically prohibits him from using funds from the estate. But each of your parents had claimed to be an only child—meaning no uncles or aunts. Would you send the money?

The same principle applies here. How can we expect to motivate people to give their lives to the Lord if we cannot even convince ourselves that he exists?

The starting point for my argument is that most people, whether they will admit it or not, actually accept that there must be a creator. This is not scientific, because science by definition deals with the non-miraculous and the non-spiritual. Attempts to scientifically measure God or anything to do with spiritual matters must fail. Science deals with physical measurements and calculations based on those measurements, but the spiritual world in general and God in particular cannot be measured or calculated in physical terms.

Note: What follows here may be helpful for those who struggle with the claims of some non-believers that science and modern understanding of the events recorded in the Bible make it clear that the biblical accounts are made-up stories applicable only to more primitive times. The fact is that neither Christian nor non-Christian scholars actually have all the answers about how this universe came to be, and that the most recent suggestions from the world of science require at least as much faith in things that cannot be seen, measured, or proved as would be required to simply believe in God. The difference is that belief in God is supposed to be based on faith, while science is not. If the claims of non-Christians in this area have bothered you, you probably need to read the rest of this section. If those claims are of no interest to you, you may want to skip to Point Two – God Cares.

The primary piece of evidence for the existence of a creator God is the existence of this universe. Science has never adequately explained, nor can it ever hope to explain, how the enormous quantities of matter and energy in this universe could come into existence without a creator. I'll readily admit that saying there is a creator doesn't explain how the universe came to be—it simply puts that explanation beyond our abilities. Once we say "God is," we have argued for a being with powers we can't comprehend and whose origins we can't explain. Science no longer has any role in the matter. But if we insist on a scientific answer to where the universe came from, there is no such answer.

Now some who work in the fields of science have proposed various explanations for the existence of this universe. Some have used a rather Buddhist argument that the universe is cyclic, that this universe came from a previous universe that collapsed under the power of gravity until it finally contained so much energy in such a small location that a "big bang" occurred and this present universe resulted.

That answer is no help, because no matter how far back and through how many cycles we go, there is still no answer to the original source of all this matter and energy. Others have argued that this is just one of an unlimited number of universes, but that involves even more matter and energy with no explanation of where all this matter and energy came from initially. Somewhere there must be a source, and that source has to be far beyond our understanding. Call that source whatever you wish, you have now encountered God.

Many in the science community today argue that the matter in this universe is primarily made up of something they call "dark matter." (Stay with me here, I'm not going to get into anything that is hard to understand.) This supposed "dark matter" is something no one can see or detect by any means, but it is supposed to make up by far the majority of the matter of this universe. Furthermore, they argue that there is something called "dark energy" that makes up by far the majority of the energy of this universe. And like the "dark matter," this "dark energy" cannot be seen or detected or described in any way. In addition, to make their theories work they suppose that there is a subatomic particle that they call the "god particle" that no one has ever seen or detected in any way. In fact, the theories call for all sorts of weird things that no one has ever seen or detected and that no one can define or tell how they came into existence. Some scientists have measured things that may hint at the presence of such things as "dark matter" and "dark energy," but no one can directly see or measure these things. So these scientists believe in "dark matter" and "dark energy" and "god particles" and multiple universes and multiple dimensions and all sorts of weird things that they cannot see or detect or describe or explain where they came from, but they don't believe in God. If that seems like a strange situation—it is. Then there is life. In describing plants and animals, many who work in the fields of science will say something along these lines: "Nature has designed this plant or animal in this way to function in this specific environment." In fact, nature cannot design anything. That person has just created his or her own god and changed the spelling to "Nature."

And among the many leaps of faith required to avoid God, perhaps the largest dealing with life is the origin of life itself. Scientists universally agree that in this world, all life is based on living cells reproducing themselves. Anything that is smaller than a cell (for example, a virus) has to rely on a cell to carry out the reproduction process.

But a single cell capable of reproducing itself is an extremely complex item. It must include a cell wall that can allow just the right amount of nutrients in and waste products out; some means to convert the nutrients to the various chemicals needed by the cell; a nucleus with DNA of some sort; and specialized functions to carry on reproduction and all sorts of other processes. In fact, modern microbiology has revealed that every cell contains many internal "factories" that perform various complex processes. And new information keeps revealing more and more complexity in just one simple cell. Beyond this, the first cell to exist would have to rely on something like photosynthesis (a capability to use sunlight to convert inert materials into usable biological materials) in order to gather nourishment—there would be no other source for nourishment. But photosynthesis is an extremely complex process. In other words, a first cell could never happen by accident (though there is no way to prove this).

Some have naively assumed that some complex combination of chemicals and energy created the first cell, but that's not even close to reasonable. Nothing approaching the complexity of a single cell capable of reproducing itself could form by accident—not in a trillion billion years. And even among those who support such claims, the environments proposed for creating such a cell would almost certainly have immediately destroyed the cell before it could reproduce itself. With endless hours of experiments in carefully controlled laboratories, no scientist has ever witnessed the spontaneous generation of a single cell—not even a cell that could not reproduce itself. And no reputable scientist believes such cells are being generated now. Once again we find some people working in the fields of science claiming to believe in spontaneous generation of at least one living cell by a process that cannot be explained and has never been seen while not believing in God.

So again, belief in God is not within the scope of what science should address, but scientists should be honest about the problems with any theory. In all honesty, both the scientist and the believer in God must operate on faith in matters that cannot be demonstrated or proved. The advantage of the believer is that he or she is not supposed to be able to prove that God is real—otherwise it wouldn't be faith. Those in the science community just have much more that they must accept on faith than those in the Christian community, and less reason to do so.

A specific issue that has troubled Christians a lot is the perceived challenge of science to the Bible's account of creation in Genesis chapters 1 and 2. The scientific evidence overwhelmingly indicates that the earth is billions of years old (in spite of claims to the contrary by well-meaning Christians) and that the universe is much older than that. A traditional interpretation of the first two chapters of Genesis along with study of biblical information on when that creation occurred (primarily genealogies along with a few other references) has led many students of the Bible to conclude that the earth and the universe are only a few thousand years old, and that the earth is actually a few days older than the rest of the universe.

Almost two thousand years ago a Christian named Augustine of Hippo gave us the right way to deal with this type of paradox when he said that in such matters we should not take a stand on a specific interpretation of what the Bible says until the facts are all in and absolutely clear. In fact, there are at least three ways to interpret the biblical information in Genesis that do not conflict with the proven facts of science. We will not address those here—for the purposes of this book it is only important to understand that the traditional interpretation of the biblical account of creation has serious problems, but it is only the interpretation that has problems. The biblical account itself has no necessary problems beyond what should reasonably be expected in a document written by and for people living in a scientifically primitive culture.

So this is where I will start. There is a creator God. We cannot explain this God—we cannot even prove or disprove his existence. We can only accept this on faith or reject it on faith, and rejecting the idea of a creator God requires leaps of faith even greater than the leap of faith to accept that there is a God. I accept God on faith, and whether they admit it or not, so do most people. (I saw the results of a recent survey that indicated that 80% of those who have masters or doctorate level college degrees actually believe that there is a god.) I have a poster that I have framed and put on my wall because I love its message. It is a beautiful dawn scene with the words, "Two foundation facts of human enlightenment: 1. There is a God. 2. You are not him."

A parable—Part 2: Saying that we accept that there really is a God is equivalent to saying we believe there are diamonds in South Africa. That does not mean that an uncle we never heard of has left us diamonds as an inheritance, nor does it mean that the man who has contacted us is actually an attorney ready to deliver the inheritance. Just believing that there is a God does not necessarily motivate any real response.

Point Two—God Cares

Now the next question to address is God's interest in this world and particularly in humans. This universe is enormous beyond comprehension. We are one species living on one very small planet circling one small star in one medium-sized galaxy. The universe has galaxies beyond counting (hundreds of billions), and each galaxy has stars beyond counting (ours has about 100 billion, and others have several times that number), so what would make us think that the God who created this vast universe has any interest us? We are less than a speck in this universe.

That seems like a valid question, and once again the answer is a matter of faith because we just cannot say what God would or would not do. It's just as reasonable to believe that a creator God with power beyond our wildest comprehension might create an entire universe just to deal with one species on one planet as it is to believe that this same God might create such a universe and populate it with an almost infinite number of species of different sorts in which he would have similar (or possibly very different) interests.

The bottom line here is that either the creator does care about humans or he does not. There is no way that we could scientifically prove the case one way or another. Yes, this earth is permeated with beauty and order that would seem to indicate a creator who cares, but that's not proof to someone who demands measureable proof.

In the 17th and 18th centuries, a movement rose called Deism. Those who became Deists believed that there is a creator god, but they viewed him as having little if any interest in his creation. He had wound the universe up like a clock and then he had gone off to other interests, leaving the creation to go its own natural way. This belief became popular among many educated people, and it remains a popular view with many Americans even today, whether they admit it or not.

If you, like these Deists, choose to believe that God does not care—if you believe that we are simply an accidental occurrence in his creational hobby—then our lives have no meaning beyond what we experience in the years we live in this world. In that case, the logical thing for each person to do would be to gratify his or her desires for pleasure in whatever way is possible with no regard to others. After all, why care about others if there is no eternal judgment? Steal whatever you can get away with stealing. Murder whoever gets in your way if you can do so without being punished. If you find pleasure in sex, have sex as often as possible with as many partners as possible in as many ways as may provide you with pleasure—including rape—regardless of how many are hurt in the process because your pleasure is the only thing that matters. If there is no God and no judgment, there is no rationale for morality or ethics. Sin has no meaning. There is no right or wrong except as defined by you for your own pleasure. Laws are truly made to be broken.

I don't think there are many people who would want to live in a world like that. After all, while we're trying to get all the pleasure we can at the expense of anybody and everybody else, all other people would be doing the same, and it's unlikely that we'd always be the winners in such a contest.

Even self-proclaimed atheists rarely go this far. And those who do go this far are classified as sociopaths—people with very sick minds. But if God does not care about his creation (or if there is no God), these so-called sociopaths are the truly sane people. (That's a scary thought!)

For some reason, just about every person in the world believes there is some standard of right and wrong that goes beyond personal desire. This standard may be called morals or ethics or family values or some other name, but it still calls for a standard that goes beyond personal desire. Such standards make no logical sense unless there is some authority over all humans who cares what humans do—and that authority brings us right back to God.

I believe almost all people, and certainly all Christians, believe that there is some sort of higher power who cares what humans do and who has established standards of right and wrong and who will eventually demand a reckoning—a judgment day. No one can prove or disprove that God cares about humans; this is a matter of faith. But it's also a matter of faith accepted by almost all humans. I certainly believe that there is a creator God who does care about humans.

A parable—Part 3: We could compare this point to believing that there are diamonds in South Africa (though we have never been there or seen the diamonds) and that there actually was an uncle who moved to South Africa (though we never met him or communicated with him in any way). This still does not mean the uncle had a fortune or that he has left the fortune to you or that the man claiming to be the executor really is. There may be hope that a fortune is available, but not enough information to motivate you to send thousands of dollars to a stranger.

Point Three—God Reveals Himself

So, if there is a God, and if he does care, and if he is by nature beyond human ability to comprehend, then the only way we would really know anything about him is if he chooses to tell us about himself. Of course there are some things we could learn just by observing his creation (see Romans 1:20), but there are limits to what we can learn from the creation. The common understanding of all humans about what is right and what is wrong must have been implanted by the creator, and that reveals something about the creator. But if God really cares, it is reasonable that he would reveal himself in ways that would allow his creation to know him at some level.

This becomes even more important if we believe (and I do believe) that this God has a plan—a reason for creating that takes into account all that happens in this creation and all that will happen beyond this creation. If God has such a plan, there is no way he could expect his creation to respond to his plan unless either he programmed us like robots to respond the way he wants us to respond or he somehow revealed to his creation what he wants the creation to know. While some may believe that we have been programmed like robots, that view is an unsatisfying belief that raises a whole different set of fairly obvious logical problems.

So either God has revealed essential information about himself, or else all religions are equally false and useless because none have any real idea what God wants. (Given some experiences, many believe the second option is true—but let's hold off on that for the moment.) Once again we are dealing with a matter of faith. We cannot prove that God has revealed anything about himself. Either we accept this on faith or we reject it on faith. But there are some factors to consider.

Jews claim that the Torah and the related Jewish sacred writings are God's only revelation. Christians accept pretty much the same Jewish sacred writings, but they insist that there are additional valid revelations from God in the sacred writings of Jesus' followers. Moslems accept at least certain parts of the Jewish sacred writings and the Christian sacred writings as valid revelations (with some modifications), but they insist that the Quran (often spelled Koran) is the ultimate revelation of God (they call him "Allah") by which all other revelations must be measured. Buddhists do not specifically focus on a God of any sort, but they do have sacred writings believed to trace in some way to the words of the original Buddha. (The word "Buddha" means "enlightened one," without specifying the source of such enlightenment). Various other religions have leaders who provide or have provided self-proclaimed revelations as appropriate to the doctrines to be taught.

If we are willing to believe that this God who does care has revealed his interest in humanity in some way that would allow us to know at least some important things about him and his purpose in creating humans, we need to consider which of these competing "revelations" is actually God's real revelation. The rest of this book will bear on that question, because anyone who understands the message of this book will see that the Christian Bible and only the Christian Bible presents a reasonable version consistent with what such a revelation should be (though the Jewish sacred writings to some degree meet this same standard and are incorporated into the Christian Bible).

A parable—Part 4: We could compare this to accepting that the uncle did have a fortune. You still do not know that the uncle left this fortune to you or that the man calling is really the executor. Hope may be stronger, but there is still not enough information to motivate you to send thousands of dollars to a stranger. Similarly, just knowing that there is a God and that he probably has somehow revealed his will does not mean that Christians have the correct revelation.

A Side Point about Buddhism and Hinduism

It is appropriate here to briefly consider the tenets of Buddhism (and Hinduism as a related note). A man named Siddhartha Guatama was the original Buddha (self-proclaimed "enlightened one"). He taught that speculation about any god or gods or afterlife or any other area that could not be known through human experience is inappropriate. His teachings were more agnostic (no knowledge of whether there is or is not a god) than either religious or atheistic (denying that there is a real god). However, modern Buddhists generally deny the existence of any creator God. The interesting thing is that Buddhists do teach certain moral standards as appropriate in imitating the original Buddha, though the only justification for these standards is to alleviate human suffering. These teachings do not generally address why an individual should want to alleviate the suffering of others if causing such suffering would bring this individual pleasure.

For a motivating factor, Buddhists and Hindus universally teach reincarnation: when any animal (including humans) dies, that animal is always brought back to life, but generally in some other form. If the animal has been faithful to its nature, that animal comes back as a higher form of life. If the animal has not been faithful, it comes back as a lower form of life. This creates a serious problem for the beliefs of Buddhists, Hindus, and any other religion teaching reincarnation as the motivation for morality. Since the form of the reincarnated life depends on how well that life-form fulfilled its appropriate role before encountering death, this implies some sort of judgment. But judgment by whom if there is no god? Who decides whether a specific death should be rewarded with reincarnation into a higher life form or should be punished with reincarnation into a lower life form? Who decides what is a higher life form and what is a lower life form? If this works consistently, such reincarnation must imply a single God who is judge over all. After all, if there are many gods (as Hindus teach) making these decisions, the results would not be consistent. And doesn't the rewarding of those who do good and the punishment of those who do evil imply a loving God?

Saying that this cycle is somehow just inherent in the universe does not deal with the issue. How did it become inherent in the universe? This goes back to the earlier question: How did the universe get here at all? Long explanations cannot make these basic issues disappear. The very basic doctrines of Buddhism and Hinduism lead logically to belief in one loving God.

Even the designation of "Buddha" or "enlightened one" implies enlightenment by some outside source. No doubt Siddhartha Guatama did teach some very real and valuable truths, but how could he be the source of his own enlightenment? Any teaching that uses reincarnation to motivate morality necessarily implies that there is one and only one supreme God and that he is a loving God who cares about his creation. (That does not mean that reincarnation is true, it just means that the religions based on that teaching do not really work.)

Point Four—Only One God

In considering which of the religions that do accept the reality of one or more gods actually has received some form of true divine revelation, I would begin by maintaining that if there is a creator God, there can ultimately be only one. While we might imagine many underlings, the order and detail of this universe cannot be the product of a committee unless the members of the committee share a single mind-meld of some sort. In any successful organization there must be one point of final decision, and in the creation of a universe, that final arbiter would be the one and only true God.

In fact, if one argues for multiple gods, which god decided the details of how the universe would work? And if where God comes from is beyond human understanding, how can we deal with trying to comprehend where multiple gods came from and to which one or ones we should listen? The one Master Creator God might have an unlimited number of created helpers who contributed in one way or another, but there has to be one who is over all others.

Of course, no created thing can be the creator God. If there is a god, he must be the source of everything else. And I can't find any reasonable way to accept more than one creator God, regardless of how many of his creations (angels, cherubim, seraphim, or others) may have received delegated power to work in his creations.

So if we accept that there is a Creator God and that he does care about us and that he does want to reveal himself in ways that would draw people to him, the next question has to be, "Which of the different religions has the right message?" If we cannot answer that question, we are left with no strong motivation to follow any of them, for they routinely contradict each other.

If we accept that there is only one God (and nothing else is reasonable), and if we accept that this God wishes to reveal certain things about himself to humans, and if we believe this God has done so in a way that is at least somewhat successful, there are only three religions that would qualify as candidates to be the true religion: Judaism, Christianity, and Islam. These are the only three that teach one creator God with any degree of success.

A parable—Part 5: We could compare this to knowing that the uncle we've been using as an illustration had no living relative other than yourself. This makes the inheritance seem much more likely, but you still do not know that the uncle left this fortune to you or that the man calling is really the executor. Hope keeps getting stronger, but once again there is not enough information to motivate you to send thousands of dollars to this stranger.

Point Five—The Primacy of Judaism

If there is only one God and if he wants to reveal himself to humans and if he has always wanted to do so, then clearly the oldest religion still being practiced that recognizes just one God has the best claim to being true—and that religion is Judaism. The Hebrews accepted just one God many centuries before any other people, and they managed to somehow maintain this belief in the face of universal opposition from others for well over a thousand years.

Some have argued that since the Jewish Torah (known by Christians as Genesis, Exodus, Leviticus, Numbers, and Deuteronomy) does not specifically state that there is only one God until somewhere in Deuteronomy, there may be reason to question whether earliest Judaism actually practiced a belief in just one God. However, any reasonable study of the earlier books of the Torah would reveal that a single creator God is assumed in every one of them.

We might stop right there and say that is the end of the matter if it were not for one important point: Judaism is the only religion that accepts sacred writings that repeatedly prophesy its own replacement. So if Judaism is the true revelation of God it claims to be, then at some point it must be replaced.

Prophecies of Replacement

What follows here may get a little deep, depending on the reader's familiarity with the Bible. The Jewish sacred writings are found in the Old Testament, and the following paragraphs discuss four cases where the sacred writings of the Jews specifically predicted the replacement of four aspects of the Jewish religion: 1) the replacement of Moses as the ultimate prophet; 2) the replacement of the Jewish priesthood with a new priest; 3) the replacement of the covenant of law with a covenant of the heart; and 4) the replacement of the greatest Jewish king (King David) with a new king from among his descendants. The details may seem a little deep, but they only serve to clarify that these four prophecies existed and were accepted by the Jews as revelations from God.

These are not the only such prophecies. Many other passages clearly imply or state that the God of the Jewish religion planned to replace that form of worship at some point in time. So while the Jewish religion must be true if any religion is true, this opens three possibilities: 1) the Jewish religion is still true and has yet to be replaced; 2) the Christian religion is the proper fulfillment of the Jewish prophecies; or 3) Islam is the proper fulfillment of the Jewish prophecies. Let's begin by looking at the four specific prophecies mentioned above.

The first prophecy we will consider is found in Deuteronomy 18:15 where Moses, the prophet who received God's law for the Jews and had it written down, is quoted as telling the Jews, "Jehovah[2] your God will raise up a prophet like me for you. He'll come from among your people, from your brothers[3]. You are to listen to him." This clearly taught (and was understood by the Jews to teach) that there would be a Jewish prophet who would come after Moses whose words would lead the people into new paths beyond what Moses had been able to provide. There was to be a Messiah who would bring new and better revelations. Of course these new and better revelations would have to be consistent with the morality that Moses taught since they would still come from God, but they would have to go beyond what Moses taught. Modern Jews who accept the Torah as revelation still look for this Messiah to come. Christians need to know that he has come, and that he is Jesus Christ.

Second, in Psalm 110:4 the psalmist says, "The Lord has sworn and will not relent, 'You are a priest forever according to the order of Melchizedek.'" Please don't let the big name confuse you, let's just call him Mel. For the Jews, every priest had to come from the Jewish tribe of Levi—they were all descendants of one man named Levi. No one else was supposed to be a priest. But this guy Mel did not qualify as a Jewish priest because he was not a member of the tribe of Levi. In fact, Mel lived years before Levi, and as far as we can tell from the Bible, he was a priest because of how he served God and not because of his ancestry. So a priest "according to the order of Melchizedek" would mean a priest who was not a member of Levi's family and who deserved the priesthood because of what he did, not because of his ancestry. Jews understood this Psalm to be another prophecy concerning the coming Messiah—that he would be a priest in spite of his ancestors not being from that tribe.

It's important to understand that the psalmist's prophecy of a new "priest forever" was written long after Moses had established the Jewish priesthood. In the New Testament, the author of Hebrews points out that what this meant was that the Jewish religion with its priesthood and its laws would be replaced. After all, if the Jewish priesthood continued, what need could there be for any other

2 Jehovah is an approximation of the name meaning "I AM" which was revealed to Moses as an appropriate name for God and for which the true pronunciation has been lost. The pronunciation is not important—the meaning is what matters. The appropriate name for God implies his eternal unchanging and all-encompassing existence.

3 In other words, the coming replacement for Moses must be from among the Hebrews, later known as Jews.

priest? But if another priest were coming who was not from the tribe of Levi, then the Jewish priesthood would be obsolete. This new priest must replace the Jewish priesthood or there would be no reason for a new priest—you don't want two different priesthoods. Jesus Christ is the new High Priest, and shortly after his coming, the purpose of the Jewish priesthood—to serve in the temple—ended for good when the Romans completely destroyed the temple where they were supposed to serve.

Third, the prophet Jeremiah wrote:

> Jehovah says, "Behold, the days are coming when I will make a new covenant with the people of Israel and with the people of Judah—not like the covenant that I made with their ancestors in the day I took them by the hand to lead them out of the land of Egypt—my covenant, which they broke though I was a husband to them. But this is the covenant that I will make with the house of Israel after those days: I will put my law in their minds, and write it on their hearts; and I will be their God, and they shall be my people. No more shall every man teach his neighbor, and every man his brother, saying, 'Know the LORD,' for they all shall know me from the least of them to the greatest of them. And I will forgive their iniquity, and I will no longer even remember their sins" (Jeremiah 31:31-34).

In this passage the prophet clearly states that God planned to replace the religion established by Moses with a subsequent religion more attuned to the focus of one's heart and life than to the laws Moses had delivered. A brief review of the Sermon on the Mount (Matthew chapters 5, 6, and 7) easily makes the point that this is exactly what Jesus Christ came to do.

Fourth, the Bible quotes God as saying to King David, the greatest king of the Jewish nation, "If your sons give proper attention to their way of living and walk before me in truth with all their heart and with all their soul, you will never be without a man of your family on the throne of Israel" (1Kings 2:4). Long years later Isaiah prophesied, "There shall come forth a rod from the stem of Jesse, and a branch shall grow out of his roots. The Spirit of Jehovah shall rest upon him" (Isaiah 11:1-2). Now you need to understand that Jesse was the father of King David, so Isaiah was predicting that someone from that family would one day arise and that God's Holy Spirit would live in him. From ancient times, and especially after the nation of Israel was deported from their homeland, Jews understood this to mean that the Messiah would be a descendant of King David (and therefore from the tribe of Judah rather than Levi), and that he would take over as ruler of all Israelites. Throughout his ministry, Jesus was known as the "Son of David," clearly indicating that even in his lifetime, people accepted him as the fulfillment of this prophecy.

A parable—Part 6: At this point let's assume that another man has contacted you claiming to be the true executor of your uncle's will and also asking for thousands of dollars for expenses. Let's assume that you now know that there was an uncle, that he did have a fortune, that he did leave a will, and that you are named as primary heir in the will. Now your problem is that you have two men claiming to be the executor, and you must consider the possibility that neither one is the executor.

Similarly, if two religions both claim to be the heirs of Judaism, and if Jews claim that there is no need for an heir since Judaism is still the true religion, the motivation to choose one over the others must depend on still more information.

Point Six—Christianity as Fulfillment of Jewish Prophecy

Christianity, of course, claims to be the proper fulfillment of these prophecies, and the evidence is impressive.

First, any replacement of Judaism should obviously accept the teachings of Judaism as true revelations from God. While there has never been total agreement among all Jews as to exactly what constitutes the Jewish sacred writings, Christianity accepts as valid revelations the writings agreed to by practically all Jews as sacred—certainly all that Jews accept as making up the Law and the Prophets. Of course Christians view the revelations provided by Christ and his followers as superseding certain aspects of the revelations in the Jewish sacred writings, but from the very beginning Christians have always pointed to the Jewish sacred writings as establishing the truth of Christianity. While Christians teach that certain ceremonial and civil aspects of the Jewish system have been superseded, Christians also teach that even these aspects have important meaning for Christians as symbols or types of things that came through Jesus.

Second, anyone familiar with Jesus' ministry must see that he accepted the role of the prophet[4] to supersede Moses found in Deuteronomy 18:15 as discussed above. This is especially obvious in Jesus' Sermon on the Mount found in Matthew chapters 5, 6, and 7 where Jesus specifically deals with how he will "fulfill" the Law given through Moses with the principles of Christian love that go beyond the letter to the spirit of the law.

Third, Jesus clearly taught that his sacrificial death was for the sins of humanity (see such passages as Matthew 26:26-29), making him the new High Priest prophesied in Psalm 110:4 (discussed above) replacing the Levitical priesthood under its High Priest. Because Jesus is viewed by Christians as replacing the Levitical priesthood, Christians consider the ceremonial laws related to that priesthood under Christ, to be superseded. Beyond this, Christians from earliest times viewed themselves as the new priesthood ministering under Christ, to the whole world (see 1Peter 2:9).

Fourth, the passage mentioned above in Matthew 26:26-29 and many, many other passages make it clear that Jesus thought of himself as establishing God's new covenant with humanity as prophesied in Jeremiah 31:31-34 (discussed above) superseding the covenant given to the Jews through Moses. Jesus' covenant fulfilled the Jewish covenant with a covenant based on love for God and for each other. Jesus taught a religion of the heart rather than a system of laws, just as Jeremiah had predicted. The Christian insistence on salvation by grace through faith exactly fulfills what Jeremiah prophesied.

Fifth, Jesus Christ was humanly a descendant of King David, and he claimed to be establishing an eternal kingdom with himself as king, fulfilling the prophecies of 1Kings 2:4 and Isaiah 11:1-2 (discussed above) that a descendant of King David would establish such an eternal kingdom. (See Matthew 1:1; 2:1; 9:27; 15:22; 20:30-31; 21:9, 15; 27:11; Luke 1:32, 69.) And since Jesus is viewed as the new king, Christians consider the civil laws (including dietary and hygienic laws) related to the Jewish covenant to be superseded. As for the moral laws, Christians maintain that these too are superseded by

4 In this age, many associate prophecy with foretelling the future, but prophecy is essentially delivering a message given by God. If God reveals some truth to any person, when that person delivers this revelation to others, he fulfills the role of a prophet. Jesus fulfilled the role of a prophet both in delivering a message given by God and in foretelling the future.

the higher spiritual standards of unselfish, generous, caring, forgiving, active love taught by Jesus. As Jesus himself taught, this standard of love covers and exceeds all the standards of the moral law[5].

Sixth, within about 40 years of the resurrection of Jesus, strict Judaism could no longer be practiced. Much of the Jewish Torah deals with the sacrificial system to be practiced under the care of the Jewish priesthood. This sacrificial system was to be centered first on the portable Tabernacle as the place of worship and later on the more permanent Temple as the place of worship. But about 40 years after Jesus' resurrection, the temple was completely destroyed—the Romans tore down the walls stone by stone. And from that time to this, there has been no place for offering the required sacrifices—not for almost 2000 years. So just when it became impossible to practice the Jewish religion as required in the Torah, Christianity arose to take its place.

A parable—Part 7: We now know that the claims of one man to be the executor of your uncles will seem valid, but what of the other man who claims to be the executor? Until this is fully resolved, you will not be motivated to send money to either man. Thus, while Christianity seems to pass the test as the heir to Judaism, we need to consider Islam's similar claim.

Point Seven—Islam Fails as Fulfillment of Jewish Prophecy

In contrast to Christianity, Islam does not measure up as being the fulfillment of these prophecies. Islam arose over 500 years after the destruction of the temple in Jerusalem—creating a major break between the end of practical Judaism and the beginning of this new religion. The origin of Islam traces to a man named Muhammad—a man who was in no way a descendant of King David and who never made any claim or performed any actions to indicate that he should be considered a priest. Rather than a religion of the heart, Islam is largely a religion of strict laws (very similar in many ways to the Jewish religion), thus not fulfilling Jeremiah's prophecy. And Islam accepts

5 The moral law (including the Ten Commandments) provides guidance for Christians in understanding how to end our rebellion against God, and this law is indeed a standard of judgment for those who have heard the message of the law and not the message of Christianity, but Christians need to focus on the commandments of love as the primary way to end the rebellion and meet the real intent of the Law.

Jewish and Christian sacred writings only with significant restrictions, denying key points in both Jewish and Christian sacred writings.

Unlike Judaism, Christian leaders and Jesus himself insisted that Christianity would be the final revelation from God. Islam claims to accept certain Christian teachings, but must reject the Christian claim to be God's final revelation and the Christian claim that Jesus came as God incarnate. Islam claims to be an improvement on Christianity (and indeed it may be seen as an actual improvement on the Christianity practiced by many at the time Islam arose), but it will be obvious to anyone who understands the message Jesus brought that the legalism of Islam is a poor substitute for Christianity.

In fact, Islam is a return to a religion of law, and stricter laws than those of Judaism. Islam is a return to that which has already been proved inadequate. Jesus made it very clear that no human could earn salvation or even contribute to the price of his or her salvation. Any religion—Judaism, Islam, various perversions of Christianity, or any other—that teaches the need for humans to somehow contribute to the cost of their salvation is false. (This does not mean that Christians can accept God's salvation without seriously changing how they live—that is the point of repentance.)

In fact, by every reasonable test, Islam fails to be a valid replacement for Judaism, and it is hard to imagine that God wanted to reveal himself to humans but decided to wait hundreds of years after the end of effective Judaism until the time of Mohammad to do so. The better one understands the real message of Christianity presented in the Bible, the more clearly it may be seen to fulfill Judaism; and the better one understands the real message of Islam, the more clearly it may be seen to fail this standard.

A parable—Part 8: Back to the illustration of the inheritance, let's say that now you know who the real executor is and you know that the will states that the entire estate must go to the heir. That means the executor must get paid by the heir, not from the estate. But let's assume that you have received conflicting instructions concerning how the payment should be made and how much money is actually required. Until the details get worked out, you still will not be motivated to send thousands of dollars.

Point Eight—No Perfect Christians

If we accept that there is a creator God, that this creator God does care about and reveal himself to humans, and that there is only one creator God, then Christianity stands out as the obvious candidate to be called the one true religion. Granted, Judaism came first, but Judaism itself predicted its replacement, and Christianity fulfills those predictions very well.

This must raise the question of which branch of Christianity is the right one. The truth is that none are and many are. There are branches of so-called Christianity that have practically nothing to do with what Christ taught—that even teach against the very things Christ taught. We will simply consider these as not Christian at all. They are like Islam in that they are late-comer imitations that fall short of the stature of true Christianity.

However, no one individual or group can ever be fully right about God or about what Christ taught—there are too many opportunities for error and too many pressures to influence us away from this or that truth. There is a poem about seven blind men who went to "see" an elephant. Each of these blind men sensed some important truth about the elephant. One thought the elephant was like a fan, for he had chanced to contact an ear. One thought the elephant was like a rope, for he had contacted the tail. One thought the elephant was like a tree trunk, another thought it was like a wall, and another thought it was like a spear, etc. Each had caught some valid truth about the elephant, and each insisted that his truth must be the only truth, but none could see the real truth that united all their limited truths.

Similarly, individual Christians and Christian organizations tend to perceive some set of truths that are indeed valid and to proclaim those truths as exclusive truth or at least as more important than other truths, but in doing so they miss the larger picture. Even those willing to accept the validity of the perspective of others run into serious difficulty selecting which perspectives are true and which are serious errors. No human individual or group can ever comprehend the whole perfectly. But God's Holy Spirit works in those individuals and organizations that truly try to serve him to bring about wonderful results

Many variations of Christianity accept enough of the key basic truths to carry on God's intended mission—and that is what God wants. The tragedy is when such Christians fight with each other over whose perception is the real truth when none really is. How much better if each of us would eagerly seek to learn from others and to seriously challenge our own beliefs to make sure they really are valid? (You can be sure that Satan has been working on any truth that has been held for some time to nudge the understanding of those who hold this truth away from actual truth.)

In this book we will try to find some of the important truths that must apply for all Christians—truths that help motivate us to be what God intends. These will be mainly "big picture" items. Once we grasp the big picture items, the key principles of Christianity, as long as we are open to his guidance, we can trust God's Holy Spirit to guide us in the details he wants us to know.

So while Christianity is the only religion with a reasonable claim to be the one true religion, there is no one true group of Christians. This is consistent with how God works. He will guide those who sincerely seek his will to serve him as he sees fit, providing guidance to all those who seek his guidance regardless of which group they choose to join.

But most of the world has never really heard the message of Christianity. What is the fate of these billions of people? How will God judge them? If people are condemned for not being Christians when they never knew anything about Christianity, how can God be a just judge? And beyond this, given terrible things God is often accused of, how can anyone trust him to be a just judge?

A parable—Part 9: Later we will see how Christians can know that they are really doing what God considers acceptable service—it's not that hard to understand. This would be like finding out exactly what is required to receive your uncle's inheritance. But first we need to consider more about who this God is and what he is really like.

CHAPTER THREE: GOD—THE ULTIMATE GOOD

God is love – 1John 4:8

This chapter may be summarized by saying that the God of Christianity is just one and only one God and that he is truly good and loving, that his description of himself as merciful, gracious, forgiving, patient, kind, and truthful is accurate. Everyone experiences things in this life that tend to make us question this description. Some of these things need to be addressed here as a foundation for what follows. If you are a Christian who is already fully convinced of these truths, you may want to just skim through this chapter. But if you are not a Christian or if you are a Christian with serious questions in these areas, I encourage you to read this chapter carefully. Again, if you are a teacher or leader, you can be sure that some in your flock need this information, so I would strongly encourage you to read this carefully. This chapter is important for the reader as a background for the rest of this book.

Sadly, many churches provide various perspectives on God that either are not motivating or are actually negative motivators. Even translations of the Bible too often present negative perspectives on God through poor translation practices (some worse than others) or by not providing at least a note about possible alternate understandings where confusion is obviously possible. And a tendency to look at an account in the Bible without considering information clearly provided in other parts of the Bible causes serious misunderstanding of what God has done and is doing. On top of this, we all tend to approach the biblical message with a human, worldly-focused perspective and generally with some preconceived ideas derived from family or acquaintances, but these worldly focused perspectives are not God's perspective nor are any of them the perspective he wants us to gain. God looks at everything from the perspective of eternity, and if we were wise we would try to do the same. After all, this worldly life is nothing compared to eternity. If God were to put us through the worst possible conditions in this life in order to give us a truly wonderful, exciting, joy-filled eternity, in the end we would be very glad for what he had done. What loving parents would not put their child through the pain of surgery and extensive physical therapy if that process were needed to give the child a chance for a full and wonderful life?

But it's hard to be motivated and to focus on God and live for God if you believe that God arbitrarily sends to hell people who never had a chance to gain heaven. It's hard to be motivated to focus on God and live for God if you believe that God is only interested in punishing you for what you have done—or worse yet—for what your parents have done. It's hard to be motivated to focus on God and live for God if you believe that God just doesn't care about you. It's hard to be motivated to focus on God and live for God if you believe that God is some kind of genocidal maniac. It's hard to be motivated to focus on God and live for God if you believe that God's demands on you are beyond the capability of any human. It's hard to be motivated to focus on God and live for God if Christian leaders proclaim that there is only one God and then teach as if there were three gods.

Yet these are false images of God that we intentionally or unintentionally accept and communicate to the world around us far too often. Generally we do not discuss such perspectives in terms that are this direct and blunt.We'd rather ignore the implications of our beliefs, but in the back of our minds we know these things cannot be right. We may say things like, "You just don't see it from God's perspective." Yet if we don't offer anything that could serve as God's perspective and turn what seems so wrong into something that could at least pass the test of our God-given sense of right and wrong, our words are cold comfort.

A parable—Part 10: God created us with this innate sense of what is right and what is wrong. If God then comes to us with a message that violates this sense of right and wrong that he gave us, our motivation to serve him must be seriously damaged. This might be like learning that the fortune left by your uncle was obtained by a combination of theft and abusive slave labor, that much of this fortune is still tied up in criminal activities of one sort or another, and that by the terms of the will the principle must remain invested in such activities. Of course there are many who would still want the inheritance, but the motivation to get that inheritance would be damaged by such considerations. In fact, more people than many of us might expect would actually turn down such an inheritance.

Similarly, if the one true religion teaches a God who violates his own principles of right and wrong, the motivation to serve such a God must be severely damaged. Many people would reject such a God, no matter what benefits he might claim to offer for the future. In fact, many Christians (or people who claim to be Christians) present God in exactly that light, and for this reason, many others reject the God these Christians present. And many who do accept the idea of such a God do so with minimal enthusiasm.

In this chapter we will look at all of these perspectives on God and we will find that in each case the biblical message offers a different and much better perspective. We will learn why those who do manage to experience this God have found that serving him is indeed motivational and that he is always true to himself and to the sense of right and wrong that he has given us.

An Arbitrary God

As a first order of business we need to consider the teaching that only people who have heard of Jesus and accepted him as Lord (or at least as savior) can be saved—that God arbitrarily condemns anyone who has not heard the message of Jesus. At this present time, most people in this world have not even heard the name of Jesus, and huge numbers of those who have heard of him have been given such a distorted concept of who he is and what he asks of us that they have no true concept of Jesus. So having established the reasons to be at least willing to believe that there is a God, that he has revealed at least something about himself, that he is a caring and loving God, and that the most reasonable identification of him is as the Christian God, we need to deal with the question of how God deals with those who never hear the message of Christianity—which would be the vast majority of all people who have ever lived in this world.

Jesus did say, "I am the way and the truth and the life. No one can come to the Father except through me" (John 14:6). The apostle Peter told the Jewish Council, "There just is no salvation in any other person, for no other name under heaven has been given to mankind by which we must be saved" (Acts 4:12). Over and over the New Testament makes clear that Jesus is uniquely the only savior who can bring us the salvation we need. So what happens to people who really try to do right to the best of their knowledge and ability but who never hear of Jesus or who hear severely distorted ideas about Jesus?

An Arbitrary God—Jesus' Perspective

This is an area where it can be hard for Christians to accept what their own sacred writings teach because so many of us have been taught something wrong for so long. Let's start with what Jesus taught. The 19th chapter of Matthew tells about a wealthy young man's visit with Jesus. This young man came asking what he needed to do in order to gain eternal life. Jesus began by telling him to follow certain commandments in the Law of Moses (which had not yet been fulfilled since Jesus had not yet been resurrected). The young man argued that he had always lived up to these commandments—though it later became evident that he had not. Jesus, perceiving that his biggest problem was his selfishness, told this young man to sell his possessions and give the proceeds to the poor. The young man simply walked away sadly, unwilling to make such a sacrifice.

At this point Jesus commented to his disciples on how hard it is for wealthy people to be saved. His disciples were astonished. They had always assumed that wealth was a sign of God's approval and blessing. They asked Jesus, "Who then can be saved?" Jesus replied that being saved is always beyond human capability—people cannot earn or purchase their own salvation, "but with God, all things are possible" (Matthew 19:26).

Now, that last phrase has often been quoted and misused out of context. Jesus was not saying that God can do even things that the Bible elsewhere tells us God cannot do (such as lie). We need to take his statement in the context of the subject he was discussing.

What Jesus was saying is that God can save whomever he chooses to save, regardless of any other circumstances. That was the point Jesus was making, and that point is still valid. Any time we say who God will or will not save, unless we have a very specific revelation supporting the claim, we have moved into doing God's job—and we have no business doing that. We certainly do not have the right or the capability to make such judgments. Even when we have what appears to be a specific supporting revelation, we need to be certain that we understand the real intent of the message. For example, while Jesus said that no one could come to God except through him, he did not say that a person would necessarily have to know anything specific about him (such as his name) or about the gospel message in order for him to bring that person to God.

The question becomes, "What is God's standard?" And to answer that, we need to carefully consider what the Bible says. Ultimately, we need to remember that God's standard is God's business—not ours. He decides the standard for who will or will not enter his eternity, we do not.

John's Gospel records a confrontation Jesus had with some Pharisees. During the conversation, the Pharisees were offended that Jesus seemed to imply that they might be spiritually blind. The Pharisees responded by asking, "Are you saying that we are blind too?" (John 9:40). To this Jesus responded, "If you were blind, what you have done would not count as sin. But now you're saying, 'We see.' Therefore what you have done is counted as sin" (John 9:41). Later in Jesus' ministry John records how Jesus said, "If I had not come and talked to them, they wouldn't really be sinners, but now they have no excuse for their sin. If someone hates me, that person must hate my Father too. If I had not done things right in their midst that no one else has ever done, what they have done would not count as sin. But now they have experienced my presence and they have come to hate me and my Father" (John 15:22-24).

Notice that in both cases Jesus makes it clear that a person's actions are only sin when that person knows better. With God, the sin is not the action but the rebellion against God's authority. The implication is that no matter what a person does, if he or she does not know that it is wrong or against God's will, there is no sin. As we will see (and as we should have expected), this teaching from Jesus matches very well with what Paul taught.[6]

6 I realize that there are teachings about unintentional sin in the Bible. Using the Bible to interpret the Bible, I believe what happens here is another language problem. The way I am using "sin" here and the way Jesus and Paul and James use it, sin is only sin when it is rebellion against what we understand to be God's will. However, when a person does what is truly wrong without realizing that it is wrong, it is still wrong, it just is not rebellion. If we define sin as doing something wrong, then that person has sinned. And the Old Testament teachings about sacrifices for unintentional sin are valid lessons in the point that we need to be aware of the fact that all of us do wrong without realizing it, and that it is important for us to grow in understanding God's will for our lives so that we can repent of such sins.

An Arbitrary God—Paul's Perspective

If we look at Paul's letter to the Christians in Rome, in the very first chapter Paul says of the gentiles (that is, all those who are not Jews and would therefore not be living by the Law of Moses and who would normally not even know anything about Moses),

> Since the creation of the world his [God's] invisible attributes (his eternal power and his Godhead) have been clearly visible because they can be understood by the things that he made. So they [the gentiles] are without excuse, because, although they knew about God, they did not glorify him as God, nor did they give him thanks. But their reasoning became empty, and their hearts were darkened through lack of intelligent thought (Romans 1:20-21).

Now, for Paul to say that the gentiles were "without excuse" strongly implies that if they had done what they knew to do (however limited the revelation they had through the creation might be), God would have accepted them. If God condemned the gentiles for not living up to a revelation they did not have, they would at least have had a valid excuse—and God would be unfair. But Paul's argument is that the gentiles were justly condemned because they did not live up to the revelation they did have through creation itself.

In the next chapter of this letter Paul addressed the circumcised (Jews) and the uncircumcised (gentiles) and said,

> Circumcision is certainly profitable if you keep the Law of Moses, but if you are one who breaks that law, won't your circumcision be counted as uncircumcision? Therefore, if an uncircumcised man keeps the moral requirements of the Law of Moses, won't his uncircumcision be counted as circumcision? And won't the physically uncircumcised, if he fulfills the moral requirements of the law, judge you who, even with your written code and circumcision, are a law breaker? For the outward evidence of circumcision does not necessarily make a man a Jew, nor is true circumcision before God limited to the outward evidence in the flesh. But a real Jew is someone who in his heart is faithful to what it

> means to be a Jew, and real circumcision is that of the heart, in the Spirit, not just keeping the letter of the law. Such a man's praise is not from men but from God (Romans 2:25-29).

So Paul holds that even if a person were not a Jew, if he or she did what God wanted, God would consider that person as equivalent to a Jew and as even better than a Jew who found loopholes in the law and violated the clear intent of the law.

The real argument Paul makes in chapter one of this letter is that gentiles in general are under God's condemnation, not because they failed to live up to the Law of the Jews about which most of them knew nothing, but because they did not live up to what they did know about God from the world he had created. In chapter two Paul's argument is that similarly, Jews are under God's condemnation because, while they knew the Law God had given them through Moses and generally lived by a higher moral standard than the gentiles, they had a much better revelation from God, and like the gentiles, they too did not live up to what they knew God wants.

Then at the end of the second chapter Paul makes the argument that those gentiles who did live up to what they knew of God's standards would be accepted by God as if they were good Jews, and those Jews who did not live up to what they knew of God's will would be rejected by God as if they were gentiles.

Later in this same letter Paul says, "You can't be guilty of sin if there are no rules" (Romans 5:13). (Literally Paul is saying that if there is no target, you can't be guilty of missing the bull's eye.) In other words, God does not ask of a person that he or she meet some standard about which that person knows nothing. God only demands that each person live up to the Revelation that person has received and should know. Sin is always rebellion, treason against God and his kingdom. And rebellion against God is always sin. But a person cannot be in rebellion against God if he or she does not know what God wants. (You may also want to look at Romans 7:7 in this context.)

One of the implications of these passages in context is that if a person has access to a revelation and does not bother to consider or pay attention to that revelation, that person is guilty of rebellion as surely as if he or she had known the revelation and rebelled against it. That person had the revelation. His or her failure to take advantage of this access is rebellion, and rebellion is always sin—the one who rebels is a traitor to God's kingdom.

But it's not just Jesus and Paul who held this view. Let's look now at what James said.

An Arbitrary God—James' Perspective

Jesus had a half-brother named James, and this man became a leader of the church in Jerusalem after Jesus' resurrection. James wrote a brief but very powerful letter addressed generally to all Christians. In this letter James said, "Therefore, to him who knows to do good and does not do it, to him it is sin" (James 4:17). Again we see the point that sin involves going against what a person knows to be God's will. Ignorance does not make the sin OK, it just means there can be no guilt—there was no intent to sin. However, intentionally ignoring God's word or any revelation from God is a sin in itself. A person cannot avoid sin by refusing to find out God's will. As Paul pointed out, any person with any amount of intelligence will have enough information to know certain things about God if only by observing the creation around that person—so ignorance is never a complete excuse for sinful living. But God does not hold a person responsible to live up to a standard that he or she could not reasonably have understood.

An Arbitrary God—The Reality

From these and other inputs, it should be clear that God can and will save anyone he chooses to save. And a person who seriously tries to live up to what he or she knows about God's will, regardless of how little or how much of God's revealed will that person has access to, is far better off than a person who is very familiar with the sacred writings of Jews and Christians but does not live in accordance with that knowledge. This does not mean that it is better to know less—no, the more we know, the easier it is to live up to God's standards (though sometimes it may not feel that way). Besides that, since God wants us to know his will (as is obvious from the fact that he has bothered to reveal it), neglecting to learn God's will is rebellion and therefore sin. Ultimately, we all have rebelled and we all must rely on God's grace, but God's grace is for those who at least seriously try to do his will.

It is my understanding (well supported by the Bible) that God will save anyone who honestly tries to serve him, and that God will condemn anyone who does not do that. As we will see, this is the essence of saving faith as defined in the Bible. Paul's argument in Romans 4 about Abraham is to clarify that the message of Christianity is not something altogether new—God has always saved people based on their willingness to submit to him in faith.

Remember, Noah, Abraham, Isaac, Jacob, and many others were saved without ever knowing anything about the Law given through Moses or about Christianity[7]. And the God who saved them is the same God who saves people today. Why would he demand more of a person today who never heard of Jesus or Moses than he demanded of Noah or Abraham who lived before Jesus or Moses? God is the same always. We misrepresent God when we argue that he will not save someone because that person did not do what he or she had no idea was the right thing to do.

So why should we bother telling the world about Jesus? First, because that's what God told us to do—we do not really need to understand more than that. Second, we need to carry the message to others because hearing the gospel message as Jesus taught it will provide motivation not otherwise available for people to follow God. Third, the gospel message provides guidance in areas that will prepare people for God's eternity, and that is an important ministry. Fourth, how can we hold back telling such good news to others?[8] And fifth, if Christians truly live as Christians, they will necessarily attract others to their Lord—real Christianity is that attractive!

Along this line, there are some very important warnings in the Bible. Jesus said, "Whoever causes one of these little ones who believe in me to sin would be better off if a millstone had been hung around his neck and he had been drowned in the deepest part of the ocean" (Matthew 18:6). Ezekiel recorded God's words to him as follows:

> "Son of man, I've made you a watchman for the house of Israel. Therefore, listen to what I have to say and give them warning from me. When I say to a wicked person, 'You shall surely die,' and you do not warn him or if you do not speak up in order to save his life, that same wicked man will certainly

7 No person in history has ever been saved by anything but the sacrificial death of Jesus Christ. However, a person need not know anything about Jesus in order to be saved by his blood (as is the case with these men). The key is ending the rebellion against the Creator, regardless of how much a person does or does not know about what that means.

8 I realize, we have not come to the really good news yet. By the time we get through Chapter 5 I believe you will find the news is far better than most Christians have realized.

> die in his wickedness, but I will hold you guilty for his death. But if you warn that wicked person and he does not turn from his wickedness, that same wicked man will still die in his wickedness, but you will have rescued your own soul. In the same way, when a righteous man turns from righteousness to sin and I lay a trap for him, he will certainly die in sin because you did not give him warning—his righteousness from the past shall not count—but I will hold you guilty for his death. But if you warn that righteous man not to sin and he accepts the warning, he will surely live because he accepted your warning, and you also will have rescued your own soul" (Ezekiel 3:17-21).

Finally we have a warning from James: "My brothers, do not allow many of you to become teachers. You know that we shall receive a stricter judgment" (James 3:1). Once again we see that God expects us to live up to the Revelation we have, and if we claim to be teachers, we agree to a higher level of responsibility because we claim to know more than those we are teaching.

Thus God does hold us responsible for carrying his message to others. If we pass along the wrong message or if we just fail to pass along the message, we will be held responsible for the sins of others who might have avoided those sins if we had done our job. That's right, we can be held guilty for the things others do wrong even though they are not guilty because they did not know it was wrong. God holds us responsible for the wrongs that occur due to our failure to do our jobs. Thank God for grace! But as we will learn, that grace is dependent upon our willingness to really try to do God's will.

A Vengeful God

Does God seek vengeance on those who turn against him or intentionally ignore him? Yes, he certainly does. But too often we see the vengeance and miss the awesome grace. In truth, we need to see both.

There have been many cases, more so in the past but still present in these times, when preachers have sought to frighten their congregations into what they have defined as correct thinking or correct behavior. The case of a person who has not submitted to God's authority over his or her life is extremely frightening, and this fear is almost always the first motivating factor that causes a person to seek God. But in too many cases this approach has involved continued graphic descriptions of God just waiting to punish each person for any deviation from whatever the specific preacher might be defining as the "true path," regardless of whether a person is or is not a Christian. Such preaching can be very motivating for legalistic and external obedience, but its results rarely include the change of heart and the focus on living in Christian love that make up saving faith. And while this approach may provide legalistic motivation for people who are members of the group, it generally repels most outsiders.

Make no mistake, God really is a jealous God—he says so himself (see Exodus 20:5 and similar passages). That means that he will not put up with those who claim to serve him but actually keep their focus on this world and its treasures and pleasures. He will judge each person in a final judgment, and he will send those who choose to live in rebellion against him to an eternity in torment. God does reserve to himself the right of vengeance against anyone who rejects his authority.

But contrary to what some teach and what even some Bible translations indicate, God rarely if ever punishes us for our sins in this life and he definitely does not punish children for the sins of their parents or ancestors. Sin itself brings enough pain and suffering without God having to add to that. But isn't it God who established the nature of sin such that it would cause such pain and suffering and death? The Bible seems to teach this, and it is entirely reasonable for God to want sin to bring suffering in order to teach us how dangerous sin really is, but it is also possible that as sin separates us from God, that very separation from our creator brings with it all the pain and suffering and death associated with sin. It is also possible that there is some combination of these causes. The point is, in this world the distribution of pain and suffering is not fair—judgment and ultimate reward (whether good or bad) are for eternity. The final judgment that brings righteous resolution for all the deeds of this life does not come in this life.

Children do suffer because of their own sins and the sins of their parents or ancestors. Sin brings all sorts of suffering both to the family of the sinner and to everyone else in the world. Again, sin is not fair in the suffering it brings. But this suffering is something we ourselves bring on our own world and everybody in it, including our families; it is not something God imposes individually to punish us for our sins or the sins of our ancestors.

In Exodus we have a record of God revealing himself to Moses. This revelation was not as a physical form, but in the form of a spiritual revelation of who God is. (That should not be surprising since God is spirit.) In this passage in Exodus, God reveals himself as "merciful and gracious, longsuffering, and abounding in goodness and truth, keeping mercy for thousands, forgiving iniquity and transgression and sin, by no means clearing the guilty, visiting the iniquity of the fathers upon the children and the children's children to the third and the fourth generation" (Exodus 34:6-7 New King James Version or NKJV). Unfortunately, the last phrase in this passage too often receives primary attention, and the meaning seen is generally the wrong meaning. The New International Version (NIV) translation renders the last phrase of this passage as "Yet he does not leave the guilty unpunished, he punishes the children and their children for the sin of the fathers to the third and fourth generation."

The NIV translation is not supported by the original wording and is wrong—and from the context that should be very clear. In the NIV translation, the sentence begins with "Yet he does not leave the *guilty* unpunished [my emphasis]." If we accept the NIV translation, punishing children of the fourth generation would normally have no effect on the guilty because they would have died before seeing that suffering. The NKJV and many other translations leave the interpretation open to another perspective, but many people assume the NIV concept as the correct meaning, even if they have only read something like the NKJV translation.

Notice that the context of the whole passage is about God's mercy, grace, patience, goodness, truth, and forgiveness. Later God inspired Ezekiel to write that God would not punish the sons for the sins of their fathers (see Ezekiel 18), making it clear that the NIV translation must be wrong. So how should we interpret this passage? In fact, the final phrase is another expression of both God's mercy and grace and his resolve to have vengeance on the truly guilty. To understand the real meaning, we need to understand that God does not look at things the same way we do and we need to try to see this from his perspective. In order to do this, let's rephrase the translation maintaining an interpretation consistent with the actual words originally written here. In this case God describes himself as "merciful, gracious, longsuffering, and abounding in goodness and truth—keeping mercy for thousands by forgiving iniquity and transgression and sin; yet in no way clearing the truly guilty, visiting upon them the penalty for the sins they cause in their children and their children's children to the third and fourth generation."

This interpretation is exactly reverse of the NIV translation, but it is a viable way of interpreting the original words of the passage and it is consistent with the context and with what Ezekiel recorded. It is also consistent with Jesus' teaching that it would be better to have a millstone tied around your neck and be thrown into the sea than to cause little children who believe in him to be misled.

Only God can make this backward interpretation work. No one else could even think of holding someone's great-great-grandfather (who is already dead) accountable for the sins he caused in the life of his great-great-grandson. But for God this is no problem at all. When a person sins, God holds that person responsible for his or her sin but he also holds the people responsible who influenced the person to sin.

With God, the real guilt is not in what a person does but rather in why he or she does it. Is an action rebellion, or is it simply ignorance. If it is ignorance, is that ignorance excusable or intentional? Only God can always truly judge these things, so only God can always place the blame exactly where it belongs.

Seeing God as a vengeful tyrant is a negative motivational factor, but seeing God as placing blame for sins exactly where it belongs is motivating. It is motivating to know that God does not hold us accountable for what we unwittingly do, and it is motivating to know that we will be held responsible for how we influence our children and anyone else whose life we affect.

An Uncaring God

Many people experience traumatic events in their lives. When these traumatic events come, a typical response is to ask, "Where was God? Why didn't he protect me from this trauma?" And strangely, that response is actually more common in those who are not Christians or are marginal Christians than among serious Christians. Put slightly differently, the question is, "If there is a God, why didn't he help me with a miracle." After all, what good is a God who doesn't help? This question seems especially appropriate when someone has seen the trauma coming and has earnestly prayed to God, asking that the trauma be miraculously prevented.

I am convinced that God works in and through traumatic events to accomplish his will and that his will is ultimately tied to our own best interests when we take an eternal view, but for now I want to focus on the response of many churches and many individual Christians to questions like these. What many Christians do is not helpful. Sometimes we talk about our inability to see things from God's perspective, but that is not entirely true because God has given us the information to allow adequate insight into his perspective. We can see at least enough of God's perspective to understand something of the role God has for trauma in our lives. Sometimes we simply say that "Everything happens for a reason." as if that were helpful. In fact, there is not a good logical reason why the general effects of human sinfulness should cause one person to suffer unbelievable trauma while another person seems to be immune to such suffering. Sin is never fair.

So responses like these are not very comforting. From the perspective of the one suffering the trauma, this sounds like platitudes with no substance—perhaps because it is. We need to understand that in most cases the traumas of this life will continue without God's interference because it is exactly these traumas that should teach us how bad sin really is—and that lesson is certainly among the most important lessons God wants us to learn. I am convinced that if we do not learn to hate sin, we cannot hope to inherit heaven.

Given this view, what should we do as Christians? Whether or not we understand the details about God's perspective, we can with absolute confidence declare that God does love, God does care, and God will provide the strength needed for each trauma if we will only trust him. And if we understand at least the aspects of God's perspective that should be obvious, we can with absolute confidence declare that while God did not cause this trauma (the environment of sin we have created did that), he will work through it for the good of anyone who is willing to trust him. Further, I believe we can with absolute confidence declare that once through the trauma, the reasons for the trauma can almost always be understood if we honestly let God reveal them. We can state with confidence that at the proper time, God will show the good that can come from the trauma to anyone willing to trust him.

When people are experiencing trauma, they tend to ask "Why?" But rarely if ever do they really want to know the answers while dealing with the trauma. In the past, I made the mistake of offering to provide answers to those who were asking, "Why?" Without exception, when I tried to provide answers to the questions being asked, the person asking the questions simply ignored the answers. He or she would sometimes change the subject immediately, offering no opportunity to even give the answers requested. In other cases I provided the answers, but the person asking responded as if no answer had even been offered. In each case the person did not reject or deny the answers, he or she just was not interested in the answers.

I finally realized that people facing trauma are not really asking "Why?" even when they say that they are. They are actually using this question to simply say "I am hurting" as forcefully as they can. And they want to find someone to blame other than themselves. Over and over the Psalmists asked God "Why?" And over and over the answer in the presence of the trauma was "Trust God, he does care." In the midst of the trauma, that is what we need to hear. Christians who have trusted God in the midst of trauma may not be able to say why this is true, but when trauma comes again, they always find it is easier to trust God after having experienced that his grace and comfort are sufficient.

People dealing with trauma need a hug and someone who will listen and let them vent. But they also need someone who comes with God's Holy Spirit to provide assurance that God does really care—that God is the only one who can take what truly is terrible and turn it into something good. They need to understand that their suffering is real and valid, but that beyond this suffering God truly can bring joy. "Hold on my child, joy comes in the morning—weeping only lasts for the night[9]."

A very different problem in this same general area is that we have not convincingly answered the world's argument that God could not possibly care about us. From the world's perspective, we are an almost infinitely small part of an almost infinitely large universe, so it does not make sense (from human logic) that God would have much interest in us one way or another. And as for the evidence of the Bible that God does care, the world argues that this "evidence" is a combination of myths and misunderstandings—that everything in the Bible can be explained away without reference to God. God's whole creation is explained away as the result of natural processes and random chance. What a terribly de-motivating perspective!

We as Christians have repeatedly insisted on holding to interpretations of the Bible long after they have been clearly shown to be wrong, and in doing this the world has even seen us use lies and deceit against obvious truth. No wonder the world doubts our testimony!

9 From "Joy Comes in the Morning" by Bill and Gloria Gaither, © 1974.

Furthermore, in far too many cases we have not demonstrated the Christian love God demands of us any better than people who have no association with the church. The means that God has ordained to demonstrate his love and mercy and caring to the world is through the church. But we spend most of our budgets on ourselves to purchase more and more ornate church buildings and more and more expensive entertainment and comfort.

I knew of a church whose building had been lovingly built many years ago. The love that God meant that church to lavish on the needy of the community wound up lavished on the building. The building included handmade stained glass windows that were true works of art. At the time that I was aware of this church, the attendance and financial support had dwindled to the point that almost the entire budget of the church was dedicated to insuring and maintaining those windows. I firmly believe that if Jesus had come into their midst, the first thing he would have done would have been to get rid of those windows—probably throwing bricks through them. Jesus is not against art—he invented it. And there are certainly times when art is very helpful in presenting the gospel. But when a church can no longer minister to the needs of the community because its resources are totally dedicated to works of art, it is time to either sell or simply destroy the art and get back to ministry. The greatest work of art in the world is a soul given to God's service.

Sometimes it's artworks, sometimes it's technology, sometimes it's ministers' salaries, but whenever a church's resources are not involved in active ministry in the community, the message to the community is that God does not care (see 1John 3:17). But the incarnation and crucifixion stand out over all of this to demonstrate just how much God does care!

We may be one tiny part of one small solar system in one modest-sized galaxy in one corner of an almost infinite universe, but God still cares. For him, creating an entire universe just to serve one creation is not a problem. We should never judge God by our standards, and we should boldly answer this challenge with a response of faith and love that shows the living God at work in our lives.

A Genocidal God

Is God sometimes genocidal? Absolutely! But if we learn to see this from his perspective, we will find that, as strange as it may seem, love is at the core of his actions even when he has to be genocidal.

Numbers and Deuteronomy provide a record of God's instructions to Moses and the Israelites to utterly destroy the inhabitants of Canaan, including men, women, children, and even babies. These instructions are given as God's revealed will—instructions to commit genocide. 1Samuel provides of a record of Samuel's instruction to King Saul to destroy the tribe of Amalek, again including men, women, children, and even nursing babies. And again these genocidal instructions are given as God's revealed will. In both of these cases we have men who clearly represented God—through whom God spoke. So how can we justify worshipping a God who gives such genocidal commands?

This is another case where we need to see things from God's perspective—something that we can never do perfectly, but that we can do well enough to deal with this issue. In Genesis we have a clue in a passage describing how God told Abraham that his descendants would eventually inherit the land of Canaan (what we now call Palestine or Israel). At that time God said that this would not take place until "the fourth generation" (Genesis 15:14). The reason God gives for this delay is that "the iniquity of the Amorite inhabitants is not yet total" (Genesis 15:16). Another clue to God's perspective may be found in the account of the destruction of Noah's world. In that account we read that just prior to the destruction, "Jehovah saw that man's wickedness in this world was overwhelming and that everything in people's minds was only constant evil" (Genesis 6:5). And another clue may be found in the account of the destruction of Sodom and Gomorrah. In that account we read how Abraham tried to argue against God's plan to destroy these cities, and how God agreed that if there were ten righteous men in these cities, the cities would not be destroyed. But God knew that there were not even ten people in these cities who were not in complete rebellion (see Genesis 18).

In other words, while the Bible does not explicitly state this, it seems apparent that God destroys a culture when that culture is so evil that no one born into that culture has any hope of finding God. From God's perspective, when a culture reaches that point every baby born into that culture would be doomed to hell from birth. And from God's perspective, any innocent person (baby or otherwise) who dies is far better off receiving eternity in God's paradise than if he or she were to continue to live in this world and end up in eternal torment. In other words, when God sees a culture completely given over to such absolute sinfulness, the most loving thing he can do for the infants and the unborn is to end it as quickly and completely as possible.

But no human can make this call. Only God knows when a culture has reached the point of no return. Any human who claims to have the right to call for such a "holy war" had better be performing the miracles and teaching the truths consistent with Jesus' message of love to show that he or she truly is a messenger from God. Judgment is God's job, not ours. In truth, there is never such a thing as a "holy war," but in these exceptional cases there may be a war that accomplishes what a holy God sees as necessary.

I knew a family whose small daughter suffered from a disease attacking half of her brain. Left alone, the disease would have spread throughout her brain and would have killed her. There was no medicine that could stop or cure the disease or restore the functionality of the half of her brain being attacked. Eventually the surgeons had to remove half of her brain to save her life. While she still has some minor limiting factors in her ability to move about, she is a bright, active young lady. Now, if a criminal had used a gun to destroy half of her brain, we would consider that a terrible crime, but we consider the surgeons who removed half of her brain wonderful life saving people.

Just consider how a primitive tribesman who has never seen anything but a small part of his jungle home area would react to suddenly being able to see open heart surgery. When God commands genocide, he is acting as a surgeon to remove a diseased entity that threatens to eternally destroy too much of his creation. Viewed from this perspective, that action should not surprise us. It is actually an expression of God's love.

Or think of this from a military perspective. In a war, generals may have to send soldiers into situations certain to result in the death of all of those involved in order to preserve the main military force and the nation for which they battle. Often these are heart-wrenching decisions for such officers, but in the end they must put the good of the country ahead of the good of a portion of the military.

I realize that there are groups claiming to be Christian and carrying out terrorism supposedly in the name of the God of Christianity. Humans do not have the authority to act on God's behalf in such ways. Jesus intentionally saw to it that his disciples had a sword when he knew he was about to be arrested. When the mob arrived to arrest

Jesus, a leader of his disciples named Peter pulled out a sword and tried to cut off the head of one of the leaders in the mob. (He only got the man's ear, but Peter was not a trained swordsman.) At that point Jesus made it clear that armed conflict was not to be the way of his people. He even healed the wound that Peter had caused. (See Matthew 26:51-52; Mark 14:47; Luke 22:50-51; and John 18:10-11.) We can never spread the gospel of love with weapons of destruction.

Someone may question the effects of having humans carry out the genocide as in the case of the Israelites who fought in Canaan or against the Amalekites. Why didn't God just wipe out the cultures of Canaan and Amalek like he did the cultures of Noah and the people of Sodom and Gomorrah? Again we need to consider the matter from God's perspective. The Israelites were being called to a level of righteousness unknown in the ancient world—a level of righteousness they had no way of comprehending culturally. They needed to understand that God is very serious about ending the rebellion, and having them totally destroy such completely corrupt cultures was a powerful way to teach this lesson. Even with this experience, it was a long time before the Israelites finally grasped the importance of this message, but the record of this experience eventually contributed to that understanding.

The message is that God cares about the rebellion and he will do whatever it takes to lead as many people as possible to end the rebellion. Once we end our rebellion, God is on our side and nothing and no one can stand against us. But the rebellion must end.

Yes, God has committed genocide and he has ordered humans to commit genocide. As stated above, only God can know when this is necessary. He acts as a surgeon cutting out a malignant cancer. If a person who has no medical training were to cut out vital organs from another person's body, that act would be considered a heinous crime. But if a surgeon cuts out the same vital organs knowing that they are cancerous, he is considered a life-saver. God knows when the cancer of sin becomes so malignant that it must be removed, and in his love for mankind, he will remove the malignancy. God cares about those who must die, but the malignancy must be removed.

When we see this from God's perspective, the message no longer appears so terrible. In fact, it is motivating. It is motivating because it teaches us how important it is to never allow our culture to become evil enough to require such measures, and it is motivating to know that God cares enough about us that he will do whatever is necessary to protect us from ourselves.

A Perfectionist God

Many people have a concept of God as a perfectionist who demands absolute perfection from his human followers—and since this is an impossible goal it is a negative motivational factor in the lives of people who hold this view. This view leads to a constant guilt complex, and misused passages in the Bible can add to this complex.

A typical example of an often misunderstood biblical passage that is used to support such thinking is found in Jesus' Sermon on the Mount. This sermon is found in the Gospel of Matthew chapters 5, 6, and 7. In the fifth chapter, Jesus goes over a list of things that had often been understood legalistically by religious leaders, and he then insists that in each case God wants us to focus on the intent rather than legalistic obedience. In other words, God wants us to have our hearts right first and let our actions flow from that. When we see Jesus' standard spelled out, we find that it is a standard no one could live up to perfectly. Yet the last verse of this chapter is generally translated something like this: "Therefore you shall be perfect, just as your Father in heaven is perfect" (Matthew 5:48 NKJV). If we take this verse as translated and apply it with modern English meaning, we have a command from our Lord that we must be as perfect as God. A sane response would be to give up immediately because no human could ever accomplish this.

The good news here is that the English translations do not convey to our generation the true meaning of Jesus' words. In our culture which is so focused on science, the term "perfect" implies an absolute standard with no flaws at all. But in Jesus' time that was not the case. In fact, the word Jesus used that is translated "perfect" in this passage actually means "full grown" or "mature" rather than absolutely perfect. This is a command to Jesus' disciples to have the kind of spiritual maturity that Jesus has been describing in this chapter—a maturity focused on the spiritual factors that are God's focus rather than on the worldly factors that are so often the human focus. In Jesus' culture, an animal or a fruit or grain could be described as "perfect" when it was full grown, even though there would always be some deviation from absolute perfection. Paul wrote to the Christians in Corinth saying, "Brethren, do not be children in understanding, however, in malice be babes, but in understanding be mature" (1Corinthians 14:20 NKJV). In that passage, the word translated "mature" is exactly the same as the word translated "perfect" in Matthew 5:48.

Now, an animal or fruit or grain that was full grown but badly disfigured would not normally be described as "perfect" in Jesus' culture, and that fits with this passage. Jesus does not intend to imply that serious spiritual problems are OK. Properly understood, this passage is a command to discipleship—to growing up as God's child to live in the spiritual image of God—that image for which God originally created us.

God knows that we are not perfect and that absolute perfection is beyond our capability. Jesus never commanded us to do what we cannot do. Years into his ministry as an apostle, Paul wrote,

> We know that God's law is spiritually focused, but I am flesh, sold as a slave to sin. I don't even understand what I'm doing, for what I want to do is not what I actually practice—in fact, what I truly hate is what I actually do. So if I am doing what I actually wish I were not doing, I must agree that God's law is good. So it is not the real spiritual me that is doing these evil things, but the power of the master of my fleshly nature, the sin within me. I know that there is nothing good living in my fleshly humanity—the desire to do the spiritual good is in my spirit, but I can't find a way to live up to the desire. In the end I don't do the good that I desire to do—instead I practice the evil that spiritually I do not want to do. So if I am doing the very things that I really do not want to do, it is not really me doing these things—it is the sin-master that I gave control of my fleshly life long ago. I find it a rule of life then that evil is always present with me—the very one who desires so much to do good. In my spiritual life I actually delight in God's law, but I see another law active in my fleshly self, warring against the law I hold sacred in my mind and bringing me into captivity to the law of this sin-master in my fleshly body. O what a wretched man I am! (Romans 7:14-24).

Now, it's important to understand that Paul immediately follows this with his eloquent cry of victory in Christ who has taken away the condemnation brought by our sinfulness. But the point here is that even the great apostle Paul, years after becoming an apostle and one of the greatest leaders of Christianity, was still a sinner. In our human nature, though we can and must grow spiritually, we can never completely live up to God's standards. And the apostle John, very late in his life, wrote,

> If we claim that we are not sinners, we're just adding to our sin by lying to ourselves—the truth just isn't in us. If we admit to our sins, Jesus is faithful and lives up to his promise to forgive our sins and to thoroughly cleanse us from every unrighteous thing we've done. But if we say that we haven't sinned at all, we are calling him a liar and his essence is not living in us (1John 1:8-10).

These men were apostles of God and their lives were as dedicated to God as any human's life could be, yet they knew that they were still very imperfect humans. The proper understanding of passages such as the one in Matthew 5:48 is discipleship. Salvation is a growth process. We are fully and completely saved as soon as we decide to turn our lives over to God and let Jesus be the true Lord of our daily living—no matter how imperfectly we initially implement this decision. This is the end of our rebellion, but it is not the end of our sinfulness. Satan will still overpower us over and over. We will still slide back into old sinful habits. And in our ignorance we will commit grave sins without even seeing our sinfulness at the time. Salvation is all about growth. Our acceptance of Jesus' Lordship is very imperfect at the beginning, but as we grow up spiritually we come closer to the spiritual maturity to which he calls us (see Ephesians 4:11-16, etc.). If we are not growing spiritually, he is not our Lord, and we are not Christians.

Matthew 5:48 challenges us to grow up in the spiritual image of our heavenly Father, just as we grow up in the physical image of our earthly fathers. It is a call to spiritual maturity, not a demand for absolute perfection. A better translation of this passage to communicate the meaning to our culture would be, "In light of all of this, you must mature with the same kind of spiritual maturity that you find in your Heavenly Father."

Multiple Gods

Earlier I argued that any true religion must teach the obvious truth that ultimately there can be only one God, and I limited the acceptable candidates for a true religion to only those that teach this truth. But sometimes Christians actually talk as if there are three gods—something the Bible definitely does not teach. I one time heard a minister explain in his sermon that God the Father was like the chairman of the board, that Jesus was the chief executive officer, and that the Holy Spirit was like the chief operating officer. Another time I heard a minister describe how God discussed his plan of salvation with Jesus. There is a popular gospel song about God searching all over heaven for someone willing to die for mankind. I even had a professor in seminary who clearly indicated that he thought in terms of three separate gods. None of this is right or biblical.

In fact, these teachings become a serious problem for Christians trying to reach Muslims or Jews who clearly believe in just one God. But more to the point for the purposes of this book, these teachings confuse Christians, and that damages motivation. I was present one time when a minister asked his congregation how many gods there are, and no one in the congregation felt able to answer that question. I saw almost the same thing happen in a large Sunday school class. And saying that God is three different persons but just one God is not helpful—either it is nonsense or it means that God has the mental illness called multiple personality disorder. The Bible never says anything like that.

The New Testament clearly teaches that Jesus lived on this earth as God incarnate—that is, as God living in a human body, and that his divine being is eternal from before time began and until forever. The New Testament also clearly teaches that this same God lives in Christians as the Holy Spirit. But this does not make three gods. Let's examine some things that the Bible says that can help us.

The best place to begin is with two things that Jesus said. First we need to look at how Jesus answered a scribe who had asked him which commandment from God is primary. Jesus said,

> The first commandment of all is this: "'Listen, O people of Israel. The Lord our God is the one and only God—and you must love the Lord your God with your whole heart, with your whole mind, and with all your strength.' This is the primary commandment" (Mark 12:29-30).

Notice that Jesus did not start his response by quoting the commandment itself—he started by quoting the verse before this commandment (Deuteronomy 6:4), unequivocally stating that there is one and only one God. Jesus never said or implied that there could be more than one God.

The next thing to look at is something Jesus said to a Samaritan woman. When Jesus told the woman that he knew that she had been married several times and was living with a man without being married, she tried to change the subject to something religious by asking whether people should worship in Jerusalem or on a mountain in Samaria. In his response Jesus said,

> The time has come for true worshippers to worship the Father in spirit and in truth, for the Father is looking for just such people to worship him. God is spirit, and those who would worship him must worship him in spirit and in truth (John 4:23-24).

In this statement the one point we need to understand for this discussion is that God is spirit. He may take on any form that he chooses at any time that he chooses for any length of time that he chooses, but his essential nature is spiritual, not physical. When he takes on a physical form, it is the spirit—not the physical form—that is God. And no physical form can contain all there is of God, though God can certainly be present in a physical form.

When God appeared to men like Moses and Elijah, the biblical account never mentions any physical form. The description is always spiritual. And as a spirit, God is not limited in location; he can be one and still be anywhere and everywhere at once.

In the Old Testament, God's spirit often entered humans giving them supernatural power or insight. The only difference between that and Jesus is the lack of limitation in Jesus. When God comes into a human's life, that presence must be very limited due to the sinfulness of our nature. Jesus had no sin—he never rebelled. The point of the virgin birth was a new creation free from the inherited tendency to rebel. As a human, Jesus was subject to all the same temptations as any of us are, but he did not have the same spiritual weakness and blindness with which we are born. As Paul said, Jesus was like a new Adam (see Romans 5 and 1Corinthians 15)—like starting over from the beginning.

It was obviously not Jesus' body that made him God. Otherwise either he would have to have come into the world as a full grown body or he would have to have existed as a zygote in eternity until time for him to be born. God is spirit. Jesus' body was flesh and bone. And the presence of God's Holy Spirit within Jesus did not completely overwhelm his human nature. The Bible tells of times when Jesus was surprised by someone's faith (for example see Matthew 8:10) or when Jesus wept with human emotion (see John 11:35). But beyond the human nature Jesus possessed as a human being was the unlimited presence of God's own spirit. God, the God who is spirit, spoke through the human Jesus because Jesus knew the mind of God from the Spirit of God within him and he willingly served as the conduit for God's message. As Jesus said, "The things that I'm saying to you I don't say on my own [that is, in my human capability], but the Father who dwells in me accomplishes the tasks" (John 14:10) Jesus the human was always completely in tune with God—he never rebelled at all.

But although there was no limit to God's presence in Jesus' human nature, that does not mean that all of God was present in Jesus. In fact Jesus himself said "There is more to the Father than just me" (John 14:28). At the beginning of the Gospel of John the apostle gives us a clue to Jesus' divine nature when he describes Jesus as the Word. Without going into all the background behind this usage, what this would have communicated to that culture is that Jesus embodied every aspect of God related to this creation—that the concept of creation and the power of creation and the "laws of nature" that maintain this creation were all embodied in the spiritual divine nature that we saw in Jesus, as well as everything that would be useful for us to know of God. In other words, in Jesus dwelt the very essence of God that brought about this creation. This is why Jesus could say, "Anyone who has experienced me has experienced the Father" (John 14:9).

The God who gave the law to Moses is the same as the God humans met in Jesus. The God who breathed life into Adam is that same God. The God who came into Samson and David and others came into Jesus in a manner infinitely exceeding what he had ever done before. Those humans who have experienced the presence of God's Holy Spirit in power know how powerful that presence is. But while there are similarities in this experience compared to what Jesus experienced, as sinful humans we can only experience a very small portion of what Jesus could and did experience.

Evidence of this relationship may be seen in the crucifixion. For all of his life, Jesus had never known a moment's separation from the unlimited presence of God's Holy Spirit in his life. Never once had he turned against God or rebelled in any way. Never once had he experienced any separation from his heavenly Father. Never once had he known the pain of sin that we have experienced all our lives to such an extent that we hardly notice it anymore. Then on the cross God placed the burden of all of our sins on him (see 2Corinthians 5:21). We cannot imagine the trauma of going from absolute sinlessness to absolute sin in a moment. But because God cannot be where sin is, at that same moment God's Holy Spirit left Jesus for the first time in his life. Once again there is no way we can even begin to understand the trauma. For those of us who have experienced the awesome joy of the presence of God's Holy Spirit in our lives, there is some hint of what this might have been, but we have never experienced anything that would come close to this. It's no wonder that Jesus cried out from the cross, "My God, my God—why have you deserted me?" (Matthew 27:46). I know the pain of losing my beloved wife of 31 years to cancer, and after more than 10 years that topic still brings me to tears, but that was nothing compared to the pain Jesus felt when God's spirit left him.

So Jesus was a man, but a man in whom God lived—and a man willing to give that up to die for us. Because God lived in him without any limitations, he was truly God incarnate, Immanuel, God with us. He could honestly say, "I and my Father are one and the same" (John 10:30). This is not two gods, it is one spiritual God who came in the man Jesus and walked among us. In Gethsemane the man Jesus verbalized his communication with the spiritual God who lived in him, expressing his strong desire to avoid the trauma he knew must accompany his death, but still submitting.

But what about the Holy Spirit? What has been said so far should make this easier to deal with, but there are some things Jesus said that may help even more. Very close to the time he was to be arrested and crucified, Jesus told his disciples that he was going away but that he would send "the Comforter" (sometimes translated "helper" or "counselor" and also identified in this conversation as "the Spirit of Truth" and "the Holy Spirit") to be with them (see John 14-16). But in promising this helper Jesus said, "I will not leave you orphaned—I will come to you" (John 14:18). Just before saying that, Jesus spoke to his disciples about this helper saying, "You know him because he is living with you now [in other words, he was present as Jesus] and will be in you" (John 14:17). He told the disciples that if he did not go away, this helper could not come. The point is that the Holy Spirit is simply the Spirit who lived in Jesus—in other words, God. This is why the King James Version translators used the term "Holy Ghost"—that is, the ghost of Jesus. They translated this word "ghost" only when spoken of as the "Holy Ghost." In all other cases they translated the same word "spirit." Those translators were trying to get the point across that the Holy Spirit is the divine Spirit that lived in Jesus as he ministered in this world.

In other words, the God we meet in the Old Testament is exactly the God we meet living in Jesus and is also the God who lives in us as Christians. In writing to the Christians in Rome Paul said,

> Your lives, on the other hand, are not focused on this fleshly life—you are focused on the Spirit (assuming the Spirit of God actually lives in you). But anyone who does not have the Spirit of Christ is not a Christian (Romans 8:9).

Note that the Spirit is mentioned three times in this one verse: first as "the Spirit," then as "the Spirit of God," and finally as "the Spirit of Christ." Paul clearly recognized the truth that the Holy Spirit is the Spirit of Christ is the God who is Spirit. This does not mean that there is no trinity, there truly is, but all three share the same Spirit and personality and at no time does God the Father have to explain his plan to God the son, because as Jesus said, "The Father and I are one" (John 10:30) and again "Anyone who has experienced me has experienced the Father" (John 14:9).[10]

Our fleshly human minds have difficulty with such concepts, and there are aspects of this that we will never understand and that we have no need to understand—aspects that are better left alone for this life. The important thing that we can grasp is that this one spiritual God is the only God, and that he was present in Jesus and is present in us.

We tend to think of God as limited to just one place at a time or as having to have two parts in order to be in two places at once. That just is not the case for God. We know from God's own word that no sinful human could survive a meeting with God "face-to-face" as it were (see Exodus 33:20). Our damaged nature could not stand such an encounter with God. But since God is spirit, he could come in Jesus in a way that would give us access to every understanding of

10 I know I may be accused of the heresy of Modalism here. Modalists teach that Christ Jesus is not eternally God, but that is nonsense. The New Testament makes it very clear that everything has been created through him, and that he is God from the very beginning (see John chapter 1, etc.). Modalists teach that both the Father and the Son have somehow been replaced by the Holy Spirit, but that too is nonsense. Jesus stated that he would be with his disciples to the end of the age (Matthew 28:20). But there is only one Spirit and one mind and one personality, and that divine eternal Sprit lives in Jesus and in us. And there is no passage in the Bible that even hints that there are multiple gods or that the Father, the Son, and the Holy Spirit are anything but one in Spirit and personality.

God that we could handle while limiting the experience to what we could stand. And he could also come into us as Christians in a way that would provide us with access to everything we need without destroying us in the process—a presence that can grow as we mature spiritually. We are like the blind men who cannot see that the different things they are experiencing are all part of one elephant.

An Illustration

To illustrate this, let's draw a picture. The first thing in the picture is something kind of like the sun with rays extending out in all directions. Let's think of this as the God who is spirit with his spiritual nature extending out in all directions to all places. Now, if we show one of these rays extending to a man on earth (let's say Moses), that would not be another god or a different personality, it would be Moses in contact with the one God. It would be as impossible for Moses to experience all of God as it would be for one of us to swim on the surface of the sun, but that does not mean that Moses did not experience God. However, Moses' experience of God had to be limited in duration and scope or he could not have survived.

Next, let's take away Moses and draw another man on earth, but this time instead of a single ray from our sun-like image, let's draw a wide band of light coming from the same area of our sun-like image. (Do not confuse God with the sun; this illustration is about our spiritual God, not about our sun.) Let's think of this man as Jesus who is constantly one with God with no limitations related to duration or scope. He is the eternal spiritual God walking among us in all the fullness we could stand to experience. He is not another god or a different personality of God. We might think of him as an extension of the one God or as a pipeline though whom we can see God directly. (Remember, all illustrations break down at some point. This is just to help visualize something that cannot ever be fully described in human language.)

Now let's remove Jesus from the earth and from the same area of our sun-like image let's draw a whole lot of rays reaching to a whole lot of people. These people are not experiencing another god or a different personality of God, they are experiencing the same God who inspired Moses and who lived in the human Jesus.

Thus God has revealed himself in three ways—first as the ultimate, eternal God whom no one has ever seen or experienced but who has told us of his existence through prophets like Moses; then as the God who is the very source of our universe and of all life who walked among us in the human Jesus; and finally as the very personal presence of his Holy Spirit in each of us. Each way we have experienced God adds to our knowledge of this one spiritual God, and when we come to him we need to focus on him as he has revealed himself to us in all three ways.

To help us understand, there is an interesting fact about people's concept of children in biblical times. Until fairly recent times, people knew nothing about genetics and DNA. Microscopes were not available. Most people were familiar with farming, but none were familiar with microbiology. Farmers would know how to get new crops every year: you took a seed from a plant and put it into the soil, and a plant would grow from the seed. That was easy to observe. The farmer also knew that the soil could have a significant effect on how the plant grew or whether it grew at all. If the plant did not grow, the soil must be barren.

Using this same thought process, people could easily see that in the human reproduction process, the man planted the seed in the woman. In their thinking, the woman was the soil. They knew nothing about fertilizing an egg—they never saw the egg of a human and the eggs of animals only appeared after the male planted the seed. Thus a child came from the father, not the mother. The mother was only the soil, and while the soil might affect how the child grew, the child still came from the father alone. This is why Paul wrote "For man does not come from woman, but woman from man" (1Corinthians 11:8) and "As the woman comes from the man, so also the man is born through the woman" (1Corinthians 11:12). It is why the author of Hebrews wrote about Levi being inside his great-grandfather, Abraham (see Hebrews 7) so that what Abraham did, in a sense Levi did.

Using this concept, to speak of Jesus as the son of God was to make him equal with God, an extension of God. John wrote, "That is why the Jews wanted all the more to kill Jesus, because not only was he breaking their Sabbath rules, but he was even calling God his own Father, making himself equal with God" (John 5:18). So, there are not three gods, and God does not have three different personalities. There is one God whom we have experienced through prophets who heard from him, through Jesus who personifies him, and through his own Holy Spirit.

I'll admit that I may be all wrong about this perspective, but to me it seems to fit the biblical information better than other explanations I've read. I would encourage readers to consider what the Bible says and try to find a solution that does not give people so much difficulty understanding the key point that there is one and only one God and that he is not restricted to a human body.

Summary to This Point

So there is a God, and he does reveal himself, and Christianity is the one true religion for today—though a non-Christian can be saved by faith (that is, by honestly trying to live up to what he or she knows of God's will). Conversely, as with the Jews, a nominal Christian who knows the gospel message but neglects or refuses to really try to live up to what he or she knows to be God's will is lost.

Given this, it is important for Christians, and especially Christian leaders, to know what the Bible teaches about what Christianity really is (not all the details—no one ever gets there—but the important key features). Anyone with any knowledge of Christianity should know that faith, hope, and love are central to Christian teaching, with love being the dominant theme of Christianity. In the next three chapters we'll look closely at these three areas, and I believe that many Christians and Christian leaders will find that there is more to these aspects of Christianity than most Christians have understood.

CHAPTER FOUR: LOVE—THE ULTIMATE COMMANDMENT

In whatever way you wish people would treat you, that's the way you must treat them – Matthew 7:12

Regardless of your background or the level of your faith, if you have made it this far, I strongly encourage you to read the remaining chapters carefully, preferably with a Bible by your side. Each chapter will provide insights that are important for all Christians and for any real understanding of what Christianity is all about. Before we are through, you should understand why a loving God created a world where sin is possible, gave humans the ability to sin, and then placed the one means of sin right in front of them, knowing that this must lead to Calvary. But we need to start with love.

In writing to the Christians in Corinth Paul said, "Now we have these three abiding factors: faith, hope, and love; but the greatest of these is love" (1Corinthians 13:13). Love is certainly the first key principle of Christianity. After all, God is love (see 1John 4:8). It may seem like stating the obvious to say that this is good news, but in fact it is both very good news and very bad news. Properly understood, love provides both the carrot and the stick of motivation—both motivation to want to be Christian and motivation to fear not being Christian. Before we are through with this study, we will find that Christian love is very good news indeed and we will consider some of that good news in this chapter. But while it may seem strange, in this chapter it will be important for us to look closely at how God's message of love can be bad news when we do not live up to it.

Good News—Bad News

The good news of the gospel is truly astonishing good news. The sad fact is that most Christians, when they really grasp how good the news is, will be astonished themselves—they have never really grasped what is truly their birthright. I hope and believe that each person who reads this will come to see the good news of the gospel as more awesome and wonderful than he or she had ever before realized. For anyone who understands this good news, Christianity should represent the most exciting, wonderful, and thrilling aspect of life.

Yet any good news is actually good only in relationship to something that is not as good. This is true of the gospel, and so to fully understand the good news, we must also understand the bad news. This chapter will focus more on the bad news than on the good news—we must start with the bad news or we can never fully grasp the good news. But the message of love does not end there. The following chapters will continue the focus on the Christian love that is the theme of this chapter and provide the good news side of the message from many perspectives. The bad news is sin, and only when we understand how bad that news is can we fully understand how good the good news of the gospel really is.

Sin and Rebellion

Let's start with the fundamental fact that sin—any sin—is always rebellion against God, and that any rebellion against God is always sin. These are just two ways of saying the same thing. Every time a person sins, that person has voted against God's rule in this world and for the rule of evil and Satan—and that is rebellion. An interesting facet of this is that if you believe that God wants you to do something and you decide not to do it, or if you believe God does not want you to do something and you decide to do it anyhow, even if God does not care one way or another about the specific item, your decision to go against what you honestly believed to be God's will is rebellion, and that is always sin.

When Paul wrote his letter to the Roman church, after a brief introductory section, he immediately and dramatically shifted to the concept of sin: "The wrath of God is being revealed from heaven against all godlessness and wickedness of men who suppress the truth by their wickedness" (Romans 1:18). He then continued with his demonstration that "all have sinned and fall short of the glory of God" (Romans 3:23). When Jesus began his Sermon on the Mount, the very first thing he said was, "Blessed are the poor in spirit [that is, those who recognize their spiritual poverty], for theirs is the kingdom of heaven" (Matthew 5:3). This concept is borne out throughout the Bible. We cannot get into the kingdom until we realize that we are absolutely and tragically outside the kingdom—in rebellion against the King and under his condemnation. Who cries out for salvation or rescue? Is it not those who realize that they are lost and beyond their own ability to rescue themselves? This truth applies to Christianity.

The Riptide of Sin

Let's illustrate this with a story about a man we'll call Tom living on the seashore. Imagine that he has just retired and moved to this area, and he loves to take a specially modified inner tube and float in the surf. While he floats, he reads a paperback novel and soaks up the sun. One day he gets caught in a riptide. However, from his perspective floating in the inner tube, all he notices is that clouds in the sky seem to be moving rapidly toward shore. Tom does not realize that the clouds are hardly moving, while he is being drawn rapidly out to die in the sea. In this situation, although he is being pulled to certain death, he feels no danger and would never cry out for help or seek salvation.

It's only when someone on the shore cries out to get his attention that he looks up and realizes that he is in terrible danger. Tom's first thought is to paddle the inner tube toward the shore, but there is no way he can paddle fast enough lying in the inner tube. He is a strong swimmer, so he decides to get out of the inner tube and try to swim to shore. But with his best efforts he can only hold his own against the riptide. Finally he realizes that he needs to be rescued. It is only at this point that he is ready to cry out for help—to seek salvation outside himself and his own efforts.

In the same way, until we realize that we are caught in a "riptide" of sin and that we have no hope of saving ourselves we will not cry out for rescue and we will not be saved. And our normal first reaction to an awareness of our danger will be to try to save ourselves. We may be "pretty good" people; we may be church members; we may even be leaders in the church—if we have not realized our hopeless state and felt the panic that will cause us to sincerely cry out for help, we cannot enter the kingdom of heaven, and there are very good reasons for this. In order to understand how desperately we need salvation, first we need to see the riptide of sin in which we are trapped.

Christian Love as God's Commandment

Jesus said that the first and greatest of all commandments is for a person to love God with all his or her heart, soul, mind, and strength; and the second commandment is to love one's neighbor as oneself. He then said that everything in the Law and the prophets—that is, everything God had ever revealed of his will, hung on those two commandments (see Matthew 22:35-40; Mark 12:28-31; Luke 10:25-28). In fact, in the Sermon on the Mount Jesus said that everything in the Law and the prophets could be summed up in the golden rule: "Whatever you want men to do to you, that's what you are to do to them, for this is the whole message of the Law and the prophets" (Matthew 7:12). After all, as Jesus indicated in Matthew 25:31-46, to care for the needs of others is to care for God. The best way we can show our love for God is by caring for his beloved creatures—our fellow humans. And this is not some hidden message in the Bible—this thought permeates the Bible, from Genesis to the Revelation.

It's important to understand that the love Jesus talked about is not an emotional feeling; it is a matter of the will. This love is unselfish, it cares about the needs of others, it is generous in meeting those needs and in forgiving any transgressions just as God has forgiven our transgressions, and it is active—actively responding to and providing for the needs of others. We can, and indeed Jesus commanded us to, show this kind of love to the people we emotionally hate—our enemies (see Matthew 5:44; Luke 6:27, 35).

If you consider this definition of Christian love, the key is unselfishness. This doesn't mean that a Christian has no self-interest. The unselfishness of the Christian is of this world, because the Christian knows that such unselfishness in this life brings reward beyond comprehension in eternity. This love puts its faith in God to provide the reward. If a person is selfish concerning this world's things, he or she cannot really care about the needs of others or be generous or forgiving.

Just one time in Jesus' ministry, he described the final judgment for his disciples. At that time, Jesus went over the same information four times. As far as I know, there is nothing else Jesus emphasized so strongly in his ministry. This is what he told his disciples:

> When I return as king in my glory with all the holy angels, then I'll be seated on throne of splendor. All the nations will be gathered before me, and I'll separate them one from another as a shepherd divides his sheep from the goats. I'll set the sheep on my right hand, but the goats on the left.
>
> Then I'll say to those on my right hand, "Come to me, because you've won the blessing of my Father. Now you will inherit the kingdom that has been prepared for you since the foundation of the world. This kingdom is yours because when I was hungry, you didn't just give me food, you gave me meat; when I was thirsty, you gave me drink; when I was a homeless stranger, you took me into your home; when I was naked, you gave me clothing; when I was sick, you came to care of me; and when I was in prison, you came to visit me."
>
> Then the righteous will answer, saying, "Lord, when did we see you hungry and feed you or thirsty and give you drink? When did we see you a homeless stranger and take you in, or naked and clothe you? When did we see you sick or in prison and come to you?"
>
> That's when I'll say to them, "I tell you with all my heart, whenever you did these things for one of the least of these my brothers, you did it for me."
>
> Then I'll say to those on my left hand, "Get away from me, you who are under the curse of my Father! You go into to the everlasting fire prepared for the devil and his angels. This condemnation is yours because when I was hungry, you gave me no food at all; when I was thirsty, you gave me nothing to drink; when I was a homeless stranger, you wanted nothing to do with me; when I was naked, you just turned your head away; when I was sick or in prison, you said I deserved to be there and ignored my condition."

> Then they also will answer, saying, "Lord, when did we see you hungry or thirsty or a homeless stranger or naked or sick or in prison and did not minister to you?"
>
> That's when I'll answer them, "I tell you with all my heart, whenever you didn't care enough to do these things for one of the least of these here, you failed to care for me."
>
> And these on the left will go away into everlasting punishment, but the righteous into eternal life (Matthew 25:31-46).

Notice that many of the things church leaders claim are important are not even mentioned in this passage. In essence, Jesus was saying that the judgment would be based on whether or not a person practiced unselfish, caring, generous, forgiving, active love toward others. This should not be a surprise. As we just saw, love is the first key principle of Christianity—it is the very heart and soul of Christianity. After all, it is the very essence of God, for "God is love" (1John 4:8 and 1John 4:16).[11]

So since unselfishness is the core value of Christian love and since failure to love is rebellion against God and therefore sin, then selfishness (including selfish pride) is the very heart and soul of sin. God has commanded us to take care of the needs of others, and we have committed treason by caring for our own wants instead of others' needs. And this world (especially since the advent of television) constantly encourages our selfishness. (One of the deepest pains of my life has been recognizing how Jesus' birthday has been turned into a holiday focused on the selfishness he would so strongly condemn.)

11 There are those who hold that God can only be love because he is three persons and the love is between those three persons. There is no biblical support for this, and I cannot see how that can be true unless there are such differences between them that they become different gods or else God is in love with himself. Saying the words that they are three different personalities but one God does not make this reasonable, and nothing in the Bible indicates that this is the case. Saying that they are separate but one is just a contradiction in terms. These are words made up by men to reach political goals, and I cannot find where they are supported in the Bible. The Father is the source of all divinity. The Son is simply a very powerful extension of the Father (which is consistent with the first century concept of a son being an extension of his earthly father—so well supported biblically). The Holy Spirit is that same extension of God reaching now into our human lives. In other words, there is one God who reaches out to us in multiple ways—one God whom we experience as Father, Son, and Holy Spirit, co-eternal because they are one Spirit.

One area that may need special focus here is the area of pride. In our culture we are encouraged to take pride in what we do and be proud of who we are. Pride actually has two sides, one of which is good and the other is bad. It is good to take pride in being a good steward of the gifts God has given us, but it is important to remember that God is the source of all we have. We did not choose where we would be born, who our parents would be, or what level of wealth they would have, so we have no right to be proud of those things. We did not choose the level of intelligence we would have, how good or bad we would look, how well or poorly our bodies would function, or what talents we would or would not have, so we have no right to be proud of those things. We did not choose who our teachers would be or what kind of learning environment we would have available, so we have no right to be proud of those things. It is good to take pride in being a good steward of these gifts, as long as we recall that they are gifts and that ultimately all of these gifts have their source in God. It good to be aware of the gifts God has given us and it is fine to be aware that in some areas God has given us greater gifts than he has given most others, but it is wrong to consider ourselves inherently better than others because of these gifts or because of the abilities and opportunities we have had to develop these gifts. Pride focused on faithful stewardship of God's gifts is fine, but pride focused on seeing yourself as inherently better than others is part of the worldly selfishness that is the heart and soul of sin. It steals the honor that belongs to God, and it is therefore one more part of our rebellion.

Before we take the next step in this study, just think for a moment what this world would be like if everyone practiced this kind of unselfish, caring, generous, forgiving, and active love. What could be more heavenly? This would not just mean a total absence of war and strife and crime of any sort, it would mean everyone around us was always concerned to meet our needs and do what is best for us—and we would feel the same about them. So God's commandments are getting us ready for what heaven must be. This is extremely important, and we'll come back to this point over and over.

God's Love – The Cross

The whole Bible testifies to the love, mercy, and tenderness of God. As we saw earlier, even those passages that make God appear most cruel, if seen from God's perspective, actually present awesome insights into God's love. As we have learned, when God either directly or indirectly wipes out an entire group of people, we as humans are easily tempted to think in human terms, as if God is like some bratty child who is striking back at someone who hurt him. However, I am convinced that the message of the Bible, if we will bother to notice, is that God does this when and only when a culture or nation or other group of people reaches a point where practically every child born is certain to end up in hell. Too often we view death as a tragedy and as the end, but God sees an entirely different picture.

But the greatest example of God's love is the cross. Without the death of Jesus, none of us could be saved. And we generally fail to grasp just how high a price God paid. This was not just a case of a man being tortured and crucified. If that were all that was involved, many others suffered far worse torture and far worse pain in their crucifixion or other means of death. Pain and suffering does not pay for sin, it never has, and it never will. If it could, then those in hell would have hope—and they do not.

Only one human ever lived without sin, and because he lived his entire life without sin, God was able to live in him in a way we could never comprehend. To meet Jesus was to meet with God. As Paul told the Christians in Colossae, "It pleased God that in him [Jesus] all the fullness of God should dwell" (Colossians 1:19). We already saw how the presence of God's Holy Spirit in Jesus' life is what qualified him to be Immanuel—God with us. The fact that we often think of God in bodily forms causes serious error in our thinking and in our ability to see things from God's perspective. A physical form is limited to one place, but God's Holy Spirit knows no such limitations. Jesus came among us as a human. It was not his fleshly body that was God, it was the unlimited presence of God's Holy Spirit that brought about the incarnation—God in Christ (see 2Corinthians 5:19 and many other similar passages).

Throughout his earthly life, Jesus never knew what it was like to be without God's Holy Spirit fully integrated into his life. Those of us who have experienced the presence of God's Holy Spirit in our lives, although limited by our sinful nature, can get a hint of what Jesus experienced, but only a hint. Throughout his earthly life, Jesus never knew sin or guilt. As a human Jesus could be tempted and he could be surprised, but God living in him as the Holy Spirit without limit was never tempted or surprised.

We experience sin at a very early age, it is all around us and before long we are choosing wrong over what we know to be right.

In this world we can never know the full integration of God's Spirit in our lives that Jesus experienced all his life.

When Jesus went to the cross, suddenly all of this changed. We can never understand all the details, but we know that suddenly Jesus bore the guilt of all the sins of mankind. Sin always hurts us in ways we've grown to ignore most of the time, but for Jesus, this was suffering beyond anything we could comprehend. And that was not all. God cannot be guilty of sin. At this point, God's Holy Spirit left Jesus and he cried out in agony, "My God, my God, why have you deserted me?" (Matthew 27:46). This is another case of suffering we can never comprehend. However, that is still not the whole picture because Jesus died as a man bearing the guilt of all the sin of every person who ever has lived or ever will live. The only possible result was that he would have to experience hell itself, and Peter in his first general letter confirms this (see 1Peter 3:18-20).

As William Barclay pointed out in his Daily Bible Study series, the torture and the crucifixion were just a visual illustration for us, God saying to us, "This is what your sin does to me...this is what your sin [your rebellion] has always done to me." What we can easily see is the pain of the torture and the cross. What we cannot easily comprehend is the far worse suffering of simultaneously taking on the guilt of all humanity and losing all contact with the loving God who has never before been absent for a moment. As the song says, "At the cross, in blood he wrote it: 'God is love,' O hear it, 'God is love.'"[12] Once we understand this, it is no wonder that Jesus, fully human, knelt in prayer and begged God to find another way if at all possible (see Matthew 26:39; Mark 14:36). The most amazing thing was that Jesus found the strength to go through this. For God to allow his beloved son to go through suffering of this magnitude is far, far beyond our comprehension. No wonder God is so adamantly opposed to the rebellion of sin that brought on this suffering!

Christian Love and Rebellion

"But," you may ask, "What does love have to do with sin?" In fact, it has everything to do with sin. If everything God ever told us to do or be can be summed up in commandments to love God and each

12 This line is quoted from a wonderful song that, after extensive searching, I cannot find. I wish I could credit the author.

other, then the opposite must be true. That is, the failure to live up to this standard must be the essence of sin—rebellion against almighty God. It is not murder, stealing, adultery, and lying that constitute the essence of sin. It is not the failure to go to church or study our Bibles or go through the motions of Christianity. It is, instead, the failure to show unselfish, generous, caring love toward God and the same kind of love with forgiveness added toward anyone in need. If we practice such love, all other sins just vanish. Look again at Jesus' description of the final judgment. Those who are condemned are condemned not for what they did (such as murder, theft, abuse, lying, profanity, adultery, etc.), but for what they did not do—for not showing unselfish, caring, generous, forgiving, active love—for not meeting the needs of those in need. And if you think about it, if those who are condemned had been showing this kind of love, the other sins could never have happened.

To illustrate the point, let's say that a division of the army has been ordered to take a particular section of ground from the enemy. If the commander reports back that his troops have killed a thousand enemy soldiers in areas unrelated to his orders, but that the area he was ordered to take has not been touched yet, that commander should be removed from command. Similarly, if we fight against all the popular definitions of sin (rape, murder, abuse, theft, etc.) and do not practice unselfish, caring, generous, forgiving, active love, we are still in rebellion, traitors to God's kingdom.

We need to give this some careful thought. If I get up in the morning and I treat other family members improperly (unnecessary anger, harsh words, sullen behavior, etc.) or if I just fail to be as caring and forgiving as I should, I have sinned and I am in rebellion against almighty God. I have voted for Satan to rule this world instead of God. If I treat fellow employees at work in a way that does not communicate unselfish, caring, generous, forgiving, active love, I have sinned. And my sin is just as bad as murder, because it can actually result in murder. Not that I would physically murder anyone, but that I may cause an expanding influence of ill will that results in someone else committing murder. While that other person is directly guilty, in God's eyes, I would be an accessory just as guilty as the murderer, for if I had demonstrated Christian love toward the person with whom I was dealing, the murderer might never have reached the point where he or she felt compelled to murder. I may have been just one small influence on the murderer, but if I contributed to the circumstances that brought about the murder, I am still guilty as an accomplice. From God's perspective, this is reality. (Even our human legal systems have a similar standard concerning accessories to a crime, though our legal standards cannot be implemented to the extent that God's standard is.)

Husbands, do you ever knowingly and intentionally say or do things that will hurt your wives? Wives, do you ever knowingly and intentionally say or do things that will hurt your husbands? If you do, that is rebellion against God Almighty. You probably even swore before God and witnesses that you would love, honor, and cherish your spouse as long as both of you live. How can we think that it is OK to cast aside those vows and turn them all into lies by treating our marriage partners badly—no matter how much they may deserve such treatment? Our vows said nothing about contingencies.

Parents hurt their children, children hurt their parents, brothers and sisters hurt each other, Christians hurt each other—and we do it knowingly and intentionally. All of this is rebellion against Almighty God. We who are supposed to be his beloved children become traitors—enemies of the kingdom.

And then there is road rage. Someone cuts you off in traffic, someone blows his or her horn at you in traffic, or someone just does not drive the way you think that person should drive in that situation—and suddenly you allow Satan to direct your thoughts and actions. All of this is rebellion against Almighty God. We are caught in this riptide of sin! And the riptide is pulling us into the eternal torment of hell.

Am I trying to scare people into heaven? Absolutely! Read the Bible and you will find the same approach. "The fear of Jehovah God is the very beginning of understanding, but fools despise wisdom and instruction" (Proverbs 1:7). If there were no threat of hell, few if any would ever find the blessings of Christianity and heaven. However, scaring people into conversion does not work unless there is immediate follow-up with a discipleship program that provides the positive motivations of Christianity. The threat of hell is the stick that motivates most people to come into the kingdom, but the joys of the kingdom are the carrot that keeps them growing and keeps the kingdom growing.

When we see ourselves in this perspective as rebels against God and his kingdom, when we realize that every time we react in an unforgiving or an uncaring way toward those around us, when we realize that in every such case we have really rebelled against God, we begin to understand the terrible state of our rebellion. And God's response is not gentle understanding and generous forgiveness—it is adamant rejection of our selfish worldliness. In our natural state of rebellion, God cannot and will not allow us into his eternity, because if he were to do so, we would bring the ruin of rebellion with us. And there is no middle ground. As Jesus put it, "He who is not with me is against me, and he who does not gather the harvest with me scatters it" (Matthew 12:30 or Luke 11:23).

Picture a football team on the field for an important game. The coach has sent orders that are clear, and each player knows his job. Now suppose that one of the players decides that he just doesn't feel like participating, so he stays out of the way of the opposing team to make sure he doesn't get hurt. This player likes to dress in the uniform. He loves the attention he gets from the other students and especially from the cheerleaders. He just doesn't want to risk any injury that might make him less attractive to his fans. The actions of that player would likely allow the opposing team to win the game. No coach would tolerate such a player on his team.

The same is true for Christians. In any church there are always some who enjoy looking like they are part of God's team, but they don't participate in the game (which for Christians is much more than a game). Our failure to show unselfish, caring, generous, forgiving love when we could easily have done so can result in others never accepting the gospel. So our failure to do as we have been commanded to do by our Lord results in someone whom God loves going into eternal torment. In addition, such failures can result in the enemy being able to accuse God's people of not showing love. When some of God's people do not show the love of God, they dishonor God and discredit his people as a whole—and Satan rejoices whenever Christianity gets a bad reputation.

Remember, sin is rebellion against God Almighty, and if unforgiven, it is punishable by hell (which is far worse than anything you or I can imagine). God has told us how he wants us to live, and when we decide to live in a different manner, we are in rebellion against God. We become traitors to his cause. God's anger, his wrath, is being revealed from heaven against those who are in rebellion. After all, it is those in rebellion who have caused the death of Jesus—just as surely as if they had pounded the nails in and thrown the spear. And it is those in rebellion who are sending millions to hell without a clue about the gospel message.

As Hebrews says, "It is a fearful thing to fall into the hands of the living God" (Hebrews 10:31). This is not a game. It is the most serious accusation we could face. We have been warned that we will have to stand trial before the highest court in all eternity on the charge of murder—of causing the crucifixion of the Ultimate Judge's son. There is no escape, there is no bail, and there is no defense we can offer.

Our only hope is the grace of God, and that only applies if we have decided to end our rebellion and truly join God's side.

No Hope of Payment

When we see sin this way, we should realize that each of us is guilty and in terrible trouble. Furthermore, there is nothing we can do to compensate for even one sin. Many people believe that if they do enough good deeds, the good deeds will balance the bad ones and they will get into heaven. This is just not true. Nor can pain or suffering pay for our sins. Jesus told his disciples of a slave owner (Luke 17:7-10) who sent his slave to work in the field all day and then had him prepare the evening meal and serve him. The slave had no permission to eat or rest until the master had been fed. And the master did not thank him, because the slave had just done what he was supposed to do. In the same way, Jesus told his disciples that even when they had done everything they should have done, they should still consider themselves as servants who brought their master no profit, because they had only done what they were required to do.

The lesson of this story is that even if we could do everything God ever wanted us to do, we would not have earned any credit—we would only have done what we were created to do. That might be adequate to get us into heaven if we could do that, but none of us can. And there is nothing we can possibly do for "extra credit." If we spent every moment of our lives doing everything we could possibly do for God, we would simply be "breaking even." The first failure is disastrous rebellion. With that first failure, we join Satan's side and he claims us as his own.

From God's perspective, the difference between a murderer and someone who fails to show unselfish, generous, caring, forgiving love toward others is practically insignificant. Both are in rebellion. Both have chosen Satan's side. Both are under condemnation. This is the great leveler of Christianity, and it is important for every Christian to see and understand this truth. It is the point of Jesus' story about the two debtors—one who owed more than any man could repay, and the other who owed a relatively small amount (Matthew 18:23-35). In this story, Jesus tells of a king who wished to settle accounts with his servants. One of his servants owed (in terms of late 2009) about 24 billion dollars. Since the servant could not repay this debt, the king ordered that everything the man had should be confiscated and the man and his family should be sold as slaves. But when the man begged for time to repay, the king said he would actually forgive the whole debt. In Jesus' story, the king's servant then found a fellow servant who owed him about $6,000. Since this man could not pay his debt, the servant whose debt had been so generously forgiven had this debtor thrown in prison. But when the king heard of this, he reinstated the first servant's debt and sent him to the torture chambers until he could pay the whole debt.

No one can pay for a sin against God or against anyone else. You cannot un-sin a sin. By caring for someone in need, you cannot make up for not caring for someone else when you could have. In Jesus' story, both men were debtors who could not repay their debts—the only difference was how big the debt was. Once we understand how big our debt is, there can be no excuse for not forgiving those who sin against us. When we see our debt as greater than anything we could ever hope to repay, only then can we realize how much we need the awesome grace and mercy of God. Each one of us is caught in a riptide of sin, and we all need the helicopter of God's grace to rescue us, but not one of us could ever pay for that rescue. When we realize how much God has forgiven us, we must be driven to be gracious and merciful and caring toward others. If that does not happen, we are simply adding new sins to our old sins, and God will not forgive either one because forgiving such a person would produce no benefit.

The common response of a person who refuses to forgive is something like, "But you don't know what they did to me!" Once we understand what our rebellion has done to God, how it has contributed to God's beloved creatures being condemned to hell and to the death of God's beloved son, how can we refuse forgiveness to others? How easily God could say of us, "But you don't know what they did to me!" and point to the cross.

As a part of this topic, we need to address something Peter wrote: "And above all things have fervent love for one another, for love covers many, many sins" (1Peter 4:8). This passage is often thought of as teaching that we can pay for a lot of our sins just by loving others, and the words Peter used could be understood that way. However, these same words can mean that practicing love will inherently keep us from a large number of sins. Putting this concept another way, teaching people to practice Christian love will inherently cause them to avoid a whole lot of sins—the topic of Christian love covers many of the topics of sin. Letting the Bible interpret the Bible, the latter meaning is consistent with what Jesus taught, and is also consistent with the context in Peter's letter. We cannot pay for any of our sins—not even one.

The Perspective Satan Wants

One of the most serious dangers for Christians is to think of sin the way Satan wants us to think of sin. He would have us focus on the sins of others as "real" sin, while our own sins are classified as minor or insignificant. He would have us focus on murder, abortion, adultery, homosexuality, pornography, drunkenness, dope addiction, drug pushing, robbery, idolatry, abusiveness, gambling, and profanity. He would not have us focus on gossip, arrogance, boastfulness, faithlessness, ruthlessness, deceitfulness, malice, envy, pride, greed, and the other sins we do commit, lest we see our danger and repent. Yet, when Paul listed the sins that bring God's wrath in Romans 1:29-31, he included all of the ones we don't want to think about.

And remember, it only takes one sin to bring about our condemnation before God. Just one sin puts us in rebellion against God. We are then on Satan's side and we stand under the same condemnation that he faces.

Satan also encourages us to think of our sins as something we can somehow balance with good deeds, as if our good deeds would somehow make up for our sins. Many Christians seriously believe that since their sins are "minor" sins, and since they do a lot of good things, the good things they do will pay for the few minor sins they have committed. With this mindset, people can always justify whatever they do. It is this kind of mindset that ultimately led the Roman Catholic Church to sell indulgences—allowing people to pay for their sins with money even before the sins had been committed.

We need to see the lies in Satan's arguments. We need to understand that we are truly and seriously condemned to hell on our own, and that our only chance of salvation is God's grace. And we need to understand that God's grace is dependent on ending our rebellion.

The Carrot and the Stick

So the "stick" is hell and the knowledge that each of us has far more than enough sin to his or her credit to send all of us to hell. By our own standards, we deserve that condemnation. On the other hand, the carrot begins with a community where Christian love is really practiced and ends in an eternal reward filled with that kind of love (and much, much more).

God demands of us that we be nice to each other at every single opportunity—who could argue that this is wrong? And when people experience other people being nice to them, they want to be part of this—it is motivating! God demands of us that we do the right thing for each other—who could argue that this is wrong? When people do the right thing, they attract others to them—it is motivating! God demands that we learn to forgive those who hurt us—and who could argue that this is wrong. Forgiving always heals the one who forgives and can heal the one who is forgiven, and people who experience such a forgiving community are attracted to it—it is motivating! God demands that we dedicate our lives to loving him and loving each other with unselfish, generous, caring, forgiving, active love—who could argue that this is wrong? When people experience such a loving community, they are attracted to it—it is motivating!

What God demands of us is that we live in exactly the ways that would turn this world into a paradise—for that is how we must prepare to live in the real paradise yet to come. Don't allow Satan to turn you away from something that good!

So Christian love is the first and central principle of Christianity, but if that is true, what is the role of faith and why does God demand faith?

CHAPTER FIVE: FAITH—THE ULTIMATE FOCUS

> *Without faith it is impossible to please God, because anyone who comes to him must believe that he exists and that he rewards those who sincerely seek him – Hebrews 11:6*

Let's focus once again on Paul's words to the Christians in Corinth: "Now we have these three abiding factors: faith, hope, and love; but the greatest of these is love" (1Corinthians 13:13). Love is certainly the first key principle of Christianity, but faith is a very close second. As Paul wrote to the Christians in Rome, "Therefore it's obvious that a man is justified by faith [belief], completely separate from keeping the Law given by Moses" (Romans 3:28). Faith is the key to the door into heaven, but to have the key, we must learn what Christian faith or belief really is. And surprisingly, most Christian groups get that definition wrong.

On the surface, faith seems a simple enough concept, but there is a problem that has plagued the church from the very beginning. The problem is that the word "faith" has a very wide range of meanings in English and an even wider range of meanings in the language of the New Testament, and Satan wants us to get the wrong meaning. In addition, we often find it difficult to separate between faith and belief—and we will learn in a moment how appropriate that really is. Once we learn what Christian faith is—what actually constitutes saving faith, we will find that this too is highly motivating. (God truly knows how to motivate, but Satan specializes in distracting us from the motivation God has provided.)

Just One Word for 'Faith' and 'Belief'

As just mentioned, in English the word 'belief' has a wide range of meanings. It can mean as little as a casual belief on which one would take no action, such as a belief that the coming winter will be a wet one. It can mean a firm conviction on which one will take action, but with a lack of certainty, such as belief that a certain stock one is about to purchase will increase in value. It can mean a conviction on which one will take action and which one is quite certain will prove true, such as in getting on an airplane to visit a city one has never visited before. We believe that the city is there and that the airplane will take us to that city, even though we have never seen the city and know nothing about how an airplane works.

However, a less common English meaning for "believe" is important for understanding the New Testament concept of faith or belief. In English a person may say, "You've got to have something to believe in," meaning, "You have to have some core principle on which you base every decision in your life." When we use that phrase, we are talking about something we believe so strongly that we would never willingly do anything that would violate that belief. When the belief is in Jesus, such a belief would be equivalent to saying "Jesus is Lord—and specifically Lord of my life. Everything I say, do, and think will be shaped by who he is and what he would desire."

If you are at all familiar with Christianity, you may already be ahead of the story here as you realize that this meaning is important to the task of understanding how Christian faith (or belief) and Christian works go together. We will find that this kind of belief is what Jesus taught, what Paul taught, what James taught, and, indeed, what every New Testament author taught. This so permeates the New Testament, and really the whole Bible, that once we grasp this it is hard to see how anyone could ever have missed it. In the New Testament, this kind of core belief is what is meant whenever faith or belief is mentioned relative to salvation with only one exception. That exception was specifically intended to reinforce this meaning. (We'll come to that in a little bit.)

In fact, from the beginning of Genesis to the end of the Revelation, the most consistent message of the Bible is that we as humans must accept God's divine authority over our lives if we hope to survive the judgment. Lip service will not do. Jesus said that many would call him "Lord, Lord," but he would have nothing to do with them. Appearance without substance will not do. Jesus said that many would claim to have served him in various ways including prophecy and miracles, but he would have nothing to do with them. Saving faith or belief is a refocusing of our lives, a shift in focus from ourselves and the things of this world to God and the things of his kingdom. Nothing else will do, and we will learn why before we are through.

Now it is important to understand that the Bible word translated 'belief' is always the same as the word translated 'faith.' There is absolutely no distinction between these terms in the Bible.[13] This word appears as a verb (believe or have faith) and as a noun (belief or faith), but it is clearly the same word every time. (Strangely, the translators of the King James Version of the Bible used the word 'faith' wherever the noun form appeared and the word 'believe' wherever the verb form appeared, intentionally or unintentionally implying some difference in meaning, but this does not serve well to communicate the intent of those who wrote the New Testament.)

When we understand that saving belief involves reshaping one's life around one's belief, we can understand the whole Bible message better. To believe in the gospel is to shape one's life around the message of the gospel. It involves believing God's message, and making every thought and action conform to that belief. This has a lot to do with motivation, because it involves finding our motivation in serving God.

Motivation can be either internal or external. As we studied in the last chapter, God has provided a message that is motivating. (We'll learn much more about how motivating that message is throughout this book.) The main motivation we discussed in that chapter is external (the fear of hell), something outside ourselves that influences us to act one way or another. Faith is internal motivation. Faith is us intentionally setting our sights on those external goals and then using those goals to shape our lives. For the Christian, God's will as demonstrated and taught by Jesus and his followers becomes the ultimate goal.

As I mentioned above, the New Testament word for faith or belief has an even wider range of meaning than the English. For Jesus and his followers, this one word could mean "trust," "conviction," "assurance," and various others not generally associated with the English words. A careful study of the biblical use of this term will lead you to the conclusion that the most common meaning for Jesus and his followers was the meaning we have in English when we say, "You've

13 For those who are interested, the Greek term used in the New Testament is "pistis" in the noun form (belief or faith) and "pisteuo" in the verb form (believe or have faith).

got to have something to believe in"—that core belief that shapes every action and thought in one's life. Such a belief in God is effectively an end to the rebellion of sin. We will still sin, but the sin will be in spite of our consistent effort to live for God. Our aim shifts from the worldly to the eternal, from the physical to the spiritual.

Law and Faith in Christianity

In recent years the news media have pushed some of our buttons as Christians when it comes to the Bible and God's Law. The Ten Commandments have become a real hot button issue, and in many parts of the country you may see yard signs with the Ten Commandments as if this were an essential part of Christianity. Indeed, there are ways in which this is at least partially true, but one of the strongest themes in the New Testament is that Christians are not under law—any law—as far as God is concerned. Accepting Jesus as Lord does not mean a new set of laws and more guilt for failing to live up to those laws. This does not mean that Christians can simply ignore God's will for their lives—quite the contrary. But it does mean that there is no law, not the Ten Commandments, not the Law given by God through Moses, and not any New Testament list of do and don't items. It's more like "Do your best and trust God to deal with the rest." The "do your best" part consists of ending the rebellion and focusing your life on living for God.

As God knew from the beginning, one problem with law is that people can always find a way around almost any law. For example, if God's law says "You shall not bear false witness," we find a way to say only things that are true while intentionally communicating something entirely false. (Who has not done this and then claimed, "I didn't *lie*"?) Another problem with law is that people justify their lawbreaking with the rationale that others who are supposed to be good people do worse than they are doing. (This is like claiming that you shouldn't be gaining weight when you eat too much as long as someone near you is eating more.) Or people excuse themselves because they are doing some sort of penance to make up for violating a law or rule; or people are sacrificing in some way that makes it OK for them to break the laws and rules. In over a thousand years of having God's law, by the time of Jesus' ministry, the Jews still had not come to truly honor God's law with their lives. In nearly two thousand years since that time, this is still true.

Yet another problem with law is that it encourages people to do the least necessary to keep the law. But God has no pleasure in those who seek the least—he accepts those who seek to do all they can with no regard to what the minimum is. Today, those who ask "What must I do to be saved?" often mean "What is the least I can get by with in order to avoid hell." Anyone looking for the minimum is looking in the wrong direction, and such a person is almost certainly lost. God is looking for a faith that says, "How much more can I do?" After all, if we love God, that will be our attitude—and for Christians, loving God is the first commandment.

Who does not break the laws of our country? Most of us who drive break the speed limits. Reports in the news indicate that large numbers of those who can find a way to do so somehow cheat on their taxes. Those who purchase products by mail or Internet without paying sales tax are almost always in violation of state laws. And even the most fastidious drivers almost never come to a full and complete stop at most stop signs. Whatever the laws say, we find ways to cheat on the laws. God does not want law-abiding followers; he wants followers who have given their hearts and lives to serving him in such a way that laws and rules become superfluous.

I have heard ministers and Bible professors say that God's law can be divided into two or three groups for Christian application. If the division is into two groups, it is generally something like "dispensational laws" and "eternal laws" with the implication that the dispensational laws went away when Jesus died but the eternal laws still apply to Christians. The Bible never divides God's laws into dispensational and eternal, so how can we possibly know which laws are supposed to be dispensational and which are supposed to be eternal? If we do not know, how can we ever be certain of our salvation?

For those who identify three groups of laws the divisions are generally along the lines of "ceremonial laws," "civil laws," and "moral laws," with only the moral laws being viewed as applicable to Christians. The Bible never uses these terms or teaches anything like that. Again, how can we know which laws apply to us and which do not? One minister or professor will teach one list, and another teaches a different list. How can we find peace if we cannot determine what laws apply to Christians? We can thank God that these questions are not a problem for Christians, because salvation is by faith, not by laws and rules.

At the beginning of his account of Jesus' ministry, Matthew records a lengthy and awesome sermon we call the Sermon on the

Mount. This message contains many of Jesus' most important teachings, and there can be no doubt that the topics covered in this sermon were common threads in Jesus' teachings throughout his ministry. Early in this sermon, Jesus told his followers

> Do not think that I came to destroy the Law of Moses or the message of the prophets. I did not come to destroy these, but to fulfill them. For I tell you most assuredly, until heaven and earth pass away, not the tiniest dot, not the least mark, shall by any means pass from the Law of Moses until all of that law is fulfilled. Whoever therefore breaks one of the least of these commandments and teaches other men to do so shall be called least in the kingdom of heaven; but whoever does and teaches them, he shall be called great in the kingdom of heaven. For I say to you, that unless your righteousness exceeds the righteousness of the scribes and Pharisees, you will by no means enter the kingdom of heaven (Matthew 5:17-20).

Jesus follows this statement with a list of legalistic things that were taught by the religious leaders (scribes, Pharisees, etc.) of his time, and in each case he demonstrates that the fulfillment he was talking about was a matter of the spirit of the law rather than the letter of the law. In fact, in some cases Jesus actually reversed what a specific written law said to focus on the overriding spirit or principles behind the whole Law of Moses.

For Christians there are three important keys in what Jesus said in this chapter: 1) either the entire law (down to the least mark on the page) applies to Christians, including laws of sacrifice, Sabbath laws, civil laws, and moral laws; or else all of God's Law from the Ten Commandments down to the most detailed ceremonial law has been fulfilled by Jesus' teachings about faith as focus on doing God's will (which is exactly what Jesus said he had come to do); 2) for Christians, God's Law has been superseded by a commandment to love God with an unselfish, caring, generous, active love, meaning that we will do what the spirit of the Law teaches, not because it is law, but because we have given our hearts to pleasing God; and 3) we are not expected to be fully perfect, but we are required to grow toward the spiritual maturity we find in God.

The last verse of this part of the Sermon on the Mount says, "In light of all of this, you must be mature with the same kind of spiritual maturity that you find in your Heavenly Father" (Matthew 5:48). As noted earlier, this verse is often misunderstood, but the meaning Jesus was communicating was all about discipleship—growing spiritually into the image of our Heavenly Father.

What Jesus was demanding of his followers was that they must grow and mature toward the spiritual maturity they would find in God. In other words, he was saying that we need to focus our lives on God—which is the very definition of Christian faith or belief that we have been talking about. It is ending the rebellion. We as Christians are to find our motivation in focusing our lives on God and on doing his will in this world—knowing that his will is unselfish, caring, generous, active love toward him and toward each other. We are to make God's will our motivation—and doing so will always reinforce that motivation by the rewards of peace, joy, and God's own Holy Spirit within (always provided to his followers), regardless of external circumstances. When we are willing to make this the focus of our lives, however imperfectly we live out that focus, God enters the picture with the grace to cover every failure.

What the Bible Says about God's Law for Christians

At this point, because of all the misunderstanding among Christians about the role of works vs. faith and grace, I feel we need to return for a moment to the subject of law and Christianity. When we are children or immature, we need laws to control our behavior. When the focus of our lives is selfishness and worldly interests, we need earthly laws to control our behavior. But when we live by the kind of faith presented in the Bible, laws become unnecessary. In fact, for people who have this kind of faith in God, laws tend to actually weaken that faith.

In Romans 3:20-30, Paul emphasizes strongly that justification (and therefore salvation) is a direct function of faith. One of his strongest points is that if justification were by obeying God's Law (the Ten Commandments and other related Old Testament laws), those who succeeded in obeying the law would have reason to boast about what they had accomplished, but since it is by faith (focusing one's life on God and trusting God to save), no one has anything to boast about. Faith is turning your life over to God and trusting him to rescue you. It's like grabbing the rescue harness extended from the rescue helicopter and leaving any flotation device behind.

Later in this same letter Paul says,

> What are we saying, then? Should we just keep on sinning because we are not under laws and rules since our sins are all covered by God's grace? May that thought never have existence! Don't you know that you are actually the slaves of whomever you choose to obey? So if you choose to obey sin, that obedience will lead to death. But if you choose to obey righteousness, that obedience will lead to life everlasting (Romans 6:15-16).

Paul was making it clear that the faith he talked about could not be compatible with living by our fleshly desires while insisting that we are still not subject to any laws or rules.

Saving faith necessarily leads to obedience, but not legalistic obedience—rather, obedience of the heart. A person who does not focus his or her life on living for God does not have saving faith and does not really love God. How successful this focusing will be is an individual thing, and God knows how to judge whether a person has actually focused his or her life on him or whether that person has only made a show of doing so. Hopefully you can see the link here to the prophecies of Jeremiah about a new covenant of the heart that we looked at earlier.

Notice how Paul contrasts law and grace in the passage in Romans 6, we are not under law but under grace. The point here is the very ability of God's Law to have enforcement. If we are under grace, there is no penalty for breaking a law, because any infraction is immediately covered by that grace. The force of any law is the penalty for breaking that law. For the Christian, there is no penalty, so the law has no power. The point that Paul is making and that we must understand is that if we focus our lives on our worldly selves or on the things of this world (including living up to some legal standard), we are not Christians, and therefore we are not under grace. But if we focus our lives on living for God, the law becomes an informative guide to help us understand what that should mean, but it has no hold on us when we fall short.

In writing to the churches of Galatia, Paul said, "Therefore the Law of Moses was our guide to bring us to Christ, that we might be justified by faith" (Galatians 3:24). In this passage the word "guide" (sometimes translated "tutor" or "schoolmaster") did not mean a formal teacher. Paul used the word for a slave whose duty it was to escort a child to and from a place of learning. This slave did provide instruction and guidance in general areas of life as he would lead the child to and from school, but he was not the child's true teacher. So the law functioned in the role of this slave, bringing us safely to where we could focus our lives on God, who is our true teacher. From the law we gain insight into what God wants from his people, just as the child gained general insights for living from his "tutor." But the real instructor is God, not the Law.

Later in that same letter Paul was discussing the fact that some whom he had led to Christ were being misled by others to practice circumcision as a legalistic requirement imposed on any who would be Christians. Circumcision was not one of the Ten Commandments, but it was a small part of the Law of Moses. Speaking of this or any other part of that law, regardless of how small a commandment, Paul said, "Those of you who want to be justified by keeping rules have cut yourselves off from Christ—you have fallen away from God's grace" (Galatians 5:4). In other words, if we try to gain favor with God by earning his admiration through obedience to one or more laws or rules, we cease to even be Christians. God's role is paying the price of our sins, and when we try to take over God's role, we shut God out.

But to make it clear that Christians are by definition focused on living for God, Paul told the churches of Galatia,

> Don't let anyone fool you. You cannot make a mockery of God. Whatever a man sows, that is exactly what he will reap. The man who sows what pleases his corruptible flesh will of the flesh reap corruption, but he who sows what pleases God's Holy Spirit will of the Spirit reap everlasting life (Galatians 6:7-8).

Again it should be obvious how these teachings are compatible with faith or belief as a focus of one's life on God, and with no other definition.

To the Christians in Corinth Paul wrote, "Everything is lawful for me, but some things are not helpful. Everything is lawful for me, but I will not be brought under the power of any" (1Corinthians 6:12), and then again "Everything is lawful for me, but some things are not helpful, everything is lawful for me, but some things are not useful in building the kingdom" (1Corinthians 10:23). Paul was always insistent that nothing in God's Law applies to Christians as law because God's grace would immediately cover any violation, but that this did not mean Christians could focus on selfish desires and worldly things and still be Christians. As soon as a person turns his or her back on God to focus on self, that person turns from Christianity and has fallen from grace.

Please do not misunderstand this. Falling from grace is not a simple slip or a deviation from your normal focus on God; it requires an intentional turning your back on God as defined in Hebrews 6:4-6—actual apostasy. To be guilty of this, a person must first have come to experience God's presence through his Holy Spirit and to have experienced the awesome blessings of Christianity. Only God can judge when a person has done this, and once a person truly experiences God in his or her life the risk of such apostasy is extremely low, but the door is never closed.

James wrote

> If you really fulfill the royal law according to the Scripture, 'You shall love your neighbor as yourself,' you do well, but if you show partiality, you are sinning, and are convicted by that same law as transgressors. For anyone who keeps the whole law and yet stumbles in one point, he is guilty of all (James 2:8-10).

(Remember, "You shall love your neighbor as yourself" was part of the Law of Moses [Leviticus 19:18].) Since this is true, it should be obvious that no one could possibly live a good enough life to earn salvation.

Hopefully it's clear to anyone who can understand these passages that James, Paul, and Jesus are all in agreement about this—Christians are those who focus their lives on and find their motivation in God and his supreme commandment to love each other with an unselfish, caring, generous, forgiving, active love—something that can never be fulfilled as law. Those who do not have such a focus but are instead motivated by the things of this world and the flesh are just not Christians and are therefore condemned under God's Law as delivered to Moses. And those who try to deserve or earn salvation by keeping laws and rules have no hope because they are actually trying to take over God's job.

Revisiting Popular New Testament Passages

Now that we know that "faith" and "belief" are the same in the New Testament and we know that the meaning of Christian faith or belief involves focusing one's life on living for God, let's consider how this changes our understanding of two familiar New Testament passages.

John 3:16 says, "For God so loved the world that he gave his only begotten Son, that whoever believes in him should not perish but have everlasting life (NKJV)." With the understanding we have just gained, it would be entirely legitimate to do an amplified translation that said, "For God so loved the world that he gave his only begotten Son, that whoever focuses his life on living as Jesus taught shall not perish but shall have eternal life." That translates the concept expressed by the apostle John into English, and that is certainly consistent with what Jesus always taught.

In Acts 16, Paul and Silas had just been freed from jail (along with other prisoners) by an earthquake. The jailer knew that if his prisoners escaped, he would be subject to the punishment due each escaped prisoner, and he was preparing to kill himself to avoid that punishment when Paul called out to let him know that none of the prisoners had fled. The jailer must have been somewhat familiar with what Paul had been teaching before he was imprisoned, because he called out to Paul, "What must I do to be saved?" Paul told the jailer, "Believe on the Lord Jesus Christ, and you will be saved, you and your household" (Acts 16:30-31 NKJV). Now, to properly understand what Paul said, we need to apply what we have just learned.

Again, an amplified version that translates the ideas as Paul meant them and as the jailer would have understood them might well read, "Make the Lord Jesus and his will the focus of your life, and you will be saved—you and anyone in your household who does the same." If we understand this, then the point Paul was making supports what Jesus taught exactly. Many other well-known passages need to be revisited in a similar way. The issue is, indeed, lordship. When Paul said "Believe in the Lord Jesus," he was not using the word "Lord" lightly.

More Evidence in the New Testament—From Jesus

In John 5:24-30, Jesus is quoted as saying,

> I tell you most assuredly; the one who hears my word and believes in [has faith in or implements a life focus on] the one who sent me already has everlasting life and shall not come into judgment, having already passed from death into life. Again I tell you most assuredly, the time is coming (and it is already here) when those who are dead will hear the voice of the Son of God, and those who are willing to hear him will live. For as surely as the Father has life in himself, so he has granted the Son to have life in himself, and has also given him authority to execute judgment, because he is the son of man. Do not be surprised by this, for the time is coming in which all who are in the graves will hear his voice and come out—those who have done good will experience the resurrection of life, and those who have done evil will experience the resurrection of condemnation. On my own, I can do nothing. As I hear, I judge; and my judgment is righteous, because I do not seek my own will but the will of the Father who sent me.

Notice the following two phrases in this paragraph: 1) "the one who hears my word and believes in the one who sent me already has everlasting life"; and 2) "Those who have done good will experience the resurrection of life, and those who have done evil will experience the resurrection of condemnation." In this passage, Jesus says two things of interest. First, he says that eternal life depends on believing or having faith in "the one who sent me." Second, he says that the dead will be raised to judgment, and the judgment will be based on what they have done.

These concepts would be conflicting if "believe" meant just believing facts or trusting Christ to save. If a person has eternal life just by believing God, how can that person be judged eternally based on what he or she has done? However, if "believe" means focusing one's life on the one believed in, then the passage makes sense because such a belief would cause a person to do the good things that God wants him or her to do. In God's perspective, one cannot truly believe in him if one does not live as if he or she truly believes. To claim that we believe one thing while living as if we believe something else is simply to lie.

More Evidence in the New Testament—From Paul

In Romans 3:28, Paul says, "Therefore it's obvious that a man is justified by faith [belief], completely separate from keeping the Law given by Moses." This might seem to argue that believing certain things is the basis of salvation. However, three verses later Paul says, "Do we, then, nullify the law by this faith? May that thought never even form in your mind! On the contrary, we uphold the law" (Romans 3:31). Yet, if belief (or faith) in the facts of who Jesus really is truly saves us, then we would make the law of no real significance. If a "sinner's prayer" really and permanently saves us, then we are saved whether or not we live in accordance with rules or laws. However, if the belief or faith Paul meant was a founding principle on which we make all our life decisions, if that faith means focusing our lives on God's will, then these concepts are compatible.

Our faith or belief causes us to live up to the moral principles of God's Law even though living by God's Law could never earn us anything once we break that law one time. We live up to the intent of the law not to earn anything but to live out our love for God. By this kind of faith we will simply have ended our rebellion, and then God's grace will wipe out our guilt. As Christians, we do not follow the guidance of the law because it is law and there is some penalty for disobedience, but because we love God and have entrusted our entire lives to him—his will has become the internal motivation for our lives. Believing that Jesus came as God's son and died for our sins does not "uphold the law," but reshaping our lives around the message Jesus brought does cause us to live up to the moral intent of the law.

More Evidence in the New Testament—From James

James has often been perceived as in disagreement with Paul. After all, Paul taught that "a man is justified by faith [belief], completely separate from keeping the law" (Romans 3:28), while James taught that, "In the same way, faith [belief] by itself, if it is not accompanied by appropriate action, is dead" (James 2:17). Yet, each of these New Testament authors defined how they were using the word "faith." As we saw, in Romans 3:31 Paul effectively defined the term as necessarily involving establishment of the law (therefore a core motivational belief that shapes one's life). In the New Testament, James is the one exception who does not use this definition for "faith." James said, "My brothers, what good is it if a man claims to have faith [belief] but has no deeds? Can faith [belief] like that save him?" (James 2:14). By the implication of faith that does not result in action in this context, James shows that he is using "faith" to mean "acceptance of facts as true" without a change in the focus of one's life rather than as a foundation for life that affects every action and thought.

Thus, using the definition Paul and Jesus used, faith saves us all by itself, but using the definition James used, faith as belief in facts by itself cannot save us. Don't let the definitions become too confusing. The point is that faith is not saving faith and belief is not saving belief unless that faith or belief is a motivational factor that shapes how you live.

More Evidence in the New Testament—From Hebrews

As a last example, in Hebrews we read,

> Now with whom was he [God] angry for forty years? Wasn't it with those who sinned, whose bodies fell in the wilderness? And to whom did he [God] swear that they would not enter his rest? Wasn't it to those who disobeyed? So we see that they could not enter his rest because of unbelief (Hebrews 3:17-19).

In this passage, notice how "those who disobeyed" are the same as those who "could not enter his rest because of unbelief." In this passage, disobedience and unbelief are treated as exactly equivalent. And that same usage of these terms as exactly equivalent continues in chapter 4. Once again we see that early Christians defined belief as something that would necessarily shape how we live.

In these and many other passages, we see that Jesus, James, Paul, and Christians of that period in general all agree that Christian faith, if it is to be saving faith, must motivate how we live. For those who have truly come to know the Lord, this should be no surprise. God demands that we end the rebellion; he has always demanded our hearts, a motivated focus on doing his will.

"Give me your heart," says the Father above,
No gift so precious to him as our love.
From this dark world he would call you apart,
Speaking so tenderly, "Give me your heart."[14]

God knows that we will experience many failures in our efforts to serve him, but he insists that we must try. That is the message of the first chapters of Genesis, and that is the core message of the Revelation and everything in between. As we saw earlier in Romans 6, Paul emphasizes that we belong to the one we serve as slaves—whether we serve God or Satan. In fact, the whole New Testament makes it abundantly clear that Christianity and salvation are a matter of accepting God's divine authority over our lives. **The rebellion must end**.

Now in saying that the rebellion must end, we are not saying that a Christian must stop sinning. In this world, God knows that we cannot completely stop sinning no matter how hard we try until he pulls us out of the riptide of sin that permeates this world. What God does demand is that we shift the focus of our lives from living for ourselves and our own pleasures to living for him. He knows the changes we can accomplish will be limited. He knows that we will need his forgiveness over and over. He only asks that we honestly and sincerely try to turn our lives around and trust his guidance. And what he asks us to try to learn to do is all good—love, faithfulness, doing the right thing, caring for others, being truthful, seeking peace, forgiving others as he has forgiven us, and the list of these good things goes on with everything motivated by the first thing on the list—Christian love.

To be honest, it is often difficult to determine today what Christians of the New Testament period might have understood as the meaning of a particular word or phrase, especially if that word or phrase is not used much. But from the information above, it should be obvious that Christians in New Testament times would have included the idea of focusing one's life on what one believes as the essence of Christian faith or belief. Of course, 'faith' or 'belief' must also include accepting certain truths on the testimony of others, that is an important part of the meaning, but that is not the full meaning for Christians. We would never accept God's authority over our lives if we did not believe "that he exists and that he rewards those who sincerely seek him" (Hebrews 11:6), but we must not overlook that Christian faith

14 Adapted from the hymn "Give Me Thy Heart" by Eliza Hewitt, 1898.

is not just believing that God exists—an important factor of Christian faith is to "sincerely seek" God's will for one's life.

Alternative Defintion for 'Faith' or 'Belief'

To make this point even more obvious, let's consider the alternative to this definition for faith or belief. Assume for this moment that the word 'belief' or 'believe' in the Bible applies only to certain truths we must believe.

This actually results in an impossibly difficult situation that is effectively a form of works salvation. The question becomes, "What must we believe?" If we go by Paul's answer ("Believe in the Lord Jesus, and you will be saved" [Acts 16:31]) then we must believe in Jesus. But what must we believe about him—that he was born? That he was born of a virgin? That he was God's son? That he was God in the flesh? That he was crucified for our sins? That he rose from the dead? That he ascended to heaven? Is it necessary to believe in Jesus' miracles?

Romans 10:9 indicates that belief in the resurrection is necessary. Hebrews 11:6 tells us that we must believe that God exists and that he rewards those who seek him. In Mark 1:15 Jesus said that people should believe the gospel—that is, the good news. What do these passages all mean? What should we include as part of the gospel? Must a person search the whole Bible looking for this or that passage that adds something we must believe? (And of what use can it be to say that we believe the whole Bible when we know little if anything about what the Bible says?)

There are also passages that tell us that people who believe certain things will not be saved. For example, the Galatian Christians were warned by Paul against believing that obeying the law of circumcision was necessary for salvation. What happens if we get this wrong and accidentally believe something that we were not supposed to believe?

Going further, must we believe in the Genesis account of creation or a specific interpretation of that account? Must we believe in the story of Jonah's or Daniel's experiences as actual events? (I happen to believe these, but some who claim to be Christians and who seem to be serving God to the best of their abilities do not.) Must we believe in a global flood in Noah's time? Must we believe in the inerrancy of the Bible? What if we fail to believe one of these things? Or what if we believe something that is not really on God's list of things to believe? Would we be lost?

The fact is that many different church leaders have different lists of the things they think must be believed. If the term 'believe' involves believing certain truths, then we must find out what those truths are and believe all of them and only them. So whose list should we believe?

With this approach, we must constantly be concerned lest there be something we should have believed that we have not believed or something we should not have believed that we believed. There is no security in salvation based on such a task.

However, if the "faith" or "belief" focuses on shaping our lives around the desires of the one we believe in, then the whole issue of *what* to believe disappears. The issue is not what we believe, but in whom we place our trust and confidence. In fact, as mentioned earlier, 'trust' and 'confidence' are alternate meanings of the New Testament word for 'belief.' In this way we are not responsible for a list of things to believe, but rather we are responsible for living according to what we know of God's will for our lives. Since it is the belief or faith that matters, we are not even held accountable for what we do not know—we are only accountable for what we do know and for seeking to know more. God is responsible for what he wants to reveal to us, and we can trust him to faithfully do his part as long as we remain open to his word and eager to learn.

The Evidence of Other New Testament Terms

When we look at certain other New Testament terms, we find a wonderful agreement with this definition of faith or belief. For example, the term 'repentance' means "to change one's mind, to change one's focus"—in other words, to stop following our own path in life and start following God's path. Repentance is a shift of life focus from self and worldly things to God and his kingdom; it is taking on a new set of motivations based on the love for God and love for others commanded by God. Just as repentance is the act of changing your mind from focus on self and worldly things to focus on God and heavenly things, so faith is maintaining your focus on God and heavenly things. The only way to come to saving faith is by repentance, and this kind of repentance always leads you to saving faith.

Picture repentance this way: A man is walking with his eyes closed toward the edge of a cliff with a shear drop of hundreds of feet to a rocky surface below. He has no awareness of the danger. Then he opens his eyes and sees the danger just before falling over the edge. He immediately stops, but that is not repentance. As long as he still faces the cliff, sooner or later he will fall over if only because the cliff erodes. Even if he turns around to face the other direction, if he remains where he is, he will eventually fall over. But when he turns around and starts walking the opposite direction, that is repentance, and that is when he is safe. (Faith would be continuing to walk in this new direction.)

And certainly, the term 'kingdom of God' implies that God is king. Speaking of Jesus as Lord ought to mean that we serve him as our lord. Too many Christians speak of Jesus as Lord, thinking that he is Lord of the universe and Lord of heaven and Lord of the whole creation without perceiving that he insists on being Lord of each person's life. As Jesus said,

> Not everyone who says to me, "Lord, Lord," will get into the kingdom of heaven, but only the one who does the will of my Father in heaven. On judgment day, many will say to me, "Lord, Lord, didn't we preach in your name and drive out demons and perform many miracles in your name?" Then I'll tell them, "Just get away from me, you who have no regard for God's laws, I never knew you at all" (Matthew 7:21-23).

Jesus made it clear that his lordship must affect our lives, not just outwardly in what we say or in demonstrations we put on for show, but as the central core issue of life. Prophesying and doing miracles is not the issue. Saying "Lord, Lord," is not the issue. Living for him, making him Lord of our lives, is the issue.

In fact, the very word "Christian" means "belonging to Christ." In New Testament times, this would imply that Christ has the same authority over us that a master would have over his slave. When we say that we are Christians, we effectively say that we are slaves of Christ—bought and owned by him.

The New Testament word for love also connects to this concept. Christian love deals with a servant love—a love that does for others. Thus if the first and greatest commandment is to love God with all one's heart, soul, mind, and body, this includes serving God. Once again, God's divine authority is central. Christianity is a lordship issue.

Jesus' Testimony

Jesus said this more than once, and it was probably an often repeated theme in his ministry: "If anyone really wants to come with me, he must renounce himself and pick up his own cross daily and follow after me" (Luke 9:23). It is hard to translate the real force of this passage into English. In English, all commands are given as "you do this" or "you do that." In an English sentence, the "you" may be plural or singular, but no other pronoun works in a command. Our culture does not have a concept of a command to someone who is not present to hear the command. We cannot say "he do this" or "he do that" as a command. This is not the case in the languages of the Bible, and in this passage Jesus used a command form for "renounce," "pick up," and "follow." In English we would be more likely to say, "If you really want to come with me, renounce yourself, pick up your cross, and follow after me." This is not a suggestion; it is a command from the Lord. We cannot be acceptable as Jesus' followers if we are not willing to at least try to do this, and this is the very definition of saving faith—truly putting the focus of our lives on Jesus.

Assumptions Concerning Free Will in Heaven

There is another point that demonstrates just how important this matter must be. It also answers many questions about God's purposes both in this creation and in the world to come. This point has to do with something Christians have come to believe with no biblical support, and that is the loss of our freedom in heaven. Many and probably most Christians today believe that once we reach heaven we will no longer be able to sin—sin will be impossible. Yet, the Bible never says this. In fact, the Bible provides strong evidence against this idea. Not that there will be sin in heaven (there will not), or even that we will be tempted to sin in heaven (we will not)—but there is very good reason to understand that sin would be possible in heaven.

When God created this world, he created humans with the ability to choose between right and wrong. After creating the humans with this ability, God pronounced his creation to be "very good." That "very good" included his gift of free will to humans—the ability to rebel against their creator. If this was a good gift, then why would God take it away from us when he takes us to his new eternal world? If it was a bad gift, why did God ever give it to us, and how could he pronounce the creation "very good" with this in it? Furthermore, which of us would really want to be a robot, unable to choose between right and wrong?

The implication of the creation account is that having free will is an integral part of what God wants humans to be. If God changes us so drastically that we no longer have free will, he will not really have saved us—he will have changed us into something we never were before.

And if God were going to redesign us so that we could not sin once we get to heaven, why not design us that way from the beginning so that sin would never be a threat? Why make us go through the experience of earth when we could have gone straight to heaven? Why would a loving God risk having most people lost when he could have avoided that risk? Why would he design a creation where his son would have to die if he were going to change that same creation into something that would never have required that death?

But love, the kind of real love that is the essence of Christianity, demands a choice. One cannot love with Christian love without having a choice not to love. A robot cannot love, because it is the very nature of love to be a choice, and it is the nature of a robot to be incapable of making personal choices. Thus, if there is to be love in heaven, there must be at least the ability to choose not to love. But the choice not to love, as we have already seen, is the very definition of sin—in other words, we must have the ability to rebel in order to have love, and rebellion is sin.

Love, this kind of love, is a vital factor in what will make heaven a paradise. Without such love, heaven cannot be the place of joy and fulfillment that it must be in order to be a paradise. And as long as love is necessary, the potential to sin must be equally necessary. (For more on this topic, see Appendix A.)

An Extended Illustration-Riptide

This does not mean that there will be sin in heaven, or that we will be in any danger of falling back into sin. Earlier we used an illustration of a man named Tom living beside the ocean who liked to use an inner tube to float in the surf. We talked about how this person might be caught in a riptide without ever knowing what was happening—how he might feel entirely safe while he was being dragged to his doom. We talked about how, when he realized his danger, he would likely cry out for help. We discussed how people must be aware of real danger before they will really turn to God for salvation.

Extending this same illustration, imagine that, after struggling against the riptide and finding that his condition is truly hopeless, Tom is rescued by a helicopter. The helicopter drops a rope with a safety harness, and he is lifted out of the riptide and placed on the shore. Having now perceived the danger of riptides, and having been rescued from certain death, will Tom ever go into the water again when there is a known risk for riptides? No normal, intelligent, healthy, well-adjusted person would do so. Tom will learn to watch for the riptide warnings, and he will never again be caught in that snare.

This is a relatively good illustration of what God has done on this earth. He has given us an environment where we can become familiar with the extreme dangers of sin and with the impossibility of rescuing ourselves. While we are here on earth, we can learn just how terrible sin really is. Once we learn this lesson and make a firm commitment to God's divine authority and against sin—in other words, once we end the rebellion, God can safely forgive our sin and take us to his new world. If God were to take us to heaven before we accepted his authority over our lives and rejected our rebellion, we would simply destroy the new world just like we destroyed this one.

Understanding God's Plan

This goes all the way back to the creation. This is the reason for the Tree of Knowledge of Good and Evil in the garden paradise. God knew that humans would sin before he even began this creation (see Ephesians 1:4; 2Timothy 1:9; Titus 1:2; 1Peter 1:20). He did not want them to sin, but he knew it was important for them to experience sin before he could safely give them eternal life. If that were not true, he could simply have planted a garden with no Tree of Knowledge of Good and Evil. Or if that tree were somehow necessary to the creation process, God could have planted it in some inaccessible place. But Genesis tells us that it was "in the midst of the garden." And that phrase may mean one tree in the very middle of the garden, but it may also mean one kind of tree growing throughout the garden. Either way, God made it so that Adam and Eve would see the tree routinely.

It is very likely there was nothing magical about that tree. No magic was needed in the fruit itself. God could have used anything—a line we were not to cross, a rock we were not to touch, a direction in which we were not to point—but he used a fruit we were not to eat. Eating that fruit was rebellion, and rebellion is sin. For Adam and Eve, this was the only rebellion possible. Before humans rebelled, they could not know the difference between good and evil because they had only experienced good. Once they ate the fruit, they had rebelled, and that very act had to give them the knowledge of good and evil—they had done evil for the first time.

In order to receive God's eternal reward, we must end that rebellion and commit our lives to God. God can forgive any sin except final rejection of his authority. He can forgive any amount of sin. However, he will not take away the freedom that makes it possible for us to love—and that same freedom makes it possible for us to sin. And since he will not take away that freedom, it is mandatory that we learn how bad sin is and that we make a life commitment for God and against sin before he takes us to our heavenly reward. **This is the essence of discipleship. The rebellion must end!** (Remember, this does not mean we have the impossible task of ending all sin in our lives, but God knows whether we have truly ended the rebellion and whether we are truly trying to learn to live for him.)

Understanding the Problem of Pain

This actually provides the answer to an age-old riddle—why does God allow so many bad things to happen in this world, even when his saints are praying together that one or more of these would cease. The fact is, God does not cause these things to happen, we do. The message of the Bible is clear—sin is the cause of every pain, every heartache, every death, and every other terrible thing in this world. The environment of sin that we have created is the cause of all this evil. God does not stop the evil in part because that would require that he wipe us out, but he also does not stop the terrible results of our sin because he wants us to learn to hate sin.

We tend to blame God for the results of our own sins—but he is not the one to blame. Every time we sin, we vote for evil to rule in this world and for God's will not to be done—and God honors our vote.

Then we blame God for what we have brought on ourselves. And sin is not fair. The person who sins does not necessarily suffer for his or her own specific sin or sins. Often a person who suffers for a specific sin is entirely innocent of that sin—such as the family of a murder victim suffering for the sin of the murderer. God is just, but sin is not, and we have voted to let sin rule in this world.

If we did not experience the pain and suffering brought on by our sins, we would never see a reason to leave our sins behind. We need to recognize just how dangerous the riptide of sin is. Every time we sin, we vote for the pain and suffering to continue and increase. Blaming God is like blaming the person who gave me a car for an injury I got when I drove that car recklessly.

Another Illustration-Golden Gate Bridge

Many people live in the San Francisco area near the Golden Gate Bridge. Thousands cross the bridge every day. Occasionally, one of these people has climbed the bridge and jumped to his or her death. In each case, we can be certain that the one who does something like this is either not rational, or not healthy, or not well adjusted, or under duress.

In heaven, God will take away our sin and our guilt and open our eyes so that we will know, even as we are known. Those who reach heaven will be rational, they will be healthy, they will be well adjusted, and they will never be under any duress to cause them to sin. There will be no Satan to tempt us. There will be no disease or irrationality to draw us back into the sin we have escaped. We will know the awesome joy of freedom from sin and guilt—a joy we can never really experience until we reach heaven. We will understand how sin brought every form of pain and suffering to our world.

For those who already have a commitment against sin, who have fought a losing battle against sin, who have a firm commitment to following God's will, and who have been rescued from sin, there will be no risk that they would ever return to sin. Sin must be possible in heaven, but it will be unthinkable. We will be in infinitely less risk of returning to sin than a healthy, sane, well-adjusted person would be at risk of jumping off the Golden Gate Bridge.

A Personal Illustration

When I was about 4 years old, my family lived in the little town of Saumonauk, Illinois on an unpaved street. At the time my father was a smoker and I thought of smoking as some forbidden fruit that I would probably enjoy based on how much my father seemed to enjoy it. So I was excited when I found a fresh unopened pack of cigarettes in the road in front of the house. Saumonauk was a very small town with very little traffic on our street, and the pack of cigarettes was completely unharmed. It had never even been opened. I had no matches, but I opened the pack and put my first cigarette in my mouth. This was before filters were added to cigarettes. This turned out to be two cigarettes—my first one and my last one—combined in one. At least in my memory I spent the rest of the day trying to get that taste out of my mouth. However long I spent trying to get rid of the taste, I have never been tempted by cigarettes since then.

That is what God is doing with sin in this world. If this were not the case, why would God have put humans in a world where sin is possible and then planted the tree of knowledge of good and evil where they would have to see it over and over. He saw that we needed to learn a lesson—that this lesson was vitally important for our eternal happiness.

The Good News of Faith and Love

When we combine this kind of faith with Christian love, Christians focused on doing God's will are going to be looking for opportunities to show Christian love at any and all times. This is obviously good news for those in need, but it is also astonishingly good news for the Christians. Anyone who has seriously experienced this will know how rewarding such activity is.

I recall as a teenager working on a mission project that involved sorting, packaging, and organizing a huge amount of material to be shipped to missionaries. Several adults and a few teens had volunteered to work this project. We started early that day and worked hard all day. At the end of the day we were all exhausted. But as we talked, you could just feel the excitement and joy. Every person involved was experiencing overflowing joy. It was a skippity-doo-dah feeling I had never experienced before, but I have experienced it many times since.

After years of serving the Lord, I have come to realize how true Jesus' words are when he said; "There is more joy in giving than in receiving" (Acts 20:35). This is God's Holy Spirit in us bringing joy beyond description. It's no wonder that Paul listed joy as the second of the fruits of the Spirit, just behind love (Galatians 5:22). I have worked long and hard at worldly tasks and have had a wonderful sense of accomplishment when the job was done, but never anything like the sense of joy that comes with working for the Lord. And this sense of joy is just a foretaste of what is waiting for us in eternity.

This combination of faith and love also provides good news for Christianity in general and individual churches in particular. When people see the Christians living their faith and love, they look favorably on the church. When these same people see the joy that Christians experience in living this way, they want to be part of that joy. There is no more powerful means of evangelism. When the Christians practice faith and Christian love, people come to the Lord.

Now there are a couple of important items to consider here. First, the local church needs to seriously facilitate this kind of activity in the local community. This is how discipleship works. This is how evangelism works. This is how the local community sees God's team in action and how the body of Christ demonstrates the love of Christ. This is a key factor in attracting people to the church. The local church needs to seriously look at the local community to find where there are obvious needs, and then the local church needs to get members involved in meeting those needs, carrying the love of Christ into the lives of the community.

Second, as Christians practice this kind of discipleship, they will experience the joy of God's Holy Spirit in their lives—and those around them will see this. When people see others experiencing this kind of joy, they want to be part of whatever brings that kind of joy. People are drawn to the Christians (and thus to the church) when they see this kind of joy in Christians' lives.

Many churches have mission programs in their budgets that provide funds for outreach in other countries, other states, or other areas in their state but have no assigned budget for ministry to local community needs. This is backward. Support for distant missions is biblical and good, but meeting local needs is also biblical and at least as important. Some may say that local needs are met by special offerings and special expenditures as the needs arise, but that leads to a lack of serious consideration of needs and a lack of intentional work to meet needs even before they come to the church. There is no more important focus for a church's ministry staff than finding ways to minister to the needs of the local community. (See Matthew 25:31-46.)

Whether or not the local church does intentional ministry to the needs of the local community, each Christian is called to do so. And while the ministry of Christians to the needs around them normally involves the local community, this ministry continues to apply wherever a Christian is. If Christians practiced this kind of discipleship as they travel on business, much of the work now done by missionaries would be unnecessary, freeing missionaries to do far more. If every person who claims to be Christian were to practice Christian love wherever he or she went, the world would be changed dramatically!

Avoiding Extremes

Before leaving the topic of faith, it is important to clarify how Satan can use some aspects of our faith to take us to extremes that will actually shift our focus away from living for God. The experience of God's people over thousands of years is somewhat like a pendulum. God will make his people aware of some error leading them away from him, and they will repent and turn from that error, but Satan will use that very turning process to lead many into an opposite error that is just as bad. In such cases, the extremes that Satan desires may seem like opposites, but these opposites have the same result of taking our focus off of living for God.

Some see faith primarily as a personal commitment to live for God. Faith is a commitment to live for God, but the danger in this mindset if taken too far is that it may place the focus too much on what we do rather than on what God does. Satan is pleased if people believe that they can earn or deserve God's forgiveness through their committed living, for with such a simple piece of misguidance he can get our focus back on ourselves and the things of this world rather than on God.

In many cases this emphasis on commitment may lead to thinking that we need rules to guide how this commitment should be lived out and what this commitment cannot allow. This path leads quickly to legalism, and as we have seen already, legalism always takes our focus off of God and puts the focus back on ourselves and on the things of this world. When Paul twice wrote to the Christians in Corinth that "All things are lawful" for Christians (see 1Corinthians 6:12 and 10:23), he was emphasizing as powerfully as he could that Christianity must never be about rules and laws. Churches that have succumbed to the temptation of legalism have always wound up with a form of religion devoid of the grace that makes the gospel such good news.

Often as Christians grow in faith and in understanding, they feel like they need to do more for God. Yet the teaching of the Bible is that we do not *need* to do more for God—God has already done all that is necessary. We should *want* to do more for God, but we must never forget that our salvation is of the Lord, not of our own efforts. Once we focus our lives on God, how much we accomplish for him or exactly what we accomplish for him is not the issue. God has already accomplished what needs to be accomplished. We are to simply do our best in living for him as the Lord we love and serve.

Others see faith primarily as submission to God's will. Faith is submission to God's will, but the danger in this mindset is that it may take the focus entirely off of our own role in serving God. Satan is pleased if people believe that they can simply rely on God to do everything, because he knows that such a simple piece of misguidance can very quickly cause us to lose interest, saying that the matter is entirely in God's hands, and so our focus returns to ourselves and the things of this world rather than God.

In many cases this emphasis on submission may lead to thinking that we do not need to do anything since there are no rules, that God does it all by the power of his grace. This path leads quickly to "cheap grace," and "cheap grace" always encourages people to take their focus off of God and to put the focus back on themselves and on the things of this world. When Jesus said that unless a person takes up his or her cross daily to follow him, that person cannot be his disciple (See Luke 9:23 and 14:27), he was emphasizing as powerfully as he could that Christianity must always be lived out in a person's life.

Faith does involve a commitment to live for God, and it also involves submission to God's will for our lives—regardless of what his will may be. Once we turn in repentance and focus our lives on God in faith, we need to be aware of the spiritual tension between extremes like these lest Satan catch us in one of his traps. Saul certainly believed that he was working for the Lord when he was dragging Christians to prison and condemning them to death—but he was not. Satan can use our zeal for a one-sided view of Christianity to lead us away from God, and he will do so whenever he can.

The Summary on Faith and Lordship

This is why lordship is such an important concept for Christians to understand. To be a disciple is to accept Jesus as Lord. It is also the concept Satan most desires to have us ignore or overlook. Satan would be satisfied to see Christians wage a winning battle against any sin but this one. A person can be perfectly moral and ethical without having any hope of salvation. A commitment to "family values" or "morality" or one's church and its doctrines or any other human-centered concept is worthless when it comes to salvation if it is not accompanied by accepting God's divine authority. This is why a person must turn his or her life over to God before that person can be saved.

As the author of Hebrews said, "And without faith it is impossible to please God, because anyone who comes to him must believe that he exists and that he rewards those who sincerely seek him" (Hebrews 11:6). As mentioned earlier, that phrase, "sincerely seek," involves making him Lord. And as Peter said,

> This water [the water of Noah's flood that buoyed up the boat and saved those in the boat] also symbolizes baptism that now saves you too—not because of washing the dirt from your body, but because you have committed yourself to a good conscience toward God (1Peter 3:21).

The phrase, "committed yourself to a good conscience toward God," involves making him Lord. The message of the Bible is always the same—he must be Lord! **The rebellion must end!**

Too many times we neglect this point. We may have some "plan of salvation" that jumps from one passage to another to explain God's plan, as if God could not put his own plan together in one place. Or we may teach people to "only believe" with no indication that saving belief must include an end to the rebellion—a complete change of the focus of one's life. We may teach people to pray some "sinner's prayer" that is not found anywhere in the Bible and that no one in the Bible ever practiced, and the "sinner's prayer" we use generally says nothing about Jesus being Lord. In fact, in most cases we say nothing about accepting Jesus as Lord! That is Satan's victory! And very few churches provide serious discipleship training about what it means to be a Christian. Even when we teach Christian living, we teach it as something that Christians "should" do, not as something Christians must do if they are to be Christians at all. That is absolute rebellion against Jesus' clear commandment: "Wherever you go, make disciples of all the nations, baptizing them in the name of the Father and the Son and the Holy Spirit, teaching them to observe everything just as I have commanded you" (Matthew 28:19-20). The last part of this—"teaching them to observe everything I have commanded you"—is our area of greatest weakness and greatest need.

We are in the most important battle in all eternity. It is far past time that we went on the offensive. That means training the Lord's army for spiritual battle with spiritual weapons. That means accepting Jesus as our Lord and making this the priority motivation of life. We sing, "Only Believe," and we miss what it means to believe. The tasks we have waiting for us in heaven involve our active participation and our free choice concerning what we will do for the Lord. God knows he can trust those he will take to heaven. Those he could not trust, he will not take to this eternal reward. Faith that focuses one's life on God is what brings us to the point that God can trust us. **The rebellion must end**! (Once again, this does not mean we have the impossible task of ending all sin in our lives, but God knows whether we have truly ended the rebellion and whether we are truly trying to learn to live for him.)

Up to this point we have focused on motivations largely concerned with avoiding the stick of hell. But God's motivation factors are far more than just the stick. They are far more than the carrot of the joy and peace we can know in this world. Now we need to turn to the really good stuff!

CHAPTER SIX: HOPE—THE ULTIMATE REWARD

If in this life only we have hoped in Christ Jesus, we are, of all men, most to be pitied – 1Corinthians 15:19

Remember once again Paul's words to the Christians in Corinth: "Now we have these three abiding factors: faith, hope, and love; but the greatest of these is love" (1Corinthians 13:13). Love is still the first key principle of Christianity, and faith is a very close second. But hope is what keeps us going—or at least what should keep us going. In fact, hope is really the core of Christianity. As we will learn in this chapter, the roles of love and faith must be what they are because of the hope God has prepared for us. And as we shift the focus to hope, we turn from internal motivation to the most powerful of all external motivations.

Real Christian hope is focused on heaven. Heaven is the motivating factor that can and should empower our faith and our love far beyond the threat of hell. Unfortunately, most Christians have such a distorted concept of heaven that it provides little or no motivation. This includes most Christian ministers and Bible scholars, and that is a major victory for Satan.

As long as we're trying to avoid hell, we'll be severely tempted to look for the minimum commitment needed to escape. But if we're aiming for heaven, our whole perspective changes. A man in New York City with no destination in mind may be motivated to stay out of the way of traffic by standing on the sidewalk, but if he has a particular destination in mind, while he is still motivated to stay out of the traffic, he is even more motivated to reach his destination, and the sidewalk becomes a path rather than a destination.

When Jesus said that his message was gospel—that is, good news—he meant it. We need to grasp that this news is and must be the most awesome, exciting, and thrilling news ever. And heaven is the focus of the good news—it is what makes the good news so good.

As we will address shortly, it is much more than unfortunate that most Christians do not view heaven as something to hope for. Indeed, most Christians honestly dread the very thing that will take them to heaven—their own death. It probably sounds morbid now to think that we should long for our own departure from this life, but if you can grasp the things we will cover in this chapter, you should find a very different perspective on death.

The Bad News

At this point we need to re-emphasize that Jesus came to bring good news, but in order to understand the good news, we need to first understand the bad news against which the good news can be compared. As we said earlier, any news is good only in comparison to news that is not as good. We therefore discussed sin: how pervasive it is, how deeply ensnared each of us is in our rebellion against God, how justified God's wrath is against those responsible for what Jesus had to endure, and how impossible it would be for anyone to compensate in any way for his or her own sin. All of us are hopelessly entangled in sin—in a rebellion against God that makes us accessories to the murder of God's Messiah and every other murder on earth since we first began to sin. All of us are completely dependent on God's grace and forgiveness to save us from certain damnation.

Our normal view of sin is reminiscent of Jesus' story of the man trying to remove a speck from another person's eye while he has a log in his own eye (Matthew 7:3-5). We see others as the sinners while overlooking the mass of sin in our own lives. Jesus wants us to see the bad news, the logs in our own eyes.

And in these times we rarely hear a message about hell. It is as if hell has disappeared. But hell is there, and it is very real. Hell is terrible beyond the capability of human language to describe. The word Jesus used for hell was actually the name of a valley just outside the city of Jerusalem where the city's garbage was dumped. In this valley the garbage of the city burned 24 hours a day every day. The stench was terrible. The message was this: if you do not end the rebellion, you become the waste product of this creation suitable only for the fire. Another term for hell used in the Revelation is the "bottomless pit." I learned a little about what this might mean in 1994 when I experienced a medical test call an ENG. In a room of absolute darkness, this test induces extreme vertigo. The feeling is as of falling with no way to stop the fall. It is absolute panic. I had the test in the early afternoon, and by evening I was still so shaken that I needed a cane to walk.

I do not believe we should just scare people into becoming Christians and consider the job done—the motivational effect ends as soon as they believe they are safe, but neither do I believe that we should fail to warn people of this very real danger. Those who end the rebellion will be a welcome part of a wonderful eternity; those who do not will be rejected as good only for hell. There is no intermediate purgatory where people can somehow earn the salvation they did not accept on earth. This is our one and only chance. (I don't know what ever gave people the idea that pain and suffering could somehow pay for our sins—no amount of pain or suffering can compensate for even one rebellion.)

Once we grasp that we are damned without God's forgiveness, lost in the riptide of sin and rebellion, we should be motivated to cry out for rescue. It is at that point that God says, "All you have to do is focus your life on me and my will [faith], and I will forgive your sins and remove the threat of hell."

It is at this point that Satan tries to get us to look for an easier way out. Trust me; there is no easier way out. God wants your life focused on him—nothing less will do. You owe him that because he is your creator—not to mention what he has done to forgive your rebellion. You owe him your life all over again because of his forgiveness and grace.

The Good News

Now we can turn to our hope as Christians—the very best of the good news that Jesus brought: the good news of heaven. Of all the good news Jesus brought us, this is the ultimate in good news. God's intention is that this motivating factor would provide Christians with the reason to overcome all obstacles and to bear any cost in serving him.

Yet, as mentioned above, for most Christians, their concept of heaven could not be described as awesome, exciting, or thrilling. In fact, given a choice between heaven and hell, Christians will choose heaven, but given a choice between heaven and earth, Christians choose earth with almost no exceptions.

This is evident in several areas. The story is told of a minister who asked his congregation to stand if they wanted to go to heaven. All but one man stood. The minister repeated the request, thinking the man might not have heard, but he continued to sit. Finally, he asked the man, "Do you not want to go to heaven?" The man replied, "Oh, sure, I want to go to heaven. I just thought you were getting a load up to go now." In other words, the man wanted to go to heaven, but only when he could no longer stay on earth. Of course this is only a story, but it seems humorous because it so accurately reflects reality.

While there are exceptions, most Christians view death as a tragedy. If someone dies, especially at a young age, most Christians will openly say something about how tragic that death is for the person who died. We could not make it any clearer that we do not believe what Jesus told us about heaven. In spite of Paul's instruction to the contrary, we mourn as those who have no hope. The testimony we give to the world is that we do not believe the gospel really is good news. We do not believe that heaven is something we should anticipate with joy.

Perspectives on Heaven

In part this kind of testimony indicating that we do not believe that the gospel is really such good news is caused by the fact that most Christians have a terrible concept of heaven. Examine our songs or listen to our sermons and you will find a belief that heaven involves worshipping God forever and forever—that and not much else. Maybe we believe that we'll spend eternity tending gardens or talking about the good times we used to have on earth. Perhaps this is OK for ardent gardeners, but a lot of us are not ardent gardeners. Maybe we believe that we'll worship God for all eternity, telling him over and over again how wonderful he is because of what he did back in the good old days on earth. In this concept we may be organized into angelic choirs in order to sing God's praises. In our worst concepts, we may float on clouds wearing scratchy woolen robes and playing golden harps (clunk, clunk). Perhaps we'll have wings, but we'll have nowhere to fly.

In the movie *The Preacher's Wife,* Denzel Washington plays the part of an angel sent to earth to help a struggling preacher rekindle his faith. In this movie, the angel tells the preacher that in heaven there is this very long line of angels all eager and just waiting to get a chance to go back to earth on some mission. When the angel played by Denzel Washington arrives back on earth, he is clearly overjoyed to again experience the pleasures of life on earth. The implication is that the best thing heaven has to offer is a chance to go back to earth. In other words, heaven may be OK, but earth is far, far better. If that is really the case, then God is a liar—but that is not the case!

I don't know about you or anyone else, but for me, about three months of doing nothing but telling God what a good God he is for what he did in the past on earth would turn into torment. I would be bored out of my mind. If I faced an eternity of such boredom, I might well decide that hell could be no worse. With such a "reward," who needs punishment? And what about those who do not enjoy singing? What about the tone deaf? Are we doomed to spend eternity in scratchy robes with golden harps going over and over an unlimited number of ways we can come up with to tell God what a great guy he is? Is God a narcissist, in love with himself? Is he a sycophant, only interested in having servants to tell him how great he is? (That may be your picture of God, but that is definitely not the God I know.)

In fact, our perspectives on heaven imply that God is either stupid or very cruel because he created an entire universe including a world specially designed for people, he made sure these people could rebel against him knowing that they would rebel, he paid a terrible price for their rebellion and will still have to send most of the people he created to hell, and he has no plan to do anything with the people he has saved except to put them on a very ornate shelf for all eternity. This would be like a company sending an employee to all kinds of schools and training sessions and then assigning the employee a job of just sitting in a nice corner office with nothing to do. Worse yet, it would be like that same company taking all employees who failed to learn from these courses and killing them for their failure, even though the company has no plans to do anything with the training.

What We Say

If you think this is not a problem, just listen to what we say and think what this communicates about our hope. I have heard Christians say all of the following and many more like these:

"Every day above ground is a good day."

"I'm still breathing, and that certainly beats the alternative."

"It's so tragic when a young person dies like that" (when said of a Christian).

"Of course I want to go to heaven; I just don't want to go until I have to."

"I'm trying to stay alive as long as I can." (I just heard a variation of this from an internationally known preacher.)

The World's Response

It's no wonder non-Christians would be turned off by our message. Who would want to become a Christians if even Christians don't want heaven except as a last resort? Who would want to become a Christian if the reward is eternal boredom? Maybe hell is worse, but how much worse can it be? Why not enjoy earth's fleshly enticements and take your chances with these two versions of eternal torment?

Let's hear what a person who is not a Christian might say.

> On one hand, I hear the message of Christians, but the heaven they offer does not seem very enticing. And these Christians disagree with each other about what it takes to get into their heaven. Some of them say that God would never send anyone to hell because he is too loving for that. If they are right, then there is nothing to fear. Others argue that a person has to believe in God in order to avoid hell. Well, I believe there probably is some sort of God, but I don't see much difference between the different religions. All of them seem to have both some very nice members and some members who are terrorists. Why should I pick one over any of the others? How would I know I had picked the right one? Any way I go, it looks like my chances are no better than a throw of the dice, so why not just do what gives me fleshly pleasure now and not worry about what I can't resolve.

That is not an unreasonable approach for a person who only hears the normal message of Christianity. If we hope to win the world to Christianity—if we really believe that is important, then we need to renew our understanding of the message that motivated such people to choose the Lord and die for him.

The Disciples of Jesus

From the testimony of the Bible itself, those who followed Jesus and became his closest disciples were just that kind of people. Matthew was a tax collector—viewed as a traitor to his nation and his religion. When Peter first experienced the miraculous power of Jesus, his response was, "Get away from me, for I'm a sinful man" (Luke 5:8), and apparently James and John had a similar reaction. These men were fishermen. They were not religious scholars, and they tended to talk like fishermen. Even after being with Jesus throughout his ministry, as Jesus was on trial for his life, the Bible tells us that Peter cursed and swore as he denied knowing Jesus (Mark 14:71). Clearly, he was no stranger to profanity.

These men were not heathens, but neither were they Sunday school kids or holier-than-thou. Whatever they were, somehow the message Jesus brought turned their lives around. Peter's tirade when he denied Jesus was the last gasp of the old Peter. Once these men realized that Jesus is all that he claims to be, that his message is true, there was nothing that could shake their faith in him. We need to rediscover that message.

Getting back to our present perspective on heaven, on various occasions I have asked people in a Sunday school class to mark a secret poll showing whether they would rather go to heaven soon or stay on earth as long as possible. The result is generally unanimous. No one wants to go to heaven. Yet heaven is God's primary motivation for Christians. Paul said, "If in this life only we have hoped in Christ Jesus, we are, of all men, most to be pitied" (1Corinthians 15:19). Somehow we have lost something very, very important—the real motivation of Christianity.

The Revised Good News

Well, the good news is that the typical concept of heaven is wrong. (Again, if it were not wrong, Jesus would be a liar to call his message 'good news.')

New Earth and Sky

In order to start getting a better idea of what heaven really is, we need to take a close look at some biblical teachings. As we do this, it's important to remember that the people who wrote these things were trying to put into human terms something that is completely beyond human comprehension.

First, let's consider some of the simpler things. We will not float on clouds for all eternity. This idea probably comes from misunderstanding a few things in the Bible:

1. The word "heaven" in the Bible is not a very specific word. (In fact, this word appears in both singular and plural forms and in both masculine and feminine forms when it is often not obvious why these changes occur.) The ancient concept of heaven is more a concept of "up there" in a very general sense. It included the air (as in "birds of the heavens" e.g. in Psalm 79:2); the universe of stars (as in "stars of heaven" e.g. in Mark 13:25); the abode of God (e.g. Genesis 24:7); and the reward of God's faithful (e.g., Matthew 5:12). In other words, the definition of this word would include the atmosphere and certainly it would include clouds as one of the possible definitions of "heaven." But that is not the right definition for God's eternity.

2. In Matthew 24:30, Jesus describes his second coming using words earlier used by the prophet Daniel, "and they will see the Son of Man coming on the clouds of heaven with power and great glory." Jesus repeated a very similar statement in Matthew 26:64, saying, "in the future you will see the Son of Man sitting at the right hand of Power, and coming on the clouds of heaven." This could be understood to mean that the clouds were the heaven from which Jesus would come, but it is actually more easily understood as simply saying that Jesus would come from "up there" and his coming would appear in the skies in such a way that all would see and recognize his true nature. (With our concept of a global earth, this may seem difficult to us. After all, how can he appear at the same time to those on opposite sides of the earth? But for God this is not even a problem.)

3. In Acts 1:9 we read that Jesus "was taken up from the earth, and a cloud received Him out of their sight;" and then two

men in white (apparently angels) appeared and said, "Why do you stand gazing up into heaven? This same Jesus, who was taken up from you into heaven, will come again in the same way you saw Him go into heaven" (Acts 1:11).

4. In 1Thessalonians 4:17 Paul writes that we as Christians will be "caught up" to meet the Lord and Christians who have died before us "in the clouds."

In all of this there is nothing that says that the "heaven" that is the reward of Christians is the same as the "heaven" of clouds in the atmosphere. We will not float on clouds for eternity.

I had read the Revelation several times before I noticed it, but in Revelation 21:10 John mentions the mountains in God's new earth. John also mentions a sea and a river that sparkle like diamonds because of the purity of the water. He mentions trees that grow along the banks of the river. In other words, John describes a beautiful world with high mountains, beautiful rivers, and an ocean of clean, clear water. God created us for a world, and he will give us a new world—a better one undamaged by sin.

Beyond this, we still need to be careful what conclusions we draw from what the Bible tells us. For example, the Bible mentions that there will be no night in heaven. The fact that there will be no night does not mean that God will not provide a way for us to enjoy the beauty of a night sky. John is telling us that the aspects of evil will no longer have darkness to hide in, and we will no longer need to stumble in the dark or fear what is in the dark as we enjoy the beauty of that night sky. Even in this world, the night sky is always there—the light of the sun just blinds us to its beauty. In God's new world I expect we will be able to see this type of beauty whenever we want to. Similarly, the colors of sunrise and sunset are always there, but the brightness of the sun or the darkness of night hides the colors. In God's new world, I believe we will always be able to see those colors whenever we wish to. In other words, I am convinced that the God who created this beautiful world will not give us a far less beautiful world—I believe firmly that he will give us a far more beautiful world, and I further believe that he will enhance our ability to see that beauty.

In high school most of you probably studied something called the electro-magnetic spectrum. If you remember anything about that, you may recall that one small portion of that spectrum is visible light.

Now we know that some portions of the spectrum that are entirely invisible to us are visible to certain other animals. Have you ever wondered how much more beautiful the universe might be if we could see those other "colors"?

But having a beautiful perfect world with towering mountains, sparkling seas, fruitful trees, and colors beyond imagination is hardly even the beginning. If that were all, we would eventually tire of heaven.

Pounds and Talents

Have you ever had absolutely nothing to do? Perhaps you were in a hospital or confined to bed at home. Perhaps you were in an office with all your tasks completed, but unable to leave. Perhaps you were in jail. Whatever the case, those who have experienced this know that there are few things worse than having long hours of nothing to do. Boredom can quickly become torment.

In light of this, one very important insight about eternity comes from Jesus' teachings, but before I can share this, it is important to understand that Jesus never told more of a story in his parables than what was needed to communicate the lesson or lessons he wished to convey. When he had told enough of the story to make the point or points he wanted, he stopped. Given this truth, we will look at two parables where Jesus gave us important insights into heaven as part of a parable.

Luke 19:12-27 is known as "the parable of the pounds (or minas)," and Matthew 25:14-30 is known as "the parable of the talents." These are actually two versions of practically the same parable. (Like any good teacher, Jesus certainly said the same things in different settings, changing some details to suit the particular setting.) In each parable's story, a wealthy master entrusts significant resources to each of three servants. In each case two of the servants put these resources to good use and the third simply hides what he has been given so that it will not be at risk. In each case, the master commends the faithful servants who used what he had entrusted to them and condemns the unfaithful servant who failed to provide good stewardship of his trust. In each case the unfaithful servant loses even what he had been given. Obviously these parables teach us multiple lessons. First, they teach us to be faithful stewards of the blessings God gives us. Second, they teach us that God has given different people different levels of stewardship, but that he expects every person to faithfully use whatever he or she has received. Third, they teach us that a failure to faithfully use what has been entrusted to us is as bad as misusing God's trust—doing nothing is not an acceptable response to God's gifts. Fourth, they teach us that, in the end, those who do not faithfully use God's gifts will lose everything. And others may well see additional points.

However, there is another point Jesus made in both cases when he told this story that is generally missed. When the master commended the faithful servants, it would have been enough in the parable to have him say, "Well done, good and faithful servant. Enter into the joy of your lord." Yet Jesus intentionally added another phrase: "You have been faithful over a few things, I will make you ruler over many things" (Matthew 25:21). In Luke's account, the master says, "Because you have been faithful in a very little, you have authority over ten cities" (Luke 19:17). Though Jesus varied the details when he told this story, in each case he made the point that faithful stewards will be given greater authority and responsibility.

Heaven will not be eternal boredom. God has things for us to do—things we will find great joy in doing. He knows us better than we know ourselves, and he loves us more than we can know, so the things he has prepared will be joy beyond description.

Earlier I mentioned how much joy I experience in working for God, even when the work is hard and dirty and offers no earthly reward. I am convinced that what we do in eternity will be that much more exciting and rewarding.

Judging Angels

Paul made a similar point when he said,

> Don't you know that the saints shall judge the whole cosmos? And if you're going to judge the cosmos, are you unworthy to judge the smallest matters? Don't you know that we shall judge angels? How much more should we be able to judge things that pertain to this earthly life? (1 Corinthians 6:2-3).

In this case we should not think of "judge" like an American judge sitting at a bench, passing sentence on those brought before him. The biblical world knew nothing of separation of powers in the government. In the biblical world, every judge was a political leader.

We need to think of "judge" as in the biblical book called Judges, that is, as a leader or ruler. The message a person reading Paul's words in biblical times would have received is that at least some faithful Christians would receive positions of authority and leadership in God's eternity, and if they were to have such leadership and authority in heaven, they should be able to exercise the judgment required of such leaders in this world.

The Kingdom

During his earthly ministry Jesus told his disciples, "Assuredly I say to you, that in the regeneration, when the Son of Man sits on the throne of his glory, you who have followed me will also sit on twelve thrones, judging the twelve tribes of Israel" (Matthew 19:28). Remember Jesus' description of the judgment as separation of sheep from goats? In that passage, those who have been faithful to God are told, "Come to me, because you won the blessing of my Father. Now you will inherit the kingdom that has been prepared for you since the foundation of the world" (Matthew 25:34).

This is not to say that all Christians will be leaders of some sort when they get to heaven. That's not what Paul was saying. But what he did say indicates that there will be tasks suited to the gifts of each Christian up to and including significant leadership roles.

The Eternal Creator

Now, one might ask, "What will we have authority over? After all, when we get to heaven, we will no longer have authority on earth. Further, even if we were to be given some sort of authority on earth, at some point the earth will be destroyed long before eternity is over. What then? How can all of God's children have authority?" One of the false pictures we have of heaven is of everyone wearing golden crowns. But if everyone is a ruler, then no one is a ruler because there is no one to rule over. (In fact, the crowns promised to Christians in heaven are not bejeweled golden diadems, they are the crowns made of laurel leaves that were given to victors in sport contests and after military victories, because we have emerged victorious over sin and death.)

The passages in 1Corinthians and Matthew mentioned above certainly do imply authority, and in the Revelation we read that we will reign for eternity (Revelation 22:5). So we are back to the issue of how we can reign if there is no one to reign over.

I believe the answer is simple, but it is one we generally don't consider. I believe it is also important for many reasons. The answer, in simple terms, is that God is a creator. It would be arrogant to think that the creator of the universe has created just once in all eternity, and that one creation is our own universe. In this world we see that creators create. It is in their nature. There is no reason to believe that the same would not be true of God. After all, earthly creators received their creative gifts from God. Indeed, there is every reason to believe that God has always been and always will be a prolific creator, and that his creations are practically infinite in number and variety.

There are those who reject this concept because of a human perspective. They see God's son dying on the cross, and they know that they could never willingly give their children to die for others—especially for enemies in rebellion. Based on this, they assume that God could not possibly have done this more than one time. But this neglects the infinite love of God. Before this world was formed, God knew that he would have to come to this world and suffer the agony of the cross (see Ephesians 1:3-6 or 1Peter 1:17-21). Yet he considered the creation to be worth the cost. In Hebrews we read that Jesus (God in the flesh) "for the joy that he could see ahead endured the cross, despising the shame" (Hebrews 12:2).

If God's love was strong enough to do this once, why would we conclude that it could not be strong enough to do it again? In fact, I believe it is the very defining characteristic of God's love to be willing to die for his creation.

The Bible does offer clues to exactly this scenario. Throughout the Bible, God works through angels. (The word "angel" means "messenger." There are actually places in the Bible where it is impossible to tell if the word should be translated "angel" for a heavenly messenger or just "messenger" for a human messenger—for example in Judges 2:1-4. For this topic we will be considering angels as heavenly messengers.) The Bible indicates that the angels were involved in creation (see Job 38:4-7 where God is speaking), so they were around before humans were created. So where do angels come from? Remember, there are both bad angels (messengers of Satan sometimes called demons—see Revelation 12:9) and good angels. I can see only three possibilities for the origin of angels:

1. One possibility is that God created some angels as good angels and some angels as bad angels, and the bad angels will be sent to eternal condemnation along with Satan and unrepentant sinners. The problem with this idea is that it makes God (who is love) a pretty cruel God when it comes to the bad angels. They never had a chance to avoid eternal hell.

2. Another possibility is that God created all angels as good angels, and that some good angels rebelled against God and became bad angels. But if God only provides one sacrifice for sin, then these bad angels do not have and never could have had any hope of a second chance based on repentance. While this is a little less cruel than the previous possibility, it still is not consistent with what we know of our loving and merciful God.

3. The only other possibility I can see is that angels come from another creation where they encountered sin and had the opportunity to repent and be forgiven. Those who ended their rebellion moved into God's eternity to serve him, and at least some of those who did not end the rebellion became Satan's angels with assurance of eventual eternity in hell. In other words, in this possibility angels would have experienced pretty much what we are experiencing. Actually, this is the only possibility I have come up with that is consistent with the biblical picture of God. (And this would explain the strong motivation of good angels to lead people in God's ways.)

If this third possibility is true, it gives us important insight into what may await us in eternity. Not that all of us would serve in different creations. God gave each of us our gifts and he knows where each of us would find the most joy in his service—and that is where he will use us. Some may enjoy landscaping or gardening in the new world. Some may feel that nothing could be better than singing in heavenly choirs. But for the many who would not be thrilled with such activities, God has plans that will be thrilling for them.

An important point here is that God will not change us into something entirely different. He will not take away our ability to choose. He will not change our natural abilities (though he probably will enhance them). He has promised to change us from mortal to immortal, but if he were to change us into something entirely different from what we are in our hearts and souls, he would not be saving us or giving us eternal life—because we would not be then who we are now. If changing us into something else were his plan, effectively turning us into some new and different beings, why not just create those beings and put them directly into heaven without going through the difficulties of this earth and the crucifixion of Jesus?

If this world has any meaning, it is to prepare us for heaven. We can be confident that the things we learn in God's service in this world will be used by God in the eternity he has planned in ways that will bring each of us ever greater joy in his service.

Unlimited Tasks

Given the concept of unlimited numbers of creations, at any given time there would be limitless opportunities to serve God in one or more of his creations; just as those we call 'angels' serve him in our creation. We have no idea how many angels serve God in this creation, or what all they do, but from the Bible we do know that God does much of his work through these messengers. In fact, this seems to be a characteristic of God, for in a similar way he works through Christians to carry out his will in this world (which could be seen as preparing us for angelic roles in heaven). Apparently, God finds joy in having his creations use their gifts in his service. (And anyone who has experienced it knows that we find joy in using our gifts in his service—a true win-win situation!)

When we consider what this means to us, the news is really very good. No matter what talents we may have, no matter what interests we may have, somewhere in God's infinite creations there is certain to be a place where we can serve God by doing exactly the things that bring us the most joy. Indeed, the one who knows us much better than we know ourselves and loves us with an infinite love will be the one to assign our tasks in eternity. You may not even be able to imagine what would work for you, but God knows.

A Picture of Eternity

Now, let's take a look at what this might mean. What follows here is just a story meant to illustrate some aspects of what we may experience in God's eternity based on what the Bible teaches.

A man wakes up in a beautiful meadow surrounded by tall trees. He opens his eyes to see the most beautiful scenery he has ever seen. Around him, the colors of the world seem clearer and more vibrant than anything he can remember seeing before. He sees colors and shades of color he cannot remember ever seeing before.

Lying still for a moment in this park, the man hears the sound of voices and turns to look. He sees a group of people approaching him, and before they reach him he realizes that they are all his closest friends and loved ones. Leading the group he sees his grandfather who taught him so many wonderful things as a child. As they approach him, they are all joyfully excited to see him, and they begin to share what has been happening since they last saw each other.

The man gets up and starts to talk and laugh with the group as they move off together down a pathway in the park. Among other things, they are talking about his new job. He is aware that he has this exciting new job, though he does not recall looking for it. He is already excited about it, describing to the others the things he intends to do. His mind fills with the exciting possibilities he sees, and he can already tell that there are more possibilities that he has not considered yet. Others in the group offer suggestions or encouragement.

Suddenly he realizes—these are the loved ones he thought of as dead. Dimly he recalls a crisis situation just before he woke in the park. Now he is with them. Yet he cannot bring himself to think of himself as dead. He is not dead. Those he once thought of as dead are not dead. No, where he was is more accurately described as dead than where he and these others are.

As they move down the path he sees a shining, beautiful city ahead, and more people come into view. Unlike cities he has known before, this city gleams with cleanliness and goodness. Some people along the path are working in gardens of breathtaking beauty. Some are in groups talking excitedly about this or that undertaking. Some rush by on their business, but from each one the man feels a powerful sense of love. The love is so strong, he feels he could almost float in it. He knows, beyond any doubt, that there could be no danger here. Suddenly, the idea of a lock like he used to use so often in his earthly life comes to his mind, and he can't restrain his laughter at the idea. There would be no locks here.

Then someone in a group nearby breaks into song. The song is clear, beautiful, and exciting. Others join in the song. It is a song of joy in what each one is doing. The man has never been a singer, but he finds himself caught up in the song. Though he does not sing, his soul joins in the song. What a thrill! The joy is so powerful that he can hardly contain it. How long does the song go on? Time seems to mean nothing.

When the song shifts to a background presence, the man says to his grandfather, "Is this heaven? If it is, when do we get to see Jesus?" To this his grandfather replies, "When you want to see Jesus, just open your eyes and look." The man wonders at this answer, but when he tries, he is suddenly overwhelmed by love so powerful it seems to shake the world beneath him. His eyes fill with tears of joy and wonder as he sees the Lord before him, reaching to brush the tears of joy from his face and grasp him in the most wonderful hug he has ever experienced. Among all the wonders he is experiencing, this is the most awesome. He realizes that he is meeting the one who will be his boss on his new job. It is as if waves of awe and wonder and love flow over him. What joy! Yet in his heart, perhaps the most exciting thing the man knows is that this is only the beginning.[15]

No Boredom There

While this picture of eternity is, without doubt, inaccurate in some of its details, perhaps it brings home the point just a little bit—that eternity as God has planned it is exciting, thrilling, good news. There will be no boredom in God's heaven. The Infinite Creator has more than enough to keep all of us busy at exactly the things that we would want most to do. And when one of us begins to get even close to the point where boredom might be sensed, God will be there to say, "Come with me, my child. Others are eager to do this work. I have a new assignment for you—one that you have always wanted to do." I really do not know the details of how this will work, but I am confident that heaven will work so well and be so good that if we could catch even a glimpse of what is coming, we would be more than eager to get there.

Think about this for a moment. Have you ever done hard work for the Lord, perhaps helping the needy, perhaps working on some

15 This is not a record of some actual near-death experience. I have had no such experience, and, to the best of my knowledge, I am not personally acquainted with anyone who has. I have read such accounts. Some seem to ring close to the truths revealed in the Bible. Others are clearly hoaxes. I would not want to add to the confusion. My only reason for including this picture of eternity is to emphasize some points I know are made in the Bible in a way that may make them more understandable or real.

mission project, or meeting some other need in the Lord's service? If you did it for the Lord, I am confident that you left the task feeling exhilarated! No matter how hard you work, no matter how long it takes, no matter how unpleasant the work seems from a worldly perspective, when we work for the Lord, he gives us joy in our labor. We always leave the task with that skippity-doo-dah joy in our hearts!

The Rest in Heaven

Now, this brings up an important point. The Bible says that we will rest from our labors in eternity (Revelation 14:13). Yet the ideas we have looked at here seem to say that we will have new and more challenging labors. Is this a conflict? I believe it is not. From God's perspective, real labor is our struggle against sin. That is the hardest part of this life for a Christian—and that is the labor that we will leave behind. Battling sin is depressing, difficult (impossible to win), and exhausting. Working for God is thrilling, never beyond our capability, and energizing. God's reward for those who have found joy in his service is even greater joy in even greater service. That is truly heaven!

Think about this. Boredom is not restful. When a fight that seems like it cannot be won and that goes on and on is finally won, that is true rest. When a person is at peace with who he or she is and what he or she is doing, that is true rest. God offers true rest within this environment of exciting work. Jesus said, "Take my yoke [a working harness] upon you and learn from me, for I am gentle and humble to the core, and you will find rest for your souls. For my yoke is easy and my burden is light" (Matthew 11:29-30). God does not promise us the eternal boredom of a heaven with nothing to do—he promises us release from the terrible burden of sin; he promises us unending joy in his service.

This does not mean that we won't have time to relax and enjoy heaven. The biblical teaching about resting from our labors should not just be limited to freedom from the battle against sin—although that will be our greatest area of relief. I fully expect to have the opportunity to wander the mountains of the new world and walk along the banks of the River of Life and rest in the shade of the Tree of Life on the shore of a sea that sparkles like diamonds. I fully expect to have wonderful times of reunion with loved ones and with giants of the faith. But eternal vacation becomes eternal boredom, and that is not what we will find in heaven.

Marriage and Heaven

Some Christians are worried by something else Jesus said. Jesus told his disciples that in heaven we would neither marry nor be given in marriage (see Matthew 22:30). Those who have experienced marriage as God intended it have found it to be among the most wonderful blessings in this world. They do not want to be separated from their spouses in eternity.

Once again, the news is good. I am convinced that Jesus never intended to imply that we will be separated. That makes no sense and does not fit with other teachings in the Bible. Instead, the very thing we found so wonderful in marriage will become much more universal. The strong love bonds we have formed over many years must be exclusive in this life, but in heaven there will be no reason for such bonds to be exclusive. There will be no envy or jealousy and no reason for envy or jealousy in heaven. Instead, each person will be able to find such love with each other person. As God's children, we will learn to love as God loves. We will still love those who were our spouses, and I have no doubt that, at least at first, we will have a stronger relationship with them than with most others. But the barriers will be down—and we will have no reason to resent the removal of those barriers.

Singing God's Praises

But what about singing God's praises for all eternity? First, while the Bible does mention singing for those who reach heaven (Revelation 5:9; 14:3; 15:3), there is no indication that singing will be our main activity or even a major activity. Indeed, I am convinced that those who serve God in eternity will be singing his praises for all eternity (perhaps vocally for some and in the spirit for others according to each one's gifts). But I am also convinced that the primary theme of our singing will not be what God has done in some distant past, but rather what God is doing. I am convinced that our singing will be the natural response of our souls to the joy of serving God in ways more wonderful than we can imagine and to the joy of experiencing God's Holy Spirit in more fullness than we could ever experience him in this world.

God is not a narcissist in love with himself; he is the very source of love for others. And it is this love that will bring the blessings of life—true life, eternal life that is really living—that will cause us to sing for joy with tears of joy streaming down our faces. And as the tasks and the experiences of the joy God brings are eternally varying, so the songs of joy will be eternally varying.

Fearing Death

Even if we seriously believe that heaven is wonderful and well worth eagerly anticipating, death is still a serious negative in our minds. No matter how wonderful heaven is, we have real concerns about getting there. First, the very process of dying may be long, painful, and very unpleasant. Second, there are passages in the Bible that can be confusing concerning what happens immediately when we die. Third, since we know that we are still sinful humans, for many there is still the nagging fear that things may not go our way at the judgment—that we may fall short and wind up in eternal hell rather than eternal heaven.

Worries about Being Lost

Let's handle each of these individually, starting with the fear of being lost. One of the things often misunderstood in Paul's letters known as Romans and Ephesians is the matter of predestination. Honest Christian leaders have misunderstood this concept largely by failing to see the pattern of thought in these letters. This has led to a doctrine accepted to varying degrees by different branches of the Reformation led by Martin Luther—a doctrine teaching that God chooses who will be saved and who will be lost before the people involved are ever born. This doctrine holds that God is and must be in absolute control of his creation, and that therefore there can never be a question in God's mind about who will be saved and who will not. God's will is supreme, and no man can change what God has ordained. Put in those terms, this doctrine can be made to sound pretty reasonable.

But that is not how Paul uses the terms predestined or foreordained. In Paul's usage, it is those who become Christians who are predestined to salvation—and this state of being predestined is contingent on a person's faith. Once a person comes to God in faith, there is no power anywhere that can pull that person out of the safety of God's grace. However, while nothing can pull a person out of God's grace, in Paul's reasoning that person never loses his or her free will. In other words, that person always has the choice to turn away from God, walking away from the protection of his grace. So long as the core focus of a person's life is on God and learning to live ever more fully for him, God's grace is like an impenetrable force field protecting us from every threat. But if a person who has come to know God chooses to turn his or her back on God and return to a life of worldly self-interest, that person leaves behind the protection he or she had as a Christian.

Those who argue that God predestines individuals for salvation or damnation before they are born must somehow deal with Peter's words: "The Lord is not neglecting to keep his promise (as some think of neglect) but is very patient toward us. He is not willing that anyone should perish but that all should come to repentance" (2Peter 3:9). They must also deal with the question of why God would bother creating those who will be condemned if he is truly a God of love. In fact, they must deal with why God would bother with a revelation like the Bible since it would have no influence at all on whether any individual were saved or lost. And they must deal with why God would send his son to the cross when he could have much more easily programmed those who are to be saved so that they would never be able to sin at all.

Anyhow, using Paul's definition of predestination, the matter is pretty simple. If you are really trying to live for God, God certainly knows that, and the protection of his grace shields you from every possible danger. You cannot be lost. You are predestined for salvation and an eternity of heaven. (If you are trying to live for God and for some reason you want to go to hell, you are out of luck—that cannot happen.) No one accidentally slips out of God's grace. No one is lost just because he or she fails to live up to this life focus from time to time. Satan is more powerful than any of us, and our worldly nature is weak. God knows our weakness and Satan's strength. That is why he has provided one and only one perfect sacrifice for sin. The price is already paid. There is nothing we have to do to receive forgiveness as long as the core focus of our life is still on being God's people. If you really want to be God's person, God will not let you fail. That's God's version of predestination.

But how can you really know that you are on the right track. First of all, if you are trying, it is God's job to see that you have all the support you need, and God can always be trusted to do his part. Better yet, when we learn to pray as Jesus taught we begin to experience awesome blessings that assure us of God's love and care. (The problem with far too many prayers is that they request what would obviously work against God's interests, and God will not grant such prayers.) Once a person masters prayer, there can be no doubt in that person's mind about the reality of his or her salvation. This is truly blessed assurance.

> Blessed assurance: Jesus is mine!
>
> O what a foretaste of glory divine!
>
> Heir of salvation, purchase of God,
>
> Born of his Spirit, washed in his blood![16]

The teaching of the Reformation generally emphasizes that once a person becomes a Christian, that person can never be lost. This teaching is not biblical, but it is close. In fact, all a Christian has to do is keep trying to live for God, and that Christian is eternally secure. Once we have it, we cannot lose our salvation unless we ourselves choose to turn from it. The important key is that salvation is a lifetime process, not a one-time action. We never get too old to continue being God's servant. The tasks God has for us will change with time, but he will always have some stewardship ready for each of us.

Immediately after Death

So what happens to a Christian immediately after death? As mentioned above, different passages in the Bible can give people different perspectives.

For example, Paul told the Christians in Thessalonica,

> The Lord himself will come from heaven with a shout, with the voice of a ruler of angels, and with the trumpet of God. And the dead in Christ will rise first. Then we who are alive and remain shall be caught up together with them in the clouds to meet the Lord in the air; and from there on we will always be with the Lord (1Thessalonians 4:16-17).

And throughout the New Testament there are references to Christians "falling asleep" meaning that they have died (Matthew 27:52; Acts

16 Fanny Crosby, 1873, in the public domain.

7:60; 1Corinthians 15:6, 18, 20). These and other passages could be understood to mean that Christians will be in some sort of waiting mode from the time they die until Christ returns again, but they do not necessarily say that.

On the other hand, Jesus told a friend and follower named Martha, "I am the resurrection and the life. He who believes in me, though he may die, yet he shall live. And anyone who lives and believes in me shall never die" (John 11:25-26). The last sentence is a pretty powerful statement that a Christian who dies physically would remain alive spiritually. And later Jesus told a man dying on a cross next to him, "I assure you, this day you will be with me in paradise" (Luke 23:43). Again, this seems like very strong assurance that we will not have to wait in some limbo condition until the Lord returns. Furthermore, Jesus told a story about a wealthy man and a poor beggar named Lazarus, and in this story Jesus pictures Lazarus as already rewarded and the wealthy man as already in torment (Luke 16:19-31). Now, you might say that this is only a story, but there is no case where Jesus told a story based on a wrong concept of how things work. (And in fact, the Bible never says that this was a parable as opposed to an actual account. If it was a parable, it is the only parable in which the name of a participant is mentioned.) Once again, this seems to argue that those who die do not have to wait to have their eternal destiny begin, at least in some form. And the apostle Paul said that to be absent from the body was to be present with the Lord (see 2Corinthians 5:8).

I believe both sets of passages express part of the truth, and I believe no human alive can tell the whole story of what happens between a Christian's death and the Lord's return. What I do believe is that Jesus correctly pictures what we will experience immediately after death, but I also believe that in some way the fullness of the reward is not revealed until Christ returns as Paul indicates.

The key point here from our Lord's own words is that for a Christian, death is simply a door into a wonderful eternity where we will find peace, comfort, and joy in serving God. For me, that is good enough. And it is interesting that the near-death accounts I have seen that seem to ring true to the Bible all picture something similar to what Jesus described—immediate peace, comfort, and joy.

The Process of Dying

At this point I will readily admit that I would much rather die a quick death than a long, lingering death. I would gladly take a quick death now as opposed to a long lingering death in some relatively distant future. But we do not get to make those choices. So let's address the death we would not prefer—the long, lingering, painful path to death.

For the case of a Christian who has to suffer for years before actually dying, what God promises is enough spiritual strength to endure. That may seem like not much comfort, but that is true only if you have not personally experienced that strength. Each case is different, and there is no way to scientifically measure what God does, but those who experience his Holy Spirit working in their lives will know just how powerful this can be.

The obvious question such cases raise is why God would allow his saints to suffer long years like this. For now we can leave it at this—God has very, very good reasons. We will never know all his reasons, but we can certainly understand enough to see that his reasons are good ones. (Many will be surprised at how obvious this is when we consider God's perspective. It's one of those head-smacking experiences.) And we will learn that God can take whatever suffering we go through either in life or in death and turn it to good.

The Necessary Link between Faith and Hope

The eleventh chapter of the book of Hebrews is often called the "faith chapter" of the Bible because it points out many heroes of faith from the history of the Jews. But that chapter could just as appropriately be called the "hope chapter." The chapter does focus on faith and people who demonstrated faith, but in this chapter a repeated theme deals with how this faith is motivated by hope.

Too many Christians with whom I have talked argue that we should not need some exciting concept of heavenly reward to support and motivate our faith. They do not have such a concept, and they even choose to reject such a concept. But this is not what the Bible teaches, and it is not consistent with how God has designed us. If we expect people to dedicate their lives to something, we need to provide some strong motivation. Otherwise the response is almost certain to be limited to the minimum considered necessary—often little more than lip service.

In Hebrews 11:6 we read, "But without faith it is impossible to please God, because anyone who comes to him must believe that he exists and that he rewards those who sincerely seek him." In this passage we learn that faith *should* be focused on a reward, but with just this passage we might understand the reward as earthly rather than heavenly.

In Hebrews 11:10 we read, "For he [that is Abraham] waited for the city which has foundations, whose builder and maker is God." In other words, the Bible is saying that Abraham demonstrated such powerful faith because his life was focused on something beyond this world—that is, on the hope that he understood God was promising beyond this life.

In Hebrews 11:13 we read, "These [that is Abel, Enoch, Noah, Abraham, and Sarah] all died in faith, not having received the promises, but having seen them afar off were assured of them, embraced them and confessed that they were strangers and pilgrims on the earth." Here again we see that the focus of a strong faith is motivated by a reward beyond this earth.

In Hebrews 11:16 we read, "But now they desire a better, that is, a heavenly country. Therefore God is not ashamed to be called their God, for he has prepared a city for them." Again, the focus of faith is beyond this life, in heaven. Faith is motivated by a serious focus on the heavenly reward.

In Hebrews 11:26 we read that Moses esteemed "the reproach of Christ greater riches than the treasures in Egypt; for he looked to the reward." While this passage again does not define the reward as heavenly, what has already been said in verses 10, 13, and 16 makes it clear that this is the case.

We need to stop making excuses for our weak faith that is based on nothing but a hope to avoid hell—in other words, not based on a hope that will provide real motivation. God has intentionally provided more than enough information to motivate our faith—we just need to accept what he is telling us. To say that we do not need such a motivation for our faith is to admit that we do not have it, even though God has done everything possible to provide it. When we say that we do not need a motivation, we are telling the world that we have no motivation, and the world simply turns away.

Preparing for Heaven

As we saw earlier, the fact that there must be an option to sin once we get to heaven is real—otherwise God would be a cruel monster. He hates to lose the people who refuse to end the rebellion, but he considers that cost to be worth the price to gain those who do end the rebellion. So the most important lesson we need to learn in this life is to hate sin and its effects. That is the primary reason that we were created to live in this world. God cannot take us to heaven if we do not learn this lesson.

But this world also serves as a training ground to prepare us for heaven. God does not control everything we do and every experience we have, in fact, for the most part he simply lets things run their course as he pleads with us to accept his rescue plan. But God can and does use the things that happen to us as lessons to better prepare us for eternity. And for those who end the rebellion, he does promise that he will never allow us to be tested beyond what we are able to bear (see 1Corinthians 10:13).

When we see this world and all the good and bad in it with this perspective, the concept is motivating. Even when things are at their worst, we can be confident that God will be with us, we can be confident that God will use whatever we are experiencing for our ultimate good (see Romans 8:28), and we can be confident that God will eventually bring us to joy beyond measure no matter how bad things may seem.

Summary of Hope

In summary: God's eternity involves excitement, love, beauty, joy, responsibility, stewardship, rewarding accomplishments, and, above all, the very personal presence of God. Good news indeed! If we could really accept this on faith—if we could really understand how wonderful this is—we would eagerly long for the day we could go to heaven. We would rejoice over every Christian who got to go ahead of us, and we would look forward to our turn with joyful anticipation. It really is that good!

As long as the best hope Christians have is for a heavenly reward that they hope they do not get—at least not in the near future—Christianity will struggle with the lack of motivation that characterizes the church in far too many ways. If we could ever one time catch even a partial glimpse of what God actually has in store for us, we would be eager beyond description for that reward, wanting nothing more than to prepare ourselves for that time. That is how God meant Christianity to work—an exciting race to glory and joy beyond imagination.

Any or all of the details of my descriptions of heaven may be wrong, but I trust God's word that "No eye has seen, no ear has heard, no one's heart has even imagined the things that God has prepared for those who love him" (1Corinthians 2:9). Once again recall Paul's words, "If in this life only we have hoped in Christ Jesus, we are, of all men, most to be pitied" (1Corinthians 15:19). We need a view of heaven that causes us to really long for and focus on getting to heaven, and we need that hope to shine forth from our lives. As Peter said, "But sanctify the Lord God in your hearts, and always be ready to give a reasonable response to everyone who asks you to explain the hope instilled in you, but with meekness and reverence" (1Peter 3:15).

The question I would ask each Christian is this: "Do you really have your life focused on heaven as your true hope?" If you would be motivated to serve God, you need a view of heaven that inspires you to focus on heaven. If you would communicate the gospel (a word that means "good news") to others, a concept of heaven that is truly desirable is the good news that will motivate people to truly and for their whole lives focus their lives on God.

Let's assume for the moment that you accept this, at least in its big picture perspective. (You may not agree with the details about heaven—that's not important as long as your view of heaven is truly motivating.) How would this concept change what we as Christians do? Is there something we are doing that we should not be doing? Is there something we are not doing that we should be doing? Are we allowing our traditions to work against these biblical principles of motivation, and therefore to limit our influence for the kingdom?

CHAPTER SEVEN: SALVATION—THE ULTIMATE MESSAGE

At the name of Jesus every knee must bow
– Philippians 2:10

Several years ago I had to go to Washington DC for a few days on business. I flew into Dulles International Airport and rented a car. The day I was to fly home was a cloudy, rainy day. I drove onto the beltway Interstate to get to the airport, knowing that I had plenty of extra time to make it before my flight. However, as I drove on the beltway, I realized that I had made a mistake in how long it would take to get to the airport—it was farther than I had thought. As my extra time began to melt away, I drove faster and faster, watching carefully for airport exit signs. Finally I stopped to look at the map and see how much farther I needed to go—and it was then I realized that I had been driving the wrong direction! The car was running great, and I was driving about as fast as I dared, but I was getting farther and farther from my goal. Too often that's a good picture of where we find ourselves in our efforts to spread the gospel. (By the way, I did make my flight, but not with much time to spare.)

The big question in my mind as I write this is, "Do we have the courage to do what is right, or are we so bound by tradition that we will once again reject the truth?" Satan wants to put us to sleep. In the movie *Tora! Tora! Tora!*, the Japanese admiral Yamamoto is portrayed as saying, "I fear that all we have done is to awaken a sleeping giant." Will the church be satisfied to remain a sleeping giant, or will we really respond to God's call?

The things we've already covered will hopefully provide strong motivation for renewed Christian living, but in too many cases the years of practicing Christianity without this kind of vision have resulted in an accumulation of bad habits and attitudes that have left us driving furiously in the wrong direction. The errors have been like the clouds in Washington that blocked my view of the sun and allowed me to drive so furiously in the wrong direction. To revitalize what we are doing, we need a kick-start in the right direction that seriously looks at some of the practices that have us going in entirely wrong directions. We need to go back to God's road map.

This section looks at some specific practices and attitudes prevalent in churches today and how these need to change in order to let the gospel message come across as truly good news. The question I would start out with is this: "Do we really want to be Christians—focused on bringing people to Christianity as Jesus taught and as it was meant to be in God's view, or are we really more interested in continuing the traditions of movements that have lost their vitality and are moving furiously in the wrong directions?" In this chapter we will look at some areas that I believe are especially significant areas that we need to change in order to get back on the track of revitalizing our Christianity. If Christianity is not inspiring and motivating, it's not what God intended.

Application to Conversion – The Huge Misunderstanding

I have been a Christian since childhood, and I firmly believe in the goals shared by most sincere Christians. However, with the best of intentions we have drifted away from our New Testament roots in some very important areas—one of the most important of these is the area of faith or belief. And this drift has led to all kinds of errors in doctrine and in practice. The drift is nothing new. Satan began his efforts to blow Christians and Christianity off course in New Testament times, and he has never stopped. And a misunderstanding of faith or belief has always been one of his favorite tools.

As mentioned earlier in this book, the words "faith" and "belief" in the Bible are just two different translations of the same word—a word with a wide range of meanings, but a word that the authors of the New Testament used in a very consistent pattern to mean focusing your life on living for God. In our earlier discussion of faith we focused on how we can know the biblical meaning of this term, and we went over some of the strong biblical evidence that saving faith necessarily involves focusing one's life on living for God—ending the rebellion. We also saw how this understanding of saving faith or belief makes sense in the light of eternity while competing ideas do not work. If we have not focused our lives on living for God, he cannot safely take us to heaven.

But from New Testament times, there have been those in the church—often in leadership roles—who failed to see this. Instead, they interpreted saving faith or belief as acceptance of certain facts as true and/or a willingness to accept God's salvation. This acceptance of the facts of the gospel or acceptance of the salvation God offers has generally been viewed as having no necessary connection to how a person lives out his or her life. In this view, accepting these facts makes us acceptable to God regardless of how we live. This thinking has led to various errors, some of which we will consider in this chapter.

Several years ago I saw a pamphlet on salvation provided by a major church group. This pamphlet was illustrated with sketches to try to convey the meaning. The state of a person who was not a Christian was illustrated with a circle representing the person and Christ outside that circle. Inside the circle was a throne, and a figure representing the person was on the throne. The state of a person who had become a Christian was illustrated with the same circle and the same person on the throne, but with Christ now inside the circle. Then the pamphlet talked about maturing as a Christian and illustrated this with the same circle but with Christ now on the throne and the person inside the circle bowing before him. The Bible knows of no such process. Either Christ is on the throne or he is not in the circle at all. He is King of kings and Lord of lords. He will not accept second place.

In addition (as addressed earlier), from the very earliest days of the church the concept of our eternal reward has been neglected to the point that most Christians, including most Christian leaders, have failed to see the important link between faith as taught in the Bible and this reward. While there are exceptions, as a whole we as Christians have failed to understand that this world has a very important purpose in God's mind, and that he is using this world with all its flaws to teach us eternally important things. We've already discussed the fact that most Christians have a concept of heaven that involves no responsibility—an eternity of singing praises to God for things he did in the past, reminiscing about the "good old days" on earth, and tending gardens in a perfect world where sin is impossible. With this concept of heaven, the earth has no real purpose. Why did God create a world where sin is possible, thereby making the death of Jesus necessary, when he could have simply created people in heaven where they could never sin? Why risk the certain loss of so many in this creation if he had an eternal end plan in mind where sin would be impossible? Is this world simply an entertainment for God? Is it just a puppet show in which God pulls all the strings? This perspective casts God in a very unflattering role at best, and at worst it makes him a very cruel and evil being. Either the message of the Bible is wrong, or the doctrines with this perspective must be wrong.

Looking at every major doctrinal teaching in Christianity today and many minor ones we will find these same two errors have crept into practically every doctrine. What a victory for Satan! Using a college class as an illustration, let's look at some doctrinal teachings that have serious problems and that do not match true biblical teaching.

For our first example, some doctrines present Christianity to be like a difficult college class where the professor guarantees a good grade to all students who agree that the subject matter is important and then ask for such a grade, whether or not they study or even come to class. Does that seem ridiculous? If you were taking such a class, how would you react to learning this? Would you bother to study the material? Would you bother to come to class? Or would you try to get a refund on your textbook purchase? And would it not be obvious that the professor has no concern about what his students learn or whether they will be able to use the class materials in their lives?

Other doctrines present Christianity to be like a class where the professor announces at the beginning of the course that he has already preselected who will pass and who will fail with no reference to student abilities or what the students learn. Does that seem ridiculous? If you were taking such a class, how would you react to learning this? Would you bother to study the material? Would you bother to come to class? Or would you again try to get a refund on your textbook purchase? And would it not be just as obvious that such a professor has no concern about what his students learn or whether they will be able to use the class materials in their lives?

Yet other doctrines present Christianity to be like a class where the professor requires all students to perform some magic ritual, assuring the students that those who perform the ritual will receive good grades regardless of what they learn or whether they attend class. Does that seem ridiculous? If you were taking such a class, how would you react to learning this? Would you bother to study the material? Would you bother to come to class? Or would you once again try to get a refund on your textbook purchase? And would it not be equally obvious that the professor has no concern about what his students learn or whether they will be able to use the class materials in their lives?

Still other doctrines present Christianity to be like such a class where the professor hands out the final exam at the beginning of the course and guarantees a good grade to any student who can answer the questions on this exam regardless of how much they actually learn about the subject. Does that seem ridiculous? If you were taking such a class, how would you react to learning this? Would you bother to study the material beyond what would be needed to answer these specific questions? Would you bother to come to class? Or would you try to return your textbook as soon as you found these answers? And would it not be obvious once more that the professor has no concern about what his students really learn or whether they will be able to use the class materials in their lives?

The ideas above may seem ridiculous when applied to college classes, and indeed each example indicates a professor who does not care about the ability of his students to meet the challenges of life after college, but the things we teach are far too often just as ridiculous. Such ideas are no less ridiculous when applied to God and Christianity; they present God as having a plan of salvation with no real purpose or meaning. Certainly people can find a few verses in the Bible to "prove" that "we must be right," but if we use verses taken out of the context of the whole message, we can "prove" almost anything.

Besides these there are doctrines that are obviously made up to match the worldly opinions popular at a given time, intentionally disregarding biblical teaching to allow acceptance of worldly ideas. And as the worldly opinions change, these doctrines try to maintain themselves against increasingly obvious indications that they cannot be right.

All of these doctrinal teachings have serious problems with biblical teachings. In each case, those who teach the doctrines have based their teachings on a few selected passages in the Bible, ignoring the clear intent of other passages. I will readily agree that we need to base our teachings on what the Bible says, but it is important to use the teachings of the Bible to interpret the teachings of the Bible. In some cases, a teaching that may be interpreted more than one way must be interpreted in light of other passages in the Bible, and every teaching should be interpreted in light of the whole Bible. But when a doctrinal teaching requires giving biblical passages a meaning that seems inconsistent with the context and with the way any reader would be expected to normally understand the words, warning alarms should go off in our minds—and unfortunately the alarms should be going off for every major doctrinal teaching in Christianity today. Did you think Satan was not working on your doctrine? He is working on yours and on mine and on the doctrine of anyone who seriously seeks to serve the Lord.

Do I have it right while everyone else has it wrong? I am well aware that I am as fallible as any man. All that I would ask is that you as a reader seriously consider the points made here and do as the Jews Paul met in the city of Berea who are describe in this way: "Now these [the Bereans] were more open-minded than those in Thessalonica, because they eagerly received the message we brought, examining the sacred writings daily to determine the truth of this message" (Acts 17:11).

On top of the errors discussed above, there are all kinds of mixtures. While some Christian leaders may be consistent in their doctrinal teaching, many leaders and most Christians tend to mix the errors—accepting as valid certain parts of different errors. In many cases these mixtures are self-contradictory, but we overlook the contradictions.

It should also be understood that there are many, many Christians who do focus their lives on living for God in spite of any doctrinal teachings, just as there would be some students who would be wise enough to seriously study the material in spite of a professor who indicates that such study would not be needed to pass the class requirements. The fact that so many Christians do focus their lives on living for God is clear evidence of the working of God's Holy Spirit in the lives of Christians. Even when we get the doctrines wrong, if we will let him, God will guide us into his ways. But how much better we could serve the Lord if what we teach and what we practice were both what God wants.

No Christian ever gets all the answers right—and that certainly includes me. No Christian group ever gets all the answers right. But in light of overwhelming biblical testimony, I believe there are a few things here that are right and that challenge the traditional teachings of many churches and many sincere Christians. Among those things are the following: 1) the fact that in the Bible, saving faith or belief always necessarily implies a life surrendered to God; 2) the fact that heaven is and must be far better than this earth and that God meant our concept of heaven to motivate our faith; and 3) the fact that God intentionally placed the humans he loved and created in an environment where he knew that they would sin and that most of them would therefore be lost because they needed to learn to hate sin before he could safely take them to heaven.

The Right Answer for Any Time

Now, imagine trying to convince someone that God's plan of salvation is to accept Jesus as Lord. This is like a college professor who tells the students that they will get a good grade if they focus on learning the material. The New Testament is permeated with passages that will establish this biblical teaching firmly. Paul rarely mentions Jesus by name without adding either "Lord" or "Christ" or both, and he often refers to Jesus as simply "Lord" or "Christ" without having to include his name. Rather than jumping around all over the Bible to find proofs for different points in some made-up plan we consider humanly logical or twisting a limited number of passages to get them to support something the Bible never really teaches, we can go almost anywhere in the New Testament to establish this point. And when we understand that Jesus is God incarnate so that accepting him as Lord is exactly the same as accepting God's authority in our lives, we can find that throughout the Bible—Old Testament or New. Thus saying that Jesus is Lord is the same as saying that you accept God's divine authority over your daily life.

Before going any further, it is important to stop here and point out that this does not create some new set of rules and laws we need to obey to earn our way into heaven. The change in attitude from a focus on ourselves and on worldly matters to a focus on what God wants is the key to salvation. In whatever ways we fall short of fully living up to that goal, God's grace is there to provide full and free forgiveness. God does not demand that we succeed at any aspect of Christian living—he demands that we really honestly try to live for him and that we really honestly try to treat each other with Christian love—but he does not demand that we succeed in all cases or in any one specific case. That's what grace is for. And of course he knows whether we are really trying or not.

Picture it this way: Imagine a drawing with two horizontal lines, one well above the other. Assume that the top line represents successfully living as God would want in every situation, and that the bottom line represents living for self and for worldly goals in every situation. Between these two lines, draw several arrows with some pointing up and some pointing down. Randomly place the arrows so that some of the arrows pointing down are close to the bottom, some close to the top, and some in between. Similarly, randomly place the arrows pointing up so that some are close to the bottom, some close to the top, and some in the middle. The ones pointing up are saved, and the ones pointing down are lost—where they are between the two lines does not matter. But in this illustration it is important to realize that the ones pointing up are all in process of at least trying to move upward. (The fact is—as we should already have learned—none of us are very close to the top.)

Now think about your response to a sales approach. If the sales person needs to provide a lengthy description of how and why you should logically go about obtaining his or her product, how many people do you think will stop really listening and trying to follow the logic before that sales person completes the presentation? On the other hand, if a sales person can tell how to obtain the product in three words that need no logical sequence of thought, won't that presentation be much more successful? JESUS IS LORD!

In our culture we have a hard time with the biblical concept of Lord because we do not have masters who have life and death authority over us, but that is exactly the basis for the biblical concept. As was mentioned earlier, the very word "Christian" means that we are owned by Jesus ("bought with a price" – 1Corinthians 7:23). While sensitivity about the abuses of slavery has led to most English translations substituting the word "servant," the apostle Paul actually starts three of his letters in the New Testament by calling himself a "slave" of Jesus, and Romans 6 expands on this thought.

So what's next? The response I would expect from anyone interested in finding God's salvation would be, "So what does it mean to accept Jesus as Lord?" That is a reasonable question, and the answer to that question is equally simple, "Just do what he wants you to do." When asked for the specifics of what that means, the biblical answer about what he wants you to do is just as easy: unselfish, caring, generous, active love first for God and then (with forgiving added) for others. How hard is that to understand? How hard is that to sell as something really right and good? As Micah put it,

> He has showed you, O man, what is good, and what does the Lord require of you but to do justice [i.e., do what is right], love mercy [i.e., find joy in caring for the needs of and forgiving the wrongs of

> others as God has cared for and forgiven you], and walk humbly with your God (Micah 6:8).

Doing right, caring about people's needs, forgiving others as God has forgiven us, and living humbly as God's servants—what could be wrong in this? This is God's plan, it always has been, and it always will be. It is faith as taught in the Bible.

Somewhere around 400 years after Jesus' resurrection a church leader named Augustine put it about as simply as it can be put: "Love, and do what you will." As long as the first word takes primary control and is defined as Christian love (unselfish, caring, generous, active, and forgiving), this is the whole message. Augustine went on to say, "Let the root of love be within, because nothing but what is good can grow from this root." As long as what you do is motivated by Christian love, it must be right. And the awesome good news is that once you focus your life on God, his grace covers anything except renewed and intentional rebellion. That is good news!

This is God's plan of salvation and it is biblically supportable with no gymnastics. This plan rings true to people almost as soon as they hear it (unless they have a strong prejudice to some other tradition)—it's an easy sell. What a victory Satan won when he managed to turn us from accepting Jesus as Lord to any other teaching.

True, given the extent of false teachings and misunderstandings about the real meaning of saving belief, at some point we need to explain the biblical meaning of belief or faith as a core belief that shapes every thought and action in life (in other words, accepting Jesus as Lord). As we have already seen, this can be established from many different passages in the Bible. And nothing in the Bible contradicts this definition.

Once we understand faith as the Bible teaches faith, the teaching that we are saved by faith only (not by any works) has a whole new and true meaning. Any good work becomes just a way of demonstrating and living out our faith. We must live in ways that do demonstrate and live out our faith because we have focused our lives on living for God—that's what faith is. But the things we do are not what saves us—God's grace to those who have this faith attitude is what saves us.

The wonderful beauty of this understanding of God's plan is that it does not end in this life—it does not even end with a person's death. Jesus is Lord becomes an eternal truth for a person who becomes a Christian, and that affects every action and thought of that person's life for now and for eternity. And in coming to serve our Lord, we find out how much he loves us and how wonderful it is to feel his presence and support. And that's motivating!!!

Empowering God's Saints

Power to Lead Others to God

With a plan of salvation this simple to explain and support biblically, we can empower individual Christians in a way we never could with any other formula. Who cannot tell a friend or acquaintance that salvation depends on accepting Jesus as Lord of your life? That's just so simple, anyone can carry that message. And who would have difficulty telling people that God's will for our lives is for us to love him and to love each other with an unselfish, caring, generous, forgiving, active love? As Isaiah said, "A highway shall be there, even a pathway for living, and it shall be called the Highway of Holiness. The unclean shall not pass over it, though it shall be for anyone. And among those who walk this road, even a fool shall not go astray" (Isaiah 35:8). It's that easy.

If you really care about God's kingdom and the revitalization of Christianity as God meant it to be, then this should be exciting! No longer would we need to tell our people to bring potential converts to the preacher. Anyone could lead family, friends, neighbors, acquaintances, co-workers, and even strangers to salvation. And living this kind of Christian life would draw people to us to learn why we are so loving, joyful, peaceful, and kind.

When we grasp this—when we understand that the gospel really is such good news and that Christians can communicate God's plan of salvation so simply, God's Holy Spirit can bring about an explosion of evangelism. When Christians live the gospel of love in daily life and are confident that they can easily communicate the truly important message of the gospel (Jesus is Lord), Christianity will spread like wildfire. The job is not traditional missionary work, the job is not church planting, the job is living the gospel and sharing the simple message. Until we take the focus off of the church building, the minister, and the missionary and put the focus on living and sharing the gospel, we can never see the explosive growth God has built into this message.

I don't want to over simplify this. Each person starts from a different point in his or her understanding, so each person will need a somewhat different path to accepting Jesus as Lord, and accepting Jesus as Lord will cause different people to respond in different ways. But the key in all cases is accepting Jesus as Lord. While the path that follows is unique and requires each person to learn to seek God's guidance, for the early church the key that set people on this path was "Jesus is Lord," and that is still the key today.

Power to Baptize[17]

So the next important step to consider is baptism—not so much in convincing a person who is accepting Jesus' lordship that he or she should be baptized, that should be easy, but in actually performing the baptism. As many churches are already finding out, there is nothing that can motivate a Christian in his or her efforts to evangelize others more firmly than the knowledge that this person's witness really has led someone to the Lord. And nothing makes that point more firmly than when a person either baptizes or assists in baptizing someone they have led to the Lord. This is real motivation—the sense of being a midwife at the birth of a new Christian.

Unfortunately there are many churches that do not encourage this. In the New Testament, all Christians felt empowered to convert non-Christians, baptize them, and train them in discipleship. If we want to revitalize Christianity, this is an important part of that goal. We will never see the explosive growth God intends until all Christians feel empowered by God to spread the gospel. Too often what we actually practice in our church services falsely implies that the minister is the most influential person for each conversion.

And it's a win-win situation when we do what I've suggested here, for the more a person is active in telling others about God, the more he or she learns about Christianity. The teacher always learns more than the student.

For churches that want to move in this direction and have not yet done so, there are various ways to get Christians comfortable with converting others, but an important first step can be encouraging others to participate with a minister in baptisms. Perhaps a good start

17 What follows here assumes that baptism is by immersion. The word used in the New Testament for baptism implies a washing activity performed by immersing the item washed into water. If you believe that some other form is preferable, just read this section substituting concepts as appropriate. Christianity is not about legalistic observance of rituals; it is about getting our hearts right in serving the Lord.

would be to have each convert name the most important person in his or her conversion, and then have that person on one side and the minister on the other as together they baptize the convert. (This also eases the task, especially in baptizing larger people.) As people get comfortable with this, more and more will learn to actually perform the baptisms, either as individuals or better yet as groups who worked together to bring a convert to Christ. And think how meaningful this is for the convert to have those administering the baptism be the very ones who led him or her to the Lord.

In the Bible, the person who administers baptism does not have to be a minister. In fact, this person does not have to be an officer. Actually, this person does not even have to be a Christian. When a person is ready to accept Jesus as Lord, that person is ready to be baptized—and it makes no difference who administers the baptism or what is said or sung. If we had to have a Christian perform the baptism, then we could never be certain that our baptism is valid, because only God can judge who is or is not a Christian. Thankfully, the baptizer does not matter, only the heart of the person being baptized is important, submitting to God through Jesus Christ.

Empowering the Whole Church

Based on only one or two passages in the Bible at most, and those taken out of the larger context, Christians have relegated too many fellow Christians to a secondary status, often depressing or killing any motivation these people had to develop the ministries for which God has gifted them. I am convinced that this is Satan's will, not God's will. I am convinced that we have misunderstood and misapplied a few passages used to justify this behavior because that is what Satan wants us to do—and too often we succumb to his urgings. In recent years things have been improving, but there is still a lot we need to think about. When we use biblical passages to justify what we do, let's be careful to understand what the Bible actually says and what these passages really mean.

The Divorced

While not all churches do this and the situation is improving, there are still too many churches that bar anyone who has ever been divorced from holding any leadership role in the church. I will readily agree that if God's will were being done, there would be no divorces. Divorce is always the result of some form of sin on the part of at least one of the married partners, and in almost all cases, on the part of both. But does such sin justify barring people permanently from ministries and leadership roles in the church? Are we maintaining that divorce is an unforgivable sin?

In writing to Timothy about elders and deacons, Paul said that each should be "the husband of one wife" (see 1Timothy 3:2, 12). Too often this has been interpreted to mean that a person holding such an office must not be a divorced person. But let's think of this logically. For the elder, among other things Paul says that he must be "not given to wine, not violent, not greedy for money...not quarrelsome, not covetous." So if we bar a person permanently from these roles because he or she had once been divorced, the implication would be that a man who had been involved in drunkenness, violence, greed, quarreling, or coveting but had turned from such sin could be forgiven and would be acceptable, but a man who had been divorced could not be forgiven or considered acceptable. That makes no sense, and it certainly does not match with biblical teaching about how God treats forgiven sin or about what sins God will or will not forgive!

We actually have a tendency to think God is focused on sex. I read a commentary on Paul's letter to the church in Rome. At the end of chapter 1 Paul addresses a list of sins, homosexual behavior being one of the sins addressed. The commentary devoted almost four pages to homosexuality and hardly even addressed any of the other sins. Is God a sexual pervert? Or are we the perverts? Yes, sexual sin in various forms is real, tempting, and quite prevalent and needs to be addressed appropriately. But the indication of the Bible is that sexual sin is no better and no worse than any other form of rebellion against God. Somehow we have come to see sexual sins as a different class of sin. In fact, most churches having rules barring a divorced person from leadership have no rules about barring a murderer from such leadership. We need to be consistent in our use of the Bible, not picking out just the passages we like because they focus on someone else's sins; and we need to get serious about our own sins.

The fact is, if we read the passages mentioned above carefully, all Paul is saying is that an elder or deacon must not be a bigamist or promiscuous. The reality is that in the language Paul was using, the primary meaning of the word translated "wife" is actually "woman." This is the word Jesus used to refer to his mother when he was on the cross, saying, "Woman, behold your son" (John 19:26; see also John 2:4). Similarly, the primary meaning of the word "husband" is actually "man." The use of a possessive pronoun before one of these words (e.g. "his woman" or "her man") was generally the indicator that this reference involved a husband or wife, but in these passages there is no possessive pronoun. The passage as Paul wrote it could entirely legitimately be translated to say that an elder or deacon must be, "a one-woman man." The words Paul used actually appear in exactly that order.

Do we believe in forgiveness or don't we? Once God forgives, does he hold a grudge? Does God hold a grudge against those who commit sexual sin but not against those who commit other sins? Does a divorced person somehow become less capable simply because of the divorce? Do we not understand that while divorce is always wrong, sometimes it is the lesser of two evils? Granted, a person going through the process of a divorce is probably a very poor choice for a leader of the church, and a person who cannot forgive his or her former spouse would also be a poor choice for a leader of the church. But once the divorce is over and the person has been forgiven by God for whatever wrongs have occurred and has learned to forgive the former spouse, we as the church need to agree with God's forgiveness and accept the person as a brother or sister without reservation. In fact, we need divorced leaders who have worked through this process and can help and counsel those facing marital problems. Most couples face serious problems at some point. Those who have been through the problems are scarred by them, but often they have learned valuable lessons that might help others avoid the same problems.

The church needs to be a community of forgiveness and acceptance in God's name. That will motivate people to want to be part of this community. More and more couples have come through a divorce. If our message to them is that they are second class citizens of the kingdom, our message is a negative motivational factor. Acceptance is a positive motivational factor. We need to stay with the positive motivational factors whenever possible. We need to use the lessons learned by those who have gone through a serious bout with sin and have recovered.

Women

Most of us probably know women who minister as effectively as any man, and often even more effectively than most. So why do we too often have the impression that women should be barred from certain ministries in the church? Is there some passage in the Bible that tells us that women should be marginalized? Was Paul sexist? Or is God sexist? Are the principles of Christianity and the freedom and grace Christianity offers only for men? Does God not care about motivating women?

In fact there are only two places in the New Testament that say anything that has been interpreted as restricting the role of women in the church, and at this point we need to look at both of those passages to see if such interpretations are appropriate.

The first passage to consider is from a letter Paul wrote to the Christians in Corinth where he said

> Let your women keep silent in the church meetings. They are not permitted to speak, but are to be submissive just as the Law of Moses also says. And if they want to learn something, let them ask their own husbands at home, for it is shameful for women to speak in the church meeting. Or did the word of God come from you? Did it only reach you? (1Corinthians 14:34-36).

Now at first sight this seems to say that women are not to speak in church meetings at all, period, no questions asked. If we take this passage absolutely literally and out of context, and we consider that in the New Testament a gathering of just two or three Christians would be considered a church meeting as long as the people had gathered to deal with any matter having to do with Christianity or the church (see Matthew 18:20), this would prohibit any woman from saying anything in any gathering of Christians[18]. (Only a few churches actually practice this extreme interpretation.)

18 As will be addressed in more detail later, we have a very bad habit of thinking of the church as a building. Christ died for the church—he did not die for a building. Biblically, the church is never a building—it is always people. The word translated "church" in the Bible actually means "assembly" and in biblical times this word did not have any necessary connection to Christianity or anything religious. Barring women from speaking when they are inside the building or even just when they are in the sanctuary (main auditorium) during large church meetings has been practical enough that many churches

But in this same letter, Paul wrote, "Every man praying or prophesying with his head covered dishonors his head. But every woman who prays or prophesies with her head uncovered dishonors her head, for that is just like having her head shaved" (1Corinthians 11:3-5). This particular passage has items that clearly had to do with social standards in biblical times that are no longer applicable, and those are not my point here. The point for this discussion is that in this passage Paul clearly deals with how a woman should dress when she prays or prophesies in a church meeting. It is also important to understand that the word translated "prophesies" means public speaking as inspired by God's Holy Spirit. So in chapter 11 of this same letter, Paul clearly indicates that he expects women to pray and speak publically.

Given this instruction for women speaking in church meetings in chapter 11, how are we supposed to understand the passage in chapter 14? Remember, over a thousand years before Paul's time, a woman named Miriam (the sister of Moses) appears in the Bible as a prophetess speaking out publicly (Exodus 15:20-21). She is one of at least ten women identified by the Bible as prophetesses. The role of a prophet or prophetess was to speak God's word in public (see 2Peter 1:21). So how could Paul say that women should not speak in an assembly of Christians, especially after saying how they should dress when they do speak in such an assembly of Christians?

It is important to note that what precedes the passage in chapter 14 about women not speaking is a discussion about speaking in tongues, and what follows it is more about speaking in tongues, so having a comment that women are not to talk in a church meeting right in the middle of this discussion about speaking in tongues sticks out like an elephant in a gathering of mice. There is nothing anywhere near this passage that would seem to be on the subject of women speaking in a church meeting. While Paul would sometimes shift subjects quickly, when he did so we can always see a reason for the shift—but not in this case. So what are we to think of this sudden shift in topic?

When Paul wrote that the women "are not permitted to speak," he had a choice of two words for "speak." Either word would work, but the word he used for "speak" originally implied a babbling kind of speech. This word had come to mean speaking in general, but it retained some implication of its root. Paul's choice of this particular

have practiced such a limitation. However if we use a New Testament definition of church, such a restriction would be almost impossible to put into practice.

term raises the possibility that he was saying (in context) that women are not to speak in tongues in church gatherings[19]. If that is the case, it resolves the conflict with what he said earlier in this same letter.

I have been present when modern-day Christians have practiced speaking in tongues, and I can testify that in my very limited experience, every time speaking in tongues seemed to get out of control in a church meeting, the leaders of this phenomenon were women. I believe that Paul may have experienced this same thing, and that the prohibition here was never intended as a blanket prohibition against women speaking in church meetings, but against women speaking in tongues in church meetings. I can find no other way to make this passage work given what Paul said in chapter 11.

The second passage to consider appears in a letter Paul wrote late in his career to a young disciple named Timothy. Paul wrote,

> Similarly, I want women to dress in modest clothing with propriety and moderation; not with fancy hairdos or jewelry or costly designer clothes. Rather, as is proper for women who claim to serve God, let them adorn themselves with good works. Let a woman learn in silence with all submission. And I do not allow a woman to teach or exercise authority over a man. Instead, she should be silent. After all, Adam was formed first, then Eve. Moreover, Adam was not deceived, but the woman was deceived and transgressed (1Timothy 2:8-14).

Remember, Paul was inspired by God's Holy Spirit to write the letter to Corinth quoted above long before he wrote this letter to Timothy, so we should expect anything God inspired him to write here to be absolutely consistent with what God inspired him to write earlier. And women prophesying in church meetings must be seen as a form of teaching ministry with men present. On top of this, we learn from Acts about a couple named Aquila and Priscilla with whom Paul worked very closely (see Acts 18:1-2, 18; Romans 16:3; 1Corinthians 16:19; 2Timothy 4:19). Typically in New Testament times when a married couple's names are given, the man is named first, but in Acts

19 There is also some evidence in the ancient manuscripts that these few verses were not actually even part of Paul's original letter to Corinth, but that will not be addressed in detail here. Regardless of whether this passage is a genuine part of Paul's letter or not, it cannot be a prohibition against women speaking intelligently in the church gatherings unless we want to say that Paul directly contradicted his own teaching from earlier in this same letter.

18:18, Romans 16:3, and 2Timothy 4:19 Priscilla is named first. Most serious students of the Bible agree that Priscilla had a leading role in that family and in the work they did for the church, and Paul clearly had no problem with this. In fact, while it is not specifically stated, there is a strong implication that Priscilla was the dominant factor in teaching Apollos about Christianity.

So how are we to understand this passage? Frankly, I have some suggestions, but I do not have a nice, neat, definitive answer.

Paul's argument appears to be that in the one case of Adam and Eve, it was Eve who succumbed to temptation, and therefore women must be more susceptible to temptation and cannot be trusted to teach men. But if that is the case how can they be trusted to teach women? I believe it may be significant that Paul does not argue that this is a revelation he has received from God, which would immediately silence all questions. Instead he says "I want women to" and "I do not allow a woman to." There are items in the Bible that are culturally oriented, such as Paul's discussion of head coverings in 1Corinthians 11 or the repeated commandments for Christians to greet one another with a "holy kiss." Most Christians understand that these things are cultural items that would be appropriate in New Testament times and not necessarily in modern American churches. Timothy was a young leader of a very large church in the city of Ephesus. This may have been a case where women in that area were abusing their rights as Christians, and Paul felt it best to simply prohibit anything in the church meetings that could create problems for the church. Whatever the case, Paul specifically avoids saying that this instruction is from God.

In writing to Titus, Paul said,

> In the same way, teach the older women to live reverently, avoiding slander or addiction to alcohol. But they should teach what is good. Then they can teach the younger women to love their husbands and children, to be self-controlled and pure, to be busy at home, to be kind, and to be subject to their husbands, so that no one will speak evil of the word of God (Titus 2:3-5).

Note that in this passage Paul's logic is based on the desire "that no one will speak evil of the word of God." While this passage does not prohibit women teaching men, it has been interpreted as having that implication. This clearly seems to me to be a cultural matter, as if Paul were saying, "do not do these things that would be considered unacceptable in our culture so that people will not speak ill of Christianity over something that is not that important."

Seeing these passages as efforts to maintain the focus on the Christian message rather than cultural matters would be consistent with the rest of the Bible, and it would be consistent with a very valid Christian principle—in any culture we should focus on what is important and not allow unimportant matters to create problems for the church. But our culture is well on its way to leaving gender discrimination behind, and we of the church should not be resistant to that move. God's Holy Spirit gives gifts to women as well as men.

The key point is that a couple of verses cannot override the overwhelming testimony of the Bible to God's willingness to work through women and even to urge women into leadership roles (see chapter four of Judges). One factor that needs to be considered in this context is the language of common gender. In the Bible (as in English until recently) there are many cases where masculine terms are clearly meant to apply to both women and men. Whether in English or in biblical languages, common gender terminology just does not exist, so in English and in the biblical languages masculine terminology is used for common gender applications. Examples can be found throughout the Bible where things addressed in masculine terms are clearly meant for both men and women. For the moment, just hold that point in mind.

In Romans 16:1 we read about a woman named Phoebe is named as a "servant" of the church in Cenchrea. The word "servant" is the feminine form of the word sometimes translated deacon in its masculine form. In writing to Timothy, Paul describes the role of deacons in the church. In the middle of his discussion of deacons we read, "Likewise their wives must be reverent, not slanderers, temperate, faithful in all things" (1Timothy 3:11 NKJV). Just before this passage about deacons there is a section about elders, and nothing is said about their wives, even though it is obvious that the elders hold a more responsible position. Why would Paul single out the wives of deacons and not mention the wives of elders?

In fact as discussed above, the New Testament word for a wife is also the word for a woman. If we apply this knowledge to the passage above, it is just as reasonable to translate the verse, "Likewise the women must be..." as if Paul were speaking of women deacons. Reading the passage in English, the fact that a possessive pronoun appears ("their wives") in light of what we learned earlier might lead someone to think that this has to refer to wives. But in the original manuscripts of the Bible, that pronoun is not present. The phrase actually says "the women" or "the wives" depending on which way we translate this word. If we recall Phoebe being mentioned as a "servant" or "deaconess" of the church in Cenchrea, again we find women in important roles in the New Testament church. Granted, in the New Testament the office of deacon seems to have more of a servant role (the word means "servant") than a leadership role, and the office of elder or bishop which is more a leadership role is never specifically associated with women. But the New Testament does seem to recognize a leadership role and definitely a ministry or service role for deacons, and it never specifically bars women from the any leadership role.

There is at most one verse in the whole Bible that could indicate that a woman should be barred from any role in the church that would involve teaching men, and there are many passages that would indicate that this would not be God's way. In a case like this, the only right thing to do is let the Bible interpret the Bible—and when we do that, we will find that women should be encouraged to do whatever God leads them to do (though they like men should never demand leadership roles). At one point late in Jesus' earthly ministry two of his disciples who were brothers asked their mother to get Jesus to grant that they would get the most influential positions in his kingdom. Jesus' response was that whoever wants to be greatest in the kingdom must become the servant of everyone else in the kingdom. If the focus is on human pride in an office held, the focus is not on God and his will. But if the focus is on ministry and service for God, then who are we to say who can or cannot serve?

In fact, when it comes to offices in the church, the real issue is what a person does, not what title that person is given. A deacon (male or female) is a deacon because of what he or she does in service to the church. Similarly, an elder is an elder because of what he (or she) does. While it may be practical to have a specific group defined by title to guide in the leadership of a church, the title does not make a person into a deacon or an elder if that person does not fulfill the biblical role, and the absence of a title does not keep a person from doing the job of an elder or deacon or any other ministry. If a person specifically wants the title, there is a motivational problem. Our motivation to serve should be to please the Lord, not to get worldly titles and glory for ourselves. The greatest title a Christian can have and the one that really matters is when God gives us the title of "faithful servant."

I know that there are women who will abuse this kind of openness. The reason I am so sure that this will happen is because of the number of men who already abuse their ministries. The fact that some men abuse their ministries does not keep us from urging that men take on the ministries to which God is calling them, and it should not keep us from urging women to take on whatever ministries God is calling them to fulfill.

My firm conviction is that any person who demands his or her right to a leadership role in the church is not fit for that leadership role, regardless of gender. And my firm conviction is that any person who fails to respond to God's call to ministry, regardless of gender, is in rebellion against God, and any person who forbids any other person from carrying out his or her ministry for God is in serious danger.

After saying this, I firmly believe that God did create men and women with certain general characteristics that may normally suit men better for certain ministries and women better for certain other ministries. The Bible does not give us a clear definition of where the limits are, probably because that is a matter that should be resolved between individuals and God. But as a general rule, if a woman or a man in a particular role would create problems in a particular cultural situation, a Christian must be very certain of God's call before violating the standards of that culture and thereby bringing discredit or shame on the message of the gospel.

Minorities

With far less to justify our actions, we have too often blocked minorities from church positions even including membership. All Christians are members of a single family. When we partake of the communion or Eucharist, we all share in the body and blood of Christ—we are all flesh and blood kin through Christ. Worshipping separately for cultural or language reasons may be OK as long as we diligently work at being one, but too often we simply go our own ways and discredit the unity Christ came to give us (see John 17:20-21). We need all Christians motivated to fulfill their ministries, regardless of race, gender, age, or any other factor, and we need to be united as one family, one kingdom, one people. There are not two heavens, and there will be no servant class in heaven.

In New Testament times there were many divisions. Romans looked down on non-Romans as inferiors. Greeks looked down on non-Greeks as barbarians. Jews looked down on non-Jews as pagan gentiles. Masters looked down on slaves as property rather than people. Men looked down on women as second-class humans. Such divisions were common, and one of the great revelations God gave to the apostle Paul was the vision to see that Christianity breaks down all those divisions.

Today the church in America is probably the most racially segregated aspect of American life, and there is absolutely no excuse for that. We are OK with our children marrying pagans, but too many Christians are repelled by the idea of interracial marriage even among Christians. We excuse our attitude by referring to the effect such marriages may have on the children, but if we were not practicing racial prejudice, there would be no effect on the children. Perpetuating a wrong can never make it right. Every Christian needs to intentionally work against such prejudices.

God needs every disciple functioning. We who are supposed to be his servants need to stop shutting out large numbers of Christians with no valid justification. Satan has managed to shade our Bible translations to get us to work against God. Well-intentioned Christian scholars have provided Satan with tools he can use against large numbers of potential Christian witnesses. We need every Christian serving the Lord with whatever talents and in whatever ministry God has given. The enemy is not fellow Christians! If God uses women and divorced people to accomplish his purposes, that should be his prerogative. As Paul wrote to the Christians in Rome, "Who are you to judge someone else's servant?" (Romans 14:4). It is far past time that we quit fighting about details that do not matter to God and got busy doing what God has commissioned us to do.

Summary on Salvation

So God's plan of salvation is simple and it is easily communicated. On top of this, it is the sort of thing that is obvious—a person hearing that plan without any preconceived prejudices will readily admit that it makes sense and that it is good. But once we understand this message and accept God's authority over our lives and our responsibility to live for our Lord, why do we as Christians continue to suffer? In fact, why does it often seem that the more we serve the Lord, the more we suffer? If we do not deal with the trials and struggles Satan will throw at us, we will still lose too many of our converts.

In Jesus' story about a farmer sowing seed that fell on different kinds of soil, three of the four soil types resulted in crop failure. While we cannot fully end that cycle, there are things we can do to help people maintain a firm faith in God when everything seems to go wrong—and that's what we need to address next.

CHAPTER EIGHT: SUFFERING—THE ULTIMATE TEACHER

I am convinced that the sufferings of this life are not worthy to be compared with the glory that is to be revealed in us – Romans 8:18

Answering Why

Have you ever had something that looked very wrong from your perspective but that turned out to be very right when you saw it from the perspective of the person who did what you thought was wrong? I believe almost all of us have experienced that at some time. This sort of situation applies even more to God. His perspective is very different from ours, and people often think God is very cruel or at least very indifferent because we humans fail to understand God's perspective. I have often had people tell me that we can never understand God's perspective, and to a degree that is true. However, God has revealed enough of his perspective in his word to let us understand some very important things that we often miss when we set about judging God. In fairness, we at least owe God the courtesy of trying to understand his perspective.

One of the most difficult problems Christians and churches face is the question, "Why?" Why did God do this? Why did God allow that? Why didn't God prevent this? Why didn't God do that? The answers Christians often give are very weak at best, and sometimes ridiculous. One of the common answers that irritates me a lot is that we cannot see things from God's perspective. In fact, he has revealed a lot about his perspective—we just have not listened very well. That typical answer is a motivation killer. Why should a person want to worship a God who seems to be cruel and whom he or she cannot understand?

How can we say that God is love and that he loves us with an eternal and unconditional love and then have God either ignore or even cause terrible suffering for those he supposedly loves? How can the love of God motivate people to be Christian when God seems so indifferent to our pain? Oh, certainly we can come up with accounts of supposedly miraculous cures, but when someone honestly tries to demonstrate the power of prayer by comparing cures that otherwise seem beyond human explanation among Christians and non-Christians, the result is that there are just as many seemingly miraculous cures among non-Christians as there are among Christians. In other words, when it comes to apparently miraculous cures, Christians seem to have no advantage over non-Christians and prayer seems to make no difference. (Don't despair, there is a very good answer.)

Sometimes, in spite of such non-answers to the questions of suffering, people who are hurting turn to God and find the help they need from God's Holy Spirit, even without a solution to the physical suffering. But too often it works just the other way—people who are part of a church will turn away from God or even turn against God because they do not understand why God allows such suffering, and the church offers no useful answers. I have known too many cases where intelligent people listened honestly to the answers the church provides and decided that if that is what God is like, they would never want to worship such a God. And given what these people have been told, I cannot blame them for this decision.

It's far past time we let Christians know that there are better answers, answers that can motivate Christians in their faithfulness. But to find those answers, we need to look at suffering from God's perspective as he has revealed this to us in his word. In fact, God uses the very times that cause us to ask "why" in powerful ways that work to our own benefit—but we fail to see this in far too many cases. Indeed, there are very good answers to these why questions.

However, there is an important problem. The answers to these questions are usually not very helpful once the suffering starts. If the answers are to be really helpful, we need to provide these answers before people ask the questions. You may ask how we can answer a question before we know what the question is. Obviously, we cannot deal with the details before we know what the details are, but we can deal with the general conditions. We can show Christians how God works through suffering and trouble. We can show Christians all the good things that can and do come through such times if we remain faithful to God. We can show people that God, and only God, can take the bad times and turn them into good results. And we can show Christians how in most cases the cause of our suffering is not God—it is ourselves. In other words, we can actually show people that even the worst times can be motivational for Christians.

Going back to an important point, it's no use trying to answer the why questions once a person is suffering. When a person does ask one or more of the why questions, he or she generally does not want an answer. Such a person is not really asking why—knowing why will not stop or even ease the suffering. The point of the question is actually just to express how hurt this person is and how angry he or she is about the situation. Being told why can actually increase the pain and anger, because it seems to rob the person of his or her assumed right to complain. Giving an answer at this time seems to say, "You should not be complaining or even hurting." That is entirely the wrong message, and its motivational force works in exactly the wrong direction.

In fact, even knowing the answers well ahead of time does not stop the pain—it just provides a path to get through the pain. That path is rarely available once the suffering and pain has started. It's like being lost in a maze and having someone tell you that you are in that situation because you entered the maze at the wrong point—but since you are lost you can't get back to correct your error, so what good is the information? That is why it is crucial for churches to address this point before the pain or suffering starts and to do so strongly enough to have the lesson retained when the pain or suffering comes. (And it will come.)

When Jesus faced the cross, he already knew the answers for the why questions—and he still felt the pain and suffering. He agonized in prayer, asking God to find another way if at all possible. But in the end, "for the joy that he could see ahead" he "endured the cross, despising the shame" (Hebrews 12:2). Our task as Christians is to let people know about the joy that awaits us when we come through suffering as Christians. If we are fully successful, we will find that we actually almost look forward to times of suffering because of the joy that we know lies beyond the suffering.

So let's look at some of the answers we can and should be providing to our congregations.

Drawing Closer to God

It's sad that it should be so necessary, but somehow we never draw as close to God as when we turn to him for help and comfort during times of suffering. We will learn in this chapter why we should not expect God to take away the suffering in most cases—there are very good reasons why he will not do so in this world. But what he will do is provide through his Holy Spirit the strength, comfort, and guidance to get us through whatever the problem is.

There is an important point here concerning God's perspective. God knows that the spiritual element of our nature is far, far more important than the physical element. God's primary focus is always on the spiritual because it is eternal. Our primary focus tends to be on the physical which is nowhere near eternal. Remember, this physical world is going to pass away, and our physical lives are very likely to pass away long before the world passes away. It is our spiritual nature that endures, so while it takes a serious shift in perspective, Christians need to understand that God's focus is always on eternity—and if we could see that eternity, that is exactly where we would want his focus to be.

This may seem poor comfort for a person who is suffering. "Don't worry, you're still going to suffer physically just as much, but you can know that God cares and will strengthen you spiritually." To someone who has never experienced the strength of what God does, this will probably seem like no help at all. But once you experience God's help even one time, it will start to make more sense. This is not just a case of trying to make people feel better without any substance. God's Holy Spirit actually does provide comfort and strength if we will let him in.

Whenever we are hurting, we tend to focus on ourselves. The more we focus on ourselves, the further we shift from God. But if we will intentionally focus on God, he will show himself to us in ways we could never have anticipated. And the more we focus on God, the more he will reveal himself to us, and the more we will experience the strength, joy, and peace that come with such revelation.

Trusting God is like a child in a large, scary city with heavy traffic all around. If the child focuses on the crowds of people and cars rushing by, he or she is likely to be terrified. But if that same child is holding the hand of a trusted adult and focuses on that adult, all the traffic becomes insignificant noise and bustle. As long as we hold tightly to God's hand, all the scary things of this world will fade into insignificance.

It is unfortunate that people rarely draw as close to God in times when there is no suffering as they do in times when there is suffering—but that's the way we are. As long as things are going well, no matter how often we attend church or how diligently we try to stay in touch with God or how much time we spend in prayer, our attention span toward God is limited. But when the suffering comes, suddenly our attention span increases significantly. And when we get through the suffering, although the attention span decreases, it rarely returns to its former condition. In the crises, we grow spiritually if we trust in God.

This does bring up an interesting point. When you pray, be careful about praying for spiritual growth, because what you are really doing is asking for suffering that will cause you to grow spiritually. But every time a crisis causes you to grow spiritually, it also enhances your capability to grow spiritually between the crises (though at a reduced rate). It is good and right to pray for spiritual growth—you just need to understand what to expect.

Through the crises of this life, God is always leading us step by step closer to him. This is growth we all need, and there is really no other way to get it.

Recognition of Spiritual Strength

For many years in my career, I worked an office job. People in the offices would often put up little signs to add a touch of humor to the work days. One of these signs was made up to look like a certificate of award. The certificate awarded the recipient one Attaboy and stated that some number of Attaboys (usually around 5,000) would result in some specific reward (perhaps a bonus or raise). Each such certificate also had a note in small letters that just one Awshucks (or some similar term) would cancel all the Attaboys you might have earned to that point.

This certificate highlighted two things commonly true in our society: 1) we all like to have someone appreciate what we contribute to any endeavor, even if the appreciation is only demonstrated by a pat on the back or words like "Attaboy"; and 2) in our culture, it does not take much of a mistake to have everybody forget all the good things you have done.

God has a different way of giving out Attaboys, and at least initially you may not care for his technique. But he knows what he is doing. When he sees that one of his people has the strength to endure some trial, he will often allow just such a trial to overtake that person. You may ask, "Why would he do that?" We'll answer that question shortly. The point I want to make here is that whenever God allows some trial in our lives, he always does so knowing that, if we will trust in him, we have the spiritual strength to successfully deal with the trial.

In writing to the Christians in Corinth, Paul said, "No trial has come to you except what humans commonly experience; but God is faithful. He will not allow you to be tested beyond what you are able to bear, but with each trial he will also make a way of escape so that you can bear up during that trial" (1Corinthians 10:13). In other words, whenever a trial of any sort comes into your life, you can know that God has looked into your inmost being and that he has found in you the ability to overcome. Whether you actually overcome or not will be up to you—God only promises that he will not allow you to be loaded beyond your ability. Once you see this perspective, even the trials can be motivational because they clearly tell you that God has found this spiritual strength in you.

Thus, in the midst of trial we can confidently say, "God wants to draw me closer to him, and God himself has examined me and found that I have the spiritual resources to handle this trial." That is actually pretty good news. The creator of the universe has taken the time to examine your spiritual health, and he has found something good enough for him to trust you in this situation.

Growing toward a Goal

God is love. He loves you. So when the trials do come, you can be sure that God has allowed them to come because he sees value for you. Part of that value is in the spiritual lessons people learn during such trials. God knows that when a person comes through such trials, he or she will have gained capabilities that can be used in his kingdom. That is not the whole reason that God allows suffering, but it is one significant contributor.

God's plan is about growth. Jesus told his disciples,

> The kingdom of heaven is like a mustard seed. Indeed, it is among the littlest of seeds, but when a person plants a mustard seed in his field, it grows into a plant larger than any other herb—so that birds can come and nest in its branches just as if it were a tree...The kingdom of heaven is like the small amount of yeast a woman folded into a large amount of flour and left until it all raised (Matthew 13:31-33).

While these passages may apply to numerical growth, I am convinced they apply more to spiritual growth. Paul said, "Brothers, don't be children in understanding. However your malice should be the malice of babies, but your understanding should be mature" (1Corinthians 14:20). Later he wrote,

> And he [Christ] himself gives some a gift to be apostles [messengers sent out with the message, in other words, missionaries], some prophets [those who are inspired by God to speak his message, in other words, inspired speakers or preachers], some evangelists [those who bring the good news, in other words, soul winners], and some pastors [shepherds of the flock] and teachers in order to equip the saints [Christians] for the work of ministry—for building up the body of Christ—until we all arrive at a united faith in and knowledge of the Son of God, to the perfection of humanity God intended, to stature measured by the fullness of Christ; that we may no longer be children, tossed to and fro and round about by every wind of doctrine and by the trickery of men in the cunning craftiness of deceitful plotting, but speaking the truth in love, may grow up in all things into him who is the head, even Christ, from whom the whole body, joined and knit together by what every joint supplies when every part does its share effectively working together, brings about growth of the body for building up the body of Christ in love (Ephesians 4:11-16).

(This is a long and very complex sentence Paul wrote, but it is well worth understanding.)

As mentioned earlier, after talking about what fulfillment of the Old Testament Law meant, Jesus said, "In light of all of this, you must be mature with the same kind of spiritual maturity that you find in your Heavenly Father" (Matthew 5:48). There are many other similar passages that emphasize the Christian's need to grow spiritually. Christian converts are described as newborn babies in Christ, needing to grow. Christians are encouraged to partake of both the milk and the meat of God's word. As Paul said when he wrote to the Christians in Philippi, "Brothers, I do not consider myself as having grasped the whole picture; but I focus on one thing. Forgetting the things in my past and reaching forward to the things in store, I press toward the goal for the prize of the upward call of God in Christ Jesus" (Philippians 3:13-14).

As we discussed earlier in the section on Christian hope, God has plans for us. Some of those plans deal with serving him in this world. For example, a Christian who has suffered the loss of a young child and come through this experience with God's help is far better suited to help another person going through a similar experience than any trained professional who has not experienced this tragedy. God needs such people serving him. A Christian who has gone through criminal prosecution and imprisonment can reach those in prison far better than any highly trained professional. And the same is true in countless other areas.

You may think God has abandoned you when in reality God is leading you down a path that he knows will prepare you for what he has planned. And what God has planned does not end in this world. Some of the things he wants us to learn will be for this life, but I am convinced that he has wonderful plans for us in his eternity, and I am just as convinced that part of what he is up to in this world is teaching us the things that will make eternity that much better.

No one ever learned patience and endurance except through trials and difficulties. And experience is not just the best teacher—experience is the only real teacher. God knows this, and he designed this world to teach us important lessons that we will use in his service, both in this life and in eternity. So when the trials come, as a Christian you can rejoice knowing that God has a plan to use this trial and turn it into great blessings for you and for others—if you let him.

Knowing that the trials of this world are God's tools to prepare us for the great things he has in store for us should be motivating. But there is something more—something very important.

God's Most Essential Lesson

While all the other lessons are important and all of them will bring joy and blessings in the end if we allow God to bring us through our trials and difficulties, there is one lesson that is more important than any other. The lesson we most need to learn is how bad sin really is.

The problem is that we get this lesson all backwards. (And you thought Satan was not really that big a deal.) When we are suffering, we tend to blame God either for causing the suffering or at least for not ending it. But what the Bible clearly teaches is that sin is the very root cause of all suffering and even of death. Please don't misunderstand me. I'm not saying that God is punishing you for your sins whenever you suffer. That is not the case at all.

In fact, most of us don't even get the message of Genesis 3 (the account of the first sin in the Garden in Eden). Somehow we believe that when God told Adam and Eve what would happen because of their rebellion, he was causing that to happen as punishment. But aside from an initial phrase, the whole passage could easily be read as God letting Adam and Eve know what was going to happen because of their sin—because God was not going to stop the effects of sin.

Given what we know about Hebrew, the first phrase looks like it should be translated something like "He [God] said to the woman, 'I will greatly multiply your sorrow and your conception.'" Now, what does that mean? Conception is related to becoming pregnant. Greatly multiplying Eve's sorrow might make sense, but how does greatly multiplying her conception make sense? So far as the Bible tells, up to this point Eve had never conceived. Some translators have changed the conjunction (and) to a preposition (in) so that this phrase says, "I will greatly multiply your pain in childbearing," but the Hebrew text as we have it now has the conjunction, not the preposition. And if that really is the meaning of that phrase, then why does the next phrase say almost exactly the same thing? (This kind of translating is making the Bible say what you think it should say rather than what it does say. That is not always a wrong thing to do as long as you at least include a note to explain what you have done and the basis for doing this, but it is dangerous ground.)

From that difficult phrase onward, the passage reads like an announcement.

> "You shall have pain in bringing forth children, and yet you will have an innate urge to unite with your husband to have more children. And he [your husband] shall rule over you." Then to Adam he [God] said, "Because you have heeded what your wife told you and have eaten from the tree I ordered you not to when I said 'You shall not eat of it,' the ground is cursed because of you. All the days of your life you will have to work hard just to eat what the ground produces. It will produce thorns and thistles for you. And you shall eat the herbs that grow in the field. The sweat will drip from your face every time you eat your bread until that day you return to the ground. For you were taken from the ground. You are made of dust, and you shall return to dust" (Genesis 3:16-18).

Given the beginning phrase, "I will greatly multiply your sorrow," it is clear that God was imposing a curse because the humans had sinned. It is the sin of the humans that brought the curse. The curse was imposed by God to teach men to hate sin. Our sin is the cause of all suffering.

I believe the key here is that God had only a limited number of choices when the humans rebelled. He could destroy the humans and end the rebellion, but then the creation was a failure. He could change the humans into animals incapable of rebelling against him, like all the other animals, but again that would make the creation a failure. Or he could allow the humans to live with the results of their rebellion, instituting a plan to rescue those who would end the rebellion. God chose the third option, but that option meant that he would have to back away from this creation and let the rebellion run its course.

And the only way he could safely rescue humans without risking the destruction of another creation was to draw them one by one into a faith relationship where the rebellion of individuals would end. God knew the price he would eventually have to pay was terrible, but he saw this as the only way.

This made the curse of sin all that much more important. God's object was to convince people that sin is so terrible that no one in their right mind would choose to rebel. God's object was to teach people to hate sin and what it does. And the curse that sin brings with it would be the ideal way to let people learn firsthand just how bad sin really is. Sin is not fair. People who suffer because of a particular sin may well be entirely innocent of that sin. Much of the suffering we endure in this world has nothing to do with any particular sin of ours or even of anyone with whom we have come in contact. The suffering sin brings is an environment of suffering. As God backed out, sin moved in, and sin brought suffering that was not at all a fair response to individuals' sins. As the Bible teaches, Satan became the ruler of this world (see Ephesians 2:2).

God still has the same choices. Do you really want him to stop the effects of the environment of sin in which we live? If so, he would have to either destroy us (since each of us is a sinner) or turn us into animals incapable of any moral choices.

As we have already seen, God's plan is to teach us how bad sin really is and then take us into an eternity where we will know better—where no temptation could ever draw us back into that cursed existence. While the price was higher than any of us will ever be able to understand, he paid the price to redeem us so that he could forgive the sins of this world. But that only works for those who learn this lesson. Anyone else would simply bring the rebellion into eternity. Therefore, there must be a garbage heap for those who do not learn the lesson, and that garbage heap is what we call hell.

Every time we sin, we vote for sin and evil to rule in this world and for God's will not to be done. Why should we argue that God should rescue us from what we ourselves keep causing? We blame God for what we have done. And we criticize God for not stopping the effects of our rebellion when we would not want to have him do what would be necessary to truly end the rebellion. We speak of disasters as "acts of God" when they should more appropriately be described as "acts of Satan," empowered by our actions.

God is not to blame, we are. The sooner we admit our blame and beg his forgiveness, the sooner we can begin to reap the blessings of the kingdom—his kingdom. And since the suffering and struggles and trials of this world are critical to this most important lesson—to teach us to hate the rebellion that has brought such devastation—we should not expect God to do away with the consequences of our actions just because they are not pleasant.

In most cases, God will not do away with these consequences in this world even if we are his very faithful servants. Doing so would create a situation where others could see the results of our faith and turn to God, not in faith, but because of solid evidence. Salvation must be by faith. That is a vital part of God's plan. God intends to bring those into eternity whom he can trust implicitly with important tasks, and faith is the key.

The same is true in this world's systems. When a person joins the military, the first thing the military trains that person to do is to carry out orders without questioning them—on faith that some higher authority knows what is necessary and has provided orders that are necessary in order to achieve strategic goals.

The motivational effect here is elimination of a de-motivating factor. When we can see that the sufferings of this life are not caused by God and that the reason he does not end them for Christians is because they serve important purposes in his plan for our salvation, a factor that can cause and has caused Christians to turn away from God turns into a factor God allows for the good of his children and those who may become his children.

Now, this does not mean that God does not do miraculous cures—I am quite convinced that he does (though of course I cannot prove this for the very reasons discussed earlier about the role of faith). But in order to maintain faith as the door to salvation without proof, for every miraculous cure of a Christian, he must logically cause a proportional number of miraculous cures for non-Christians so that a skeptic cannot measure some obvious difference. (Again and for the same reasons, I cannot prove this. I have seen things happen that certainly look like obvious miracles, but every scientific study I have read indicates no difference in unexplainable events between Christians and non-Christians. What I have suggested here is the only answer I have been able to suggest.) So while I believe that God does perform miracles to cure individuals, the obvious evidence is that those cures are not commonplace, and they occur for God's reasons, not ours.

CHAPTER NINE: PRAYER—THE ULTIMATE ACCESS

Whatever you ask in my name, that is exactly what I will do – John 14:13

Expectations and Results

Face it, prayer is a real issue for many Christians. In many cases, it is one of those issues that never gets intelligently addressed, but it is nevertheless constantly in the background. And it is a negative motivational factor in many, many cases.

We read in the Bible one account after another telling how this person or that person prayed for something and then received it. In our childhood, those of us who grew up in the church learned about miracle after miracle God performed to help his people. Yet when we ask for something, even something very simple and seemingly very good, we never seem to have our requests granted. Or if we do get what we prayed for, there is no evidence of a miracle—it could easily have been coincidence, something we would have received whether we prayed or not.

There is a story of a woman whose son was late getting home. As a Christian, she decided to pray and ask God to bring her son home safely. When she saw her son driving up the street, she ended her prayer by saying, "Never mind, God. He's home now."

Let's say you are on your way to a meeting with church leaders. You believe that you have important contributions to make—perhaps you are even chairperson for this meeting—and you really want to be there on time. But today the time got away from you for some reason (a flat tire, a sick child, an unexpected phone call, or whatever), and you have just enough time to get to the meeting on time if all the traffic lights are green. This is a very good cause, so you ask God for this simple favor—and over half the traffic lights are red. In fact, many of them have just turned red when you get to the intersection, so you have to wait through the whole red time. On top of that, every slow driver in the county pulls out in front of you. So you asked God for help, and you arrive at the meeting twenty minutes late—just as the meeting is breaking up.

Worse, let's say you are the minister for a local church, and your wife has come down with cancer. You have three small children, and you don't know what you will do if she dies. You really do believe that God has the power to heal, and you pray earnestly every available moment that God will heal her. In addition, churches all around the country and even in foreign lands are praying for your wife. Your congregation has special prayer meetings for her healing. Yet you watch her suffer as the cancer worsens and then you are at her side when she dies.

Where was God? Why were your prayers not granted? You have been faithful to God, why was he not faithful to you and to what seemed like very powerful promises in his word?

Miracles in the Bible

First let's deal with miracles in the Bible. This is an important starting point. The impression we often get in studying the Bible is that miracles were quite common in biblical times, and yet they are clearly not that common in our lives. Many people decide that the biblical accounts must be fictional myths, because these things just do not happen in real life.

The problem starts with how we first learn about the Bible. In many cases the lessons focus on the miracles God has done. The intent is to impress us with how great and good God is by recounting what he has done in the past, but if he no longer does those things, then perhaps he was great and good to people in those times, but he does not seem so great and good to us. We feel cheated because we do not experience these miracles.

Unfortunately, few if any are ever taught the reality of miracles in the Bible—a reality clearly presented by the Bible. Let's look at that reality. There are important things we need to see in the biblical account of miracles.

First, let's focus on major miracles. By major miracles, I mean obvious miracles that were witnessed by at least a fairly large number of people. While we may find one or two exceptions, if we look at the period of time covered by the biblical accounts, major miracles only occurred in three periods. Remember, the biblical account stretches from creation to the ministry of Jesus disciples in the first generation of the church.

The biblical account of the history of mankind from the creation to the time of a man named Abraham takes only twelve chapters in Genesis. Obviously the creation is miraculous, but there was no human present to witness the miracles of creation, so while the miracles of creation could certainly be considered major miracles by most standards, by our definition they would not fit. No human witnessed these miracles. Several years after the creation, the Bible tells that God took a man named Enoch. This passage is generally interpreted to mean that Enoch was taken to heaven without dying, which would be a significant miracle, but there is no indication that anyone saw this happen. The only other significant miracle before the time of Abraham is Noah's flood, and in this case only eight people from one family survived to tell what happened. And none of these appears to have been the result of someone praying for these miracles.

When he was about seventy-five years old, Abraham was promised descendants if he would serve God. After waiting several years, Abraham finally had his first son, born to a slave in his household—but God told Abraham that this was not the child he [God] had promised. Abraham was about a hundred years old when he and his wife Sarah had the son God had promised. While not specifically stated, it is obvious from the account that this was important to Abraham, and that he had been praying for this result for at least twenty-five years. And when the prayer was granted, a skeptic could easily say that it just took that long for Abraham and Sarah to have a child. By our definition of an "obvious miracle," this would not qualify.

While God blessed Abraham's descendants in many ways, the Bible tells of no obvious miracles witnessed by many people over the next few hundred years. Everything the Bible tells could easily be explained as just good luck anyone might have experienced.

Hundreds of years after Abraham, a man named Moses rose to lead the descendants of Abraham now known as Israelites out of bondage in Egypt. In the process of leading the people out of Egypt, two things happened of importance to this topic. 1) God worked many obvious miracles in front of many thousands of witnesses. 2)

God delivered a new revelation to Moses, including a system of laws the people were to follow, a system of worship the people were to observe, and even the details of a tent of worship where the people were to focus their worship activities.

Once Moses died, a man named Joshua took his place as leader of the Israelites. While God blessed the activities of Joshua and the Israelites, with the exception of the first battle they fought in their campaign to take a homeland for themselves, there were no more obvious miracles that could not as easily be explained by good luck or good leadership.

Hundreds more years passed. Israel had various leaders from time to time who were specially blessed by God, but the things they did would not fit the category of obvious miracles witnessed by a large number of people. Even the powerful leader, Samson, though he was extremely strong, would not fit the category. Everything he did he accomplished in his own human strength.

In fact, the next obvious period of miracles did not occur for about six or seven hundred years. At this time the first of a line of great prophets, a man named Elijah, began demonstrating significant miracles. However, by our definition of obvious miracles witnessed by a large number of people, there was only one time such a miracle occurred during a contest with a large number of false prophets. Elisha was the immediate successor to Elijah, and like Elijah, Elisha demonstrated significant miracles. But again, only one or two would actually fit our definition. We do not know how many companions were brought by a leper named Naaman when he sought a cure from the prophet, but it was probably a large enough group to qualify. Similarly, we do not know how many were present when Elisha made an iron axe-head float so the man who had borrowed it would be able to return it. We do know that a large number were involved in Elisha's being able to lead a Syrian army that had been sent to capture or kill him into the hands of the king of Israel.

Elijah and Elisha led a movement of great prophets among the Israelites. These prophets expanded on what God had revealed to Moses, refining people's understanding of what God really wants.

After the time of Elisha, there were several more prophets, but very few who demonstrated these obvious miracles witnessed by a large number of people. There was an unnamed prophet who caused the hand of the king of Israel to shrivel and then healed it. And the three companions of Daniel would qualify when they survived being publically thrown into a huge fire. But for the most part miracles were rare at best. Then for more than five hundred years before the birth of Jesus, the Bible again records no miracles at all.

When Jesus came on the scene, he and his followers demonstrated more miracles of greater power than had ever been witnessed at any time in recorded history. Jesus was by far the greatest miracle worker, but for several years after he was gone, his followers demonstrated similar miracles in his name. Jesus came to give fullness of meaning to all God's revelations. He showed how the law revealed to Moses was just a tool to help men understand what God wants, and how it can only serve as a guide because the real issue is always ending the rebellion.

Hopefully you have seen a pattern here. No obvious miracles witnessed by a large number of people for thousands of years, until the time of Moses when God wanted to deliver a major new revelation. During Moses' life, God established that the revelation given to Moses was indeed from him by working many obvious miracles witnessed by thousands. Once Moses died and his replacement was established, there were no more obvious miracles witnessed by a large number of people until the time when God saw fit to provide a significant adjustment in understanding the revelation given to Moses. Then with a few obvious miracles God established the authority of the prophets to speak for him. But after a relatively brief period of such revelations, the obvious miracles stopped again until God sent his last and best revelation through Jesus. This time there were more miracles than had ever been witnessed before. However, once the church was established and going strong, the miracles became less and less an important part of the church's life.

The pattern is simple. When God sends a new revelation, he sends miracles (also called "signs" in the Bible) to demonstrate that this new revelation came from him. While God still reveals his truth to men by the work of his Holy Spirit today, these revelations are not new revelations; they simply provide better understanding of the revelations already given. Once a new revelation is adequately established, there is no longer a need for obvious miracles. In fact, the obvious miracles soon become a detriment rather than an aid, because they affect the role of free will.

The message here is not that God does not or will not do miracles for his children. The message is that those miracles are unlikely to be obvious or witnessed by a large number of people. Such miracles serve a specific limited purpose, and since Jesus brought the final new revelation, no new age of miracles is likely (though God can certainly do whatever he sees fit to do).

Prayer in Jesus Name

Toward the end of his ministry Jesus told his disciples,

> I tell you with absolute assurance, he who believes in me will also do the works that I do and even greater works than these, because I am going to my Father. And whatever you ask in my name, I will do exactly that, in order that the Father may be glorified in the Son. If you ask anything in my name, that is what I will do (John 14:12-14).

Later in the same conversation Jesus said, "You did not choose me—I chose you. And I appointed you to go and bear fruit—fruit to last forever—so that whatever you ask the Father in my name he may give you" (John 15:16). Still later in this same conversation Jesus said,

> In the coming days you will ask nothing of me. I tell you with absolute assurance, whatever you ask the Father in my name, he will give you. Until now you have asked nothing in my name. Ask and you will receive in order that your joy may be full. I have said these things to you in figurative language, but the time is coming when I will no longer speak to you in figurative language, but I will tell you plainly about the Father. In that day you will ask in my name, and I am not telling you that I will pray to the Father for you because the Father himself loves you since you have loved me and have believed that I came from God (John 16:23-27).

Over and over Jesus insisted that his followers could have whatever they asked for as long as they asked for it "in my name." So when we pray we often end our prayers with something like "I pray this in Jesus' name, amen." But no matter how we word the ending of our prayers, the prayers still are not granted—we do not receive what we have asked for. So what is wrong here? Was Jesus wrong? Or is it that we are not his followers? Or was he talking only to the original disciples?

In fact, it was not too long after this that one of the disciples named James was arrested. There can be no doubt that the other disciples and the Christians of that time prayed that James would be released, but he was executed. So what happened to Jesus' promises? The quotations above about praying in Jesus' name are from the Gospel of John, and John wrote his gospel about sixty years after Jesus said these things to him and the other disciples. During that time the church had endured severe persecution, including the terrible years of Nero's vendetta against Christians. So how could John record these words of Jesus as if he believed that they were absolutely true?

In fact, the problem is that we do not understand the meaning of the words "in my name." And there is no real excuse for this, because the New Testament is full of examples where this phrase is used in ways that should have made the meaning very clear.

A good example is when Jesus said, "I have come in my Father's name and you do not accept me. If someone else comes in his own name, you'll accept him" (John 5:43). Another excellent example is when Paul says, "Whatever you do in word or deed, do it all in the name of the Lord Jesus giving thanks to God the Father through him" (Colossians 3:17). In these passages, the concept of "in someone's name" clearly has nothing to do with using such words. It clearly means "consistent with the nature of this person."

This is an important key to understanding how prayer works. If we ask God for something that is inconsistent with his nature, we should not expect him to grant the prayer. In items addressed above, we saw how focus on worldly self is the very heart and soul of sin, so when our prayers include requests that God sees as focused on this world and on self, he is unlikely to grant most of those—and that's the majority of most Christians' prayers!

So if our prayers are selfish in a worldly sense, we should not really expect God to grant them. And if granting our prayers would make it more likely that others would be eternally lost, the same expectation should apply. There may be (and almost certainly are) exceptions to either case, but they would be exceptions, not the rule.

Does God not care about our worldly desires and needs? Of course he does! But he cares much more about our eternity. This life lasts almost no time at all compared to eternity, so in his love for us, he puts our eternity first. That is a perspective we rarely appreciate, but one we need to learn to appreciate.

Spiritual Matters

So if God only does miracles to provide what he wants to provide, of what use is prayer? Why not just neglect prayer altogether? (Actually, as a practical matter many Christians come very close to this.)

In fact, there is enormous power available in prayer, and using prayer properly will bring rewards every time. The most important key to prayer is to focus on the spiritual. Let's look at Jesus' model prayer for a moment. Jesus taught his disciples to pray along these lines:

> Heavenly Father, may your name be kept holy. May your rightful role as king be established, and may what you desire be done here on earth just as it is done in heaven. Give us today the bread we need for this day. Forgive us where we have turned against you just as we forgive those who turn against us. And do not lead us into temptation, but deliver us from the evil one (Matthew 6:9-13).

Notice in this model prayer that the only thing that is focused on our needs in this world is a prayer for the food we need for this day. The prayer begins with a focus on God, but that focus has strong implications for the one praying. The prayer asks for God's name to be kept holy and for his will to be done as his kingdom is established. We cannot really pray for those things if we are not willing to keep God's name holy and to accept his authority over our lives. Then after a brief prayer for food (daily needs), the prayer focuses on our relationship with others, asking God to forgive us in the same way that we forgive others. This can be a very dangerous prayer for a person who is not forgiving. Finally there is a prayer for our own spiritual condition—a prayer that we may avoid temptation and be rescued from Satan.

Now, this prayer is not to be used as a memorized chant. It is a pattern that is intended to teach us the factors that are important or useful in prayer. If we pay attention to the pattern, the first step is praying that God will help us to be his faithful servants ourselves and to lead others to the same relationship. I believe there is no better place for prayer to start.

Following a serious prayer focused on God's authority being established in your life and the lives of those you influence, the next step is prayer for the things you really need. This is not a time to ask for things that God is already providing, but it would be a good time to thank him for those things. This is the time to tell God when you truly lack the needs of life—adequate food, clothing, housing, etc. God may well provide far more than just your needs, that is his prerogative and in his love for you he will often do so, but the role of the Christian is to accept what God provides with gratitude, always willing to live with far less or even to die in God's service.

Then once we have a chance to pray for our own physical needs, the next step is to pray for our relationship with others, especially with those who hurt us. One of the greatest keys to a truly good life is the ability to forgive. Someone once told me that what I needed to do was take the handle on the side of my head and just flush all those things others had done to hurt me. The more I practice forgiveness, the more I realize how good this is for me. Most of the time if I do not forgive something that someone has done to me, I suffer stress, anger, and unhappiness while the person I have not forgiven may not even know that he or she has hurt me. If I forgive, I get rid of all that stress, anger, and unhappiness. Forgiveness allows me to focus my life on the good things in my life.

Finally the model prayer calls for us to pray for our own spiritual welfare. This is an area where we can ask for God's miraculous blessings and he will pour out far more than we imagine possible. In this part of the pattern we would pray for spiritual strength and wisdom and guidance. These are blessings God is always eager to grant. And the "us" of this section applies to those we know and influence as well as to ourselves.

The more we pray for God's spiritual blessings, the greater the blessings he will give us, and the more we will find the joy and peace and excitement that God has for us when we focus on him. Until a person experiences this, there is no way to communicate to anyone what this experience is like, but it's awesome!

Now, there is another side to this that is hard for some people to deal with. The results are not instantaneous. Remember Abraham? He prayed for a son for 25 years before God said "Yes." And God had already promised to give him that son! Jesus told a story to illustrate this point. In his story, a poor widow had been wronged and kept appealing to the local judge for justice, but the judge was not concerned at all with justice. Perhaps he wanted a bribe from those he helped, or perhaps he just did not want to offend someone who was wealthier and more powerful than this widow. In any case, the widow just kept coming back to the judge day after day. The judge finally said to himself, "Though I do not fear God or care about men, yet because this widow irritates me I will avenge her, lest by her continually coming here she may wear me out just listening to her" (Luke 18:4-5). The point is, be patient and constant in prayer. Changing a worldly focused person into a God-focused person takes time, and God knows how to do this with infinite patience.

C. S. Lewis was right in arguing that prayer does not change God so much as it changes the person who sincerely prays. However, prayer does change what God will do, in part because it changes us into acceptable vessels for his blessings. And the more we allow God to change us spiritually, the more he can bless us even in worldly goods, because he knows we will use even worldly goods for spiritual purposes. When God knows that he can trust us with spiritual things, he knows he can also trust us with physical things.

Serious Prayer

When you are ready to start praying, you need to find a time to pray daily. If you are an early riser, you may find you can spend at least half an hour or more in prayer before you even get out of bed. If you are a late riser, perhaps you can go to bed a little early and spend at least half an hour in prayer before going to sleep. Somehow, if you would grow spiritually, you must find serious time to pray. As you grow, you will find half an hour is an absolute minimum, and three or four times that is not too much.

And the awesome thing about such a prayer time is that you will find your mind wanders, but if you are faithful in prayer, you'll suddenly realize that God is guiding your mind-wandering to understand spiritual things he wants you to know. At first you may think this is just coincidence, but the more it happens, the more you will know God is speaking with you. But if this never happens, you'll still find that the practice of prayer focused on spiritual matters brings spiritual growth that results in joy, peace, love, grace, and awesome living.

CHAPTER TEN: FORGIVENESS—THE ULTIMATE PEACE

If you don't forgive men when they turn against you, your Father won't forgive you either – Matthew 6:15

When we studied Christian love earlier, we defined this kind of love as unselfish (in a worldly sense), caring, generous, forgiving, and active. The emphasis until now focused primarily on unselfish, caring, generous, and active without a lot of emphasis on forgiving. In this chapter we must focus on forgiving. We are still focusing on motivation and the factors that affect a Christian's motivation to serve God, because it is almost impossible to be motivated to act in Christian love when you are focused on a grudge.

Forgiveness is a real wooly booger. We don't want to do it, no matter how much God wants us to do it and no matter how many benefits forgiving may bring to us. This is one of Satan's strongest hooks when he's out fishing for souls. We don't even want to talk about forgiveness. It's a boring, unnecessary topic we don't need to consider. After all, we know that we are very forgiving in most cases and that we have excellent justification for not being forgiving in the rest of the cases. When the sermon comes to this topic, either we tune out or we feel like the preacher has quit preaching and gone to meddling (or perhaps we convince ourselves that this does not apply to us).

I knew a woman who never wanted to go to a doctor because she was certain that she had cancer and she just did not want to have it confirmed by someone else. I don't recall what finally led to her death, but it had nothing to do with cancer. When it comes to forgiveness, we are like that. We just don't want to look at this critical aspect of our Christian lives.

Yet forgiveness is vitally important to Christians—both eternal life and our own earthly lives are determined by our willingness to forgive. When the irritation and anger and resentment you feel toward one or more people consumes your life, it is practically impossible to practice unselfish, caring, and truly generous love toward others. Satan will keep bringing the anger and the irritation back into your focus so that it will take up your full attention. Normally this irritation and anger focused at even one individual or group so consumes your life that even those you love the most are marginalized.

"But you don't know what they did to me!" How often we hear that, and too often we say it. When you have allowed people to torture and murder your own son just for jealousy, knowing that he would have to experience hell itself, and you have forgiven that, then you still would not have the right to say those words. Because that's what your sins did to God. If he can forgive you, what right do you have to withhold forgiveness from anyone?

Pay attention to what you say and do when you have a grudge against someone—no matter how justified. You will probably find that you are unable to have a long conversation with anyone without bringing up and justifying your irritation or anger toward this person or group. The more groups or individuals you resent, the more of your life is consumed by this resentment, and the more your communication with close friends, family, and loved ones is damaged by the need to constantly express your resentment and irritation and anger.

The topic of forgiving contributes to both the "carrot" and the "stick" of Christian motivation. We have already addressed that unselfish, caring, generous, active, love is a mandatory part of Christianity; and we will find in this chapter that Christian forgiveness is just as much a mandatory part of Christianity. That's the stick aspect—a person who wishes to participate in the salvation promised by God and in the grace needed to obtain that salvation is absolutely required to develop a forgiving attitude toward those who offend in any way. This is not easy and may seem impossible. In fact, it would be a lot harder than it really is if it were not for the "carrot" aspect. As we learn to forgive, we will find that the result of forgiving is a very freeing experience. No one can experience the full joy and wonder of Christianity until he or she has experienced the peace that comes with forgiving.

Back to Rebellion

Matthew's Gospel starts out with probably the most awesome sermon ever given. Based on what we know today, this is just a summary of what Jesus actually said on that occasion, but summary or not, it is a message Christians could and should study for a lifetime. No matter how often I read this Sermon on the Mount, I always find new treasures and I'm always convicted of how much I still need to work on in my life in order to have my life truly focused on God.

In the middle of this sermon, Jesus gives what must be the most well-known part of the whole sermon—a model for prayer often called The Lord's Prayer (Matthew 6:9-13). As we learned in Chapter 9, this model was never meant to be something we repeat by rote—it is a model for Christians to consider in understanding what prayer should be. It is a model from which we can learn much—a model each of us should consider over and over. But for now, I want to focus on just one portion of that model.

As a part of this model prayer, Jesus included the line, "Forgive us where we have turned against you *just as we forgive those who turn against us*" (Matthew 6:12; emphasis added by me but definitely implied by Jesus). Then, after completing the prayer, Jesus immediately said, "For if you forgive men when they turn against you, your heavenly Father will forgive you. But if you don't forgive men when they turn against you, your Father won't forgive you either" (Matthew 6:14-15). This is why I could say with confidence that the emphasis added above by me was certainly implied by Jesus. The fact that after completing the model prayer, Jesus felt it important to return immediately to this topic of forgiveness, stating basically the same point three times, demonstrates how crucial this is in God's sight. We need to understand that our failure to forgive those who hurt or offend us can send us to the judgment bar for eternity unforgiven! If we wish to be forgiven, we absolutely must learn to forgive.

Later in Matthew's gospel we read about Peter, a leader among Jesus' disciples, asking Jesus just how many times he should forgive his brother for some offence. (The whole account is found in Matthew 18:21-35.) Peter's suggestion was that he should forgive his brother up to seven times. (Seven was a number that Peter's culture saw as significant in God's sight, a number expressing completeness.) Jesus' reply to Peter was, "I'm not going to tell you to forgive him seven times, but seventy times seven times" (Matthew 18:22). Now, for some people it may be important to realize that Jesus was not telling Peter to stop forgiving at offence number 491. In his culture, what Jesus said would immediately be seen as equivalent to forgiveness with no limit. To put it another way, what Jesus was telling Peter was that true forgiveness cannot count to two.

Jesus immediately followed this answer with the story of two debtors. The first was in debt to his master for an almost unimaginable amount. Apparently he had been on very good terms with the master, and the master was extremely wealthy. Perhaps he was an ambitious man who tried to accomplish great things either militarily or in business without the expertise needed, or perhaps he had a serious gambling problem. In any case, he owed the master an immense amount of money, and the master's patience had run out. The master called the man to account, and when he could not pay, the master ordered that the man, his family, and everything he owned should be sold to pay his debt. Please don't miss the point that this man and all of his family were to be sold into slavery. However, when the man begged his master for more time, the master actually forgave the entire debt. In Jesus' story, the second debtor was in debt to the first debtor for a relatively small amount of money. After being forgiven his vast debt, the first debtor demanded payment from the second man. When the second debtor could not pay and begged for patience, the first debtor had him thrown into prison. When the master heard of this, he reinstated the first debt and threw that debtor into prison until he could pay the full amount of the debt (in other words, a life sentence).

Following this story Jesus said, "Even so my heavenly Father will do the same to you if each one of you does not forgive his brother from the heart for any trespasses" (Matthew 18:35). For Christians, forgiving those who offend us is not an option—it is mandatory if we want God to forgive us. While a new babe in Christ should not be expected to have mastered this, and while we will all fall short in this and other areas at times, focusing one's life on God and on ending the rebellion must include focusing on learning to forgive.

This applies to forgiving your wife or your husband. It applies to forgiving your parents, your children, and your siblings. It applies to forgiving that person at church whom you cannot tolerate, regardless of how wrong you believe that person to be. It applies to political leaders and religious leaders and everyone else. After all, if we have grasped the concept of our own sin and what an overwhelming debt God has forgiven us—if we have grasped how deeply our sin has hurt God in causing him to send his son to die bearing our sins—we should realize that nothing anyone has ever done to us could compare to what we have done to God and what God offers to forgive if we will end our rebellion. So part of ending the rebellion is growing up with the kind of spiritual maturity God has, and that means being willing to forgive those who hurt us just as we want God to forgive us.

In fact, Jesus even went beyond this level of forgiveness, saying "I tell you, don't resist an evil person. If someone slaps you on your right cheek, turn your face so that he can hit you on the other cheek too. If someone wants to sue you and take away even the shirt off your back, be sure to give him your jacket as well. And if someone forces you to go with him for a mile, go two miles" (Matthew 5:39-41). There are a couple of things worth noting here. First, for the average right-handed person, slapping someone on the right cheek involves a back-handed slap—meaning both injury and insult are involved. Next, at the time that Jesus said this, Roman soldiers had the right to force any non-Roman to carry any burden for one "mile" (slightly less than our American mile). At the end of the mile, the non-Roman was allowed to put the burden down. Beyond this we need to understand that the Romans were an occupying foreign power. The attitude of the local people to the Roman soldiers varied from general dislike to absolute hatred. Jesus was saying that those who would be his disciples should be willing to go the extra mile for someone they despised.

Remember, we have accepted God as our Father—we have agreed to grow up spiritually in the nature of God himself. And God defined himself to Moses as

> I AM the I AM, compassionate and gracious, slow to anger and overwhelmingly kind and faithful, holding thousands safe in my loving kindness, forgiving perversity and rebellion and sin, yet in no way allowing the truly guilty to go unpunished, even holding them responsible for the sin they foster in their children and grandchildren to the third and fourth generation after them (Exodus 34:6-7).[20]

If such mercy and grace and forgiving love is the very definition of God's nature as stated by God himself, and if we accept God as our Father, then we should grow up spiritually to be like our Father in these characteristics. If we are not growing in this way, there is good reason to believe that he is not our Father and we are lost in our sins.

In the passage just mentioned, you may have noticed that there are cases where God does not forgive. Similarly, there are some limits

20 Note: As we learned earlier, most translations do not make the final portion of this passage clear, and some like the New International Version absolutely mistranslate the passage, but the intent of the words in context is clearly as translated here.

to the forgiveness Christians are to practice. But for now, we need to consider some of the benefits of learning forgiveness as a way of life.

The Benefits of Forgiveness—The Carrot

The benefits of forgiveness to the person forgiven may seem obvious, but the benefits to the person who forgives are always far greater. Of course, as addressed above, the first benefit is forgiveness from God since God forgives only those who learn to forgive others. Without that forgiveness, we can never know true peace. That has to be the most important and significant benefit, but the benefits beyond that are still great.

The truth is that when a person harbors ill will toward someone else for some offense, the person harboring ill will suffers, and often he or she suffers much more than the person who committed the offense. The anger and resentment felt will cause stress, and that stress leads to mental, emotional, physical, and spiritual health issues. Such stress generally causes a person to vent his or her feelings about the offender in ways that are additional forms of rebellion against God's commands to love. Failure to forgive often causes a person to gossip about the offender. If the offender hears of the gossip, this results in further alienation. And even if the offender does not hear, such gossip often alienates those who do hear the gossip. "After all," such a person may think, "if you gossip about someone else, you'd probably gossip about me." And anyhow, who wants to listen to a constant complainer, no matter how justified the complaints?

On top of this, anyone who has ever gossiped knows how Satan will use our gossiping to tempt us to exaggerate the truth, leading us into lies and deceits. It's a rare gossiper who can resist embellishing the gossip with at least suggestions of additional possible wrongs. (And in many cases this temptation to exaggerate results in someone learning that the gossiper has lied—a difficult and very embarrassing situation, since now the gossiper has been revealed as the one in the wrong.)

Physically, harboring ill feelings toward someone who has offended you can lead to increased blood pressure problems, muscle tension and related headaches and muscle aches, stomach upset, and many other ailments. These ill feelings may well cause a person to avoid the offender and in the process to miss out on any good things that the offender enjoys. Spiritually the failure to forgive builds a barrier in a person's relationship with God. Mentally the failure to forgive contributes to depression and anger. And all of this can and generally does lead to emotional problems.

In America today, people spend billions on trying to keep or regain youth. There is nothing that does more for a youthful attitude and appearance than forgiving others. Wrinkles you would get from worry or stress are avoided. Attitudes associated normally with older people are avoided by forgiveness freely given. Ailments that make people feel old are avoided by forgiving as God has forgiven us. If you want to look and feel and act younger, try forgiveness (just $2.00 for a month's supply).

The fact is that in many cases the offender is entirely unaware of the offense and therefore unaware of the ill feelings someone harbors. In such cases the offender suffers no consequence, while the one offended prolongs his or her suffering.

On the other hand, once the offense is forgiven, all the bad effects of holding a grudge just go away. A truly forgiven offense cannot cause any physical, emotional, mental, or spiritual ailments. A truly forgiven offense, by itself, cannot isolate anyone just to avoid the offender (though we may legitimately need to avoid someone who continually offends). On top of this, God's Holy Spirit will always bless us with his presence in the act of forgiving, and that is an experience so wonderful it cannot be expressed in human language.

Resentment and ill will are like mental feces (in more vulgar terms, it's mental shit). I mentioned earlier that someone once told me that a person needs to learn to reach up to the imaginary handle on the side of his or her head and just flush it. Or as the character Van on the TV show *Reba* said, there is just one word that applies—"Letitgo!" (For those unfamiliar with the show, that's a very condensed version of "let it go!") But for the Christian, letting it go means turning it over to God for resolution in full faith that God can and will resolve all things appropriately in the end.

Looking the Wrong Direction

On top of all of the health issues and the issue of rebellion, harboring ill feelings about an offender always has us looking backward, and God would have us looking forward. We cannot concentrate properly on the tasks God has for us in his kingdom if we are constantly focused on past offenses. If we truly trust God, we can turn the matter over to him and know that in the end he will deal with it properly.

Forgiving is one of the most healthy and freeing experiences anyone can know. For the Christian, it is truly a matter of faith. In forgiving others, we admit that we do not have the insight to know the proper response to any offense. We do not know the factors that influenced the offender to commit the offense. We do not know in what way we may have offended the one we view as offender. Only God can know the right answer, and ultimately he will provide that answer. If the offender has been forgiven by God, we can be sure that God knows best. If the offender has not been forgiven by God, we can be sure that no punishment we could ever inflict would come close to what God's judgment will do, so why should we try to add to that and risk God's judgment on ourselves. We have no business trying to do God's job for him, and that is what is happening when we do not forgive.

This is part of getting our focus on God and the work he has ahead for us instead of on ourselves and the things of this world. With rare if any exceptions, the offenses that we resent and want to punish have to do with our worldly pride or our worldly bodies or our worldly possessions. And the punishments we want to inflict are also of this world. When we truly get our focus on God and the future he has planned for us instead of past offenses, the offenses of this world will fade into an insignificant background. We have eternity in heaven coming to us—why should we trouble ourselves over the momentary offenses of this world.

So the offender stole all your money and you are already retired and now have nothing to provide for your needs or the needs of your family during retirement. This loss seems terrible, but if you will trust in him, God can and will provide what is really needed. In addition, if you will trust in him, God will turn this terrible experience into valuable lessons learned and all sorts of good that will last throughout eternity. And even if you starve to death as a Christian, the result is only good. The Christian response is definitely a matter of faith, but for the one with such faith, God always comes through.

So the offender killed the person you held most dear. No one is ever promised even one more minute in this life, and God handles death constantly. When we see things from his perspective, we will always find that he has done right. We need to trust him. He will deal justly and mercifully with those who die, and he will deal justly and mercifully with those who live. If the one who dies has focused his or her life on God, that person is far, far better off in a death that is really a door into a life that is better in every way.

As long as we do not forgive, to the extent that we do not forgive we must be focused on what is in the past. As soon as we forgive (which does require momentary focus on the past), we can take our focus off of that past and put it on the future.

No matter how bad the offense, the Christian's calling is to forgive and turn the judgment over to God. Yes, it is good and right for Christians to learn from the offenses of this world and to seek to avoid being repeatedly offended in the future. Yes, it is good and right for Christians to turn things over to the proper earthly authorities when the offender is violating the laws of this world. But in the end, it is the Christian's responsibility to focus on God—to turn these things over to God and trust him to settle the accounts in the right way. After all, would you really want to receive exact justice for all of your offenses, including all the times you have offended God and all the times your apathy or neglect has contributed to offending others?

Phases of Forgiveness

Now forgiveness does not always imply forgetting the offense (contrary to what some would say). When a person offends you, the offender is often completely unaware of the offense. He or she often has no idea anything is wrong. In some cases it is important to address the offense with the offender to avoid future offenses both for yourself and for others. In other cases it is appropriate to simply be cautious around a person who tends to offend others. And in severe cases it is necessary to report some offenses to the proper authorities in order to assure that others do not have to suffer the same offenses.

There are at least three easily identifiable phases to Christian forgiveness.

1. The first phase is turning the offense over to God. This one is mandatory for all offenses in all cases. This is a matter of faith. If we believe that God can and will judge the world in righteousness, then any effort on our part to do his job is rebellion. This does not mean that we forget about any lessons we may have learned because of the offense or that we would not report the offense to the proper authorities if appropriate. It just means we take ourselves out of the judgment seat. This is what Jesus was talking about when he said that Christians should not

judge (Matthew 7:1-5). It is worth noting that Jesus followed this immediately by teaching that Christians can and should determine their attitudes and actions toward others based on how those others behave. In context, it is clear that Jesus was saying that we should not try to do God's job, but that it is entirely OK for us to avoid those who habitually offend.

2. The second phase of forgiveness involves re-establishing a good relationship with the offender. This phase is not mandatory. Jesus said, "If your bother offends you, tell him what he has done; and if he repents, you must forgive him" (Luke 17:3). Note that in this case this level of forgiveness is contingent on repentance. This is consistent with Jesus' teaching in Matthew 7 where he told his disciples not to try to give what is holy to "dogs" or to throw their pearls to "pigs" (Matthew 7:6) and where he told his disciples that they should be able to recognize false teachers "by their fruits" (Matthew 7:15-20). We are not to try to do God's job for him, but we can and should learn from the behavior of others and respond appropriately. However, if an offender repents, we are to trust the repentance and be willing to re-establish our relationship just as God has done for us. Obviously, if a person commits the same or similar offenses repeatedly, the level of trust in his or her repentance will be affected. This leads us to the third phase.

3. The third phase of forgiveness is forgetting the offense. This phase also is not mandatory, but when it is possible, it is a real blessing. When an offender continues an offensive pattern of behavior, forgetting the offenses could lead to even worse offenses. Even when a relationship is restored, the potential for repetition of offenses and the need to learn lessons from earlier offenses (as Jesus taught) may require that we remember the offenses or at least that we recall that offenses of this type were brought on by a person or group. But when a person repents and shows evidence of a desire to really stop his or her offending ways, the Christian's best response is to forget past offenses whenever possible. Sometimes past offenses may be just too traumatic to forget. That is part of our being human. But God's word to Jeremiah prophesying of the new covenant brought by Jesus was, "I will forgive their iniquity and I will no longer even remember their sins" (Jeremiah 31:34). When

we emulate our Heavenly Father's willingness to forgive and forget the sins of those who truly repent, we will find joy in his Holy Spirit and peace in having one less stress factor.

In the examples mentioned earlier, a thief who steals all that you have needs to be reported to the proper authorities in order to prevent similar injury to others. In the same way, a person who kills either intentionally or because of carelessness needs to be reported. A Christian may well participate in the legal process required to prevent future criminal or injurious activities. That is a valid expression of our love for those who may be injured if we do not do this. But for a Christian, personal vengeance must not be the goal—that is God's area. "Beloved, don't try to avenge yourselves. Instead, leave vengeance to God's wrath, just as it says in the sacred writings, '"Vengeance is mine, I will settle the score," says the Lord'" (Romans 12:19). The Christian's goal is to be based on the love and care for others that also cares about preventing injury to others.

A Christian is not required to live as a doormat for others to walk on. One of the keys to proper Christian forgiveness is that forgiveness deals with what is in the past, not what is yet to come. Forgiveness must involve withholding personal retribution, but it does not have to withhold whatever it takes to prevent future injury. Forgiving what someone has done in the past does not mean that we cannot take action to avoid similar problems in the future. Forgiving what a person has done does means that we will not try to even the score.

An interesting example is given in Paul's letters to the Christians in Corinth. In 1Corinthians Paul describes a man who was living with "his father's wife." (In English, the phrase "his father's wife" might cause us to think this man was living with his stepmother, but the fact that this same phrase appears twice in Leviticus and twice in Deuteronomy in a sense that would indicate any wife of one's father [including one's own mother] leaves open the possibility that the man was actually living with his own mother as if she were his wife. Paul's response is more in line with this latter interpretation.) We do not know the details of this case except that in that culture and community, Paul made it clear that this was considered especially immoral, and this man's behavior was causing the local community to gossip about Christians as if Christians permitted and approved of such behavior. Paul's instruction was for the man to be put out of the congregation and for the Christians to have nothing to do with him, but with the goal "that his spirit may be saved in the day of the Lord

Jesus" (1Corinthians 5:1-5). Note that it was what the man's behavior would do to the witness of the church (not what he had done as an immoral person) that required this judgment.

Then in 2Corinthians 2:4-11 Paul appears to deal with the same person's situation after the man repented and ended his objectionable behavior. At that point Paul instructed the church to forgive the man and take him back into the congregation. Notice the change in focus from past to present and future. As long as the man continued in his offense, the responsibility of Christians was to minimize the effect on themselves and the witness of the church, but as soon as the offense was in the past, the responsibility of Christians was to forgive and accept the penitent Christian.

Example – Road Rage

One of the most common areas where American Christians have problems with forgiveness is road rage. Perhaps one of us is driving down a road and someone who wants to go faster than we are going gets so close behind us that it is dangerous. How do we respond? Or we are in the left lane getting ready to pass a line of vehicles and suddenly the person just in front of us (who is going slower than we are and is not that close to the next vehicle) pulls into the left lane, forcing us to slow down while he or she catches up with and passes the line of traffic we were about to pass. How do we respond? Or someone insists on driving in the left lane even though there are good opportunities to move to the right lane and let us get by. How do we respond? And the list of such offenses goes on and on.

In far too many cases, the response of those who claim to be Christian is anything but Christian. In fact, in many cases the response involves driving activities that are as dangerous as or more dangerous than anything the offender has done, as if the offense somehow justifies our response—a response that in any other circumstances would obviously be as wrong as what the offender has done. And too often the one who responds in this way to an offense has some symbol or marker on the rear of his or her vehicle indicating that he or she is a Christian, thus bearing witness that this "Christian" does not act as a Christian should and thereby bringing discredit to the church and to the Lord.

For most people, road rage is one of those forgiveness issues that gets the blood pressure up, causes muscle tension that often results in headaches, stomach pains, and muscle cramps, and generally creates a negative attitude that is not compatible with love, joy, peace, or any of the other fruits of the Spirit (see Galatians 5:22). These are attitudes that shut God out of our lives—attitudes based on worldly selfish pride and arrogance. (After all, we know what great drivers we are—it's just all the idiots that make driving so dangerous.) In fact, our responses are often adequate to ruin a day that otherwise might have been very good. And in worst case, our response may lead to some kind of accident or even to an armed response from someone we viewed as an offender.

How much better it would be to immediately turn the whole matter over to God for judgment. In this way there are no blood pressure problems and no headaches or stomachaches related to stress. If the offender is driving too close behind you, why not find the first convenient place to pull over and let that person get by. (You'll often catch up with that car at the next traffic light.) While the offender may wind up in an accident caused by his or her wreckless driving, we as Christians can avoid the added risk of being involved. (If the offender is truly driving recklessly, the Christian's appropriate response may include pulling off the road and calling the proper authorities.)

Example – Family Issues

All too often we who claim to be Christians need to learn the lesson of forgiveness in our own families. Husbands and wives always hurt each other emotionally, no matter how hard they may try to avoid it (and too many do not try very hard). It is impossible for two people to live together for very long without causing some offense. With few exceptions the first offenses are not intentional, but when they are not resolved and forgiven, offenses and counter-offenses start to build. Eventually two people who swore before God and witnesses that they would treat each other with love under any and all circumstances for the rest of their lives are living in constant animosity or even hatred. Other family relationships, though not as frequently marred by long-term and compounded offenses, are still susceptible to similar problems—children and parents or brothers and sisters working against each other because neither side will push the reset button by sincerely and completely offering forgiveness.

The issues that can cause problems in the home are sometimes very serious and sometimes ridiculous. Couples fight over how to squeeze toothpaste out of a tube or how to hang the paper towels and toilet paper or which direction to hang shirts in the closet and on and on. Couples criticize each other in public over these and even less important matters. And in doing this, we bring discredit to ourselves and our Lord.

And the problems are not limited to our natural families. Church families have very similar problems. In any family situation, people will hurt one another from time to time—this is impossible to avoid in your worldly family, and it is impossible to avoid in your Christian family. The very people we should hold dearest and treat with the most consistent love are too often the ones we come to resent or even hate.

Forgiveness can bring renewed bonds of friendship and love, but who will go first? Given all the blessings for forgiving and all the curses associated with not forgiving, the right response is to eagerly desire to be first. After all, are we children of the God who is love, or would we rather be children of the devil himself? That really is the choice.

Motivating Factors

Getting back to motivation, as long as we refuse to let go of our anger, resentment, and desire to "get even," we will be a negative motivating factor for Christianity both to ourselves and to those who witness our behavior. When we demonstrate God's love and mercy by practicing forgiveness, we become a positive motivating factor. Furthermore, when we practice forgiveness God's Holy Spirit works in our hearts to bring love and joy and peace and a sense of the very presence of God. And when we remember that our willingness to forgive others brings God's willingness to forgive us, the sense of peace and joy is further enhanced.

At a level all too rarely experienced, if the people who make up a church truly practice real forgiveness, this can encourage people to open up about their spiritual weaknesses—and that can offer opportunity to help each other and encourage each other. If we can get to that level, we can experience more than ever the power of God's Holy Spirit working among us—and that is truly motivating.

This is indeed a vital aspect of ending our rebellion. As long as we insist on holding grudges and ill feelings, we continue in rebellion—we have not truly submitted to God and we are actively demonstrating a lack of faith in God's ability to deal with those who offend us. In learning to truly forgive and turn retribution over to God, we find peace and freedom and we establish ourselves as truly God's servants. And if the people who make up a church are forgiving, that forgiving nature will motivate others to learn about the Lord.

But this is not just something that motivates us individually. Practicing forgiveness is probably the most powerful witness a Christian can have. When people see the joy and peace we have because of the way we practice forgiving love, they want what we have. The more you practice this aspect of Christian love, the more you will realize that you could not really be doing this if it were not for God's Holy Spirit within you. And when others see how this changes your life for the better in every way, they will not understand how you are able to do what you do. It is at that point that God opens the door and lets you testify to something people will really want to hear—the message of how God's Holy Spirit can empower us to experience that kind of life. That is a very powerful witness.

What to Do?

So what can we do about forgiveness? Obviously, the first simple answer is to start forgiving others, but that can be such a huge task that we would give up before we ever experienced the peace and joy God has in store for us. So the first practical step is prayer. Talk to God about the whole matter. Confess the areas where you cannot bring yourself to forgive, and ask him to guide you. And keep praying that prayer day by day while you struggle with Satan's powerful effort to stop you. Understand that while we will look at a few suggestions here, every case is different.

One key to success is picking a single issue that causes you to be irritated or angry and work on that one. Try to understand why the person or people who irritate you might be doing whatever they are doing. After all, very few people are irritating just because they want to be irritating. Most irritating people are irritating for a reason: because they don't realize how irritating they are, because they don't know how to behave any other way, or because you or someone else is actually irritating them.

Once you have picked something to work on, take it to the Lord every day before you get out of bed. Explain to God why you think this should be irritating you in light of his forgiveness. Examine yourself to see if you may have behavior that is similar to what irritates you in others or that may be irritating to others. Learning to really forgive and turn matters over to God is not easy, but it is necessary and the rewards are great—beyond anything you can imagine until you start practicing this kind of grace.

CHAPTER ELEVEN: CHURCH—THE ULTIMATE FELLOWSHIP

Let everything you do be for building each other up – 1Corinthians 15:26

It's hard to be motivated as a Christian if what you experience week after week in the church meetings is not motivating. Far too often people's experiences in a church meeting are not motivating, and this is one more area where we need to learn to follow the guidance God has provided—guidance that is essentially a practice of applying what we have already learned in this study. In doing so, we will find that church meetings can and should be highly motivating. People leaving a church meeting should normally feel exhilarated, and they would if we would only do what God wants us to do. But to do this, we need to consider some things we often miss.

Before diving into this topic, it's important to admit that some churches cannot be as motivating as some might wish because of leadership problems. As Paul said, "We have this awesome treasure in jars made of clay" (2Corinthians 4:7). In other words, God has entrusted the awesome treasure of the gospel message to weak and imperfect humans (clay jars). Sometimes the clay jars who serve in leadership roles for a church actually lead in ways that prevent that church from experiencing the motivational dynamic intended by God, and there may be no way to correct that situation quickly. Replacing the leader or leaders may seem like an option, and in some cases it is, but there are not enough people with the leadership skills needed to fill all the openings—and that is true in business as well as in churches. In such cases, each Christian must do his or her best to practice individually what the church should be practicing collectively, and each one must pray diligently for God's Holy Spirit to work in this situation, patiently waiting on God to resolve the problems in his own time. Our task as Christians is to do the right thing regardless of the quality of leadership. As Jesus said, "The harvest is truly bountiful, but there are just not enough people willing and able to do the work. In that situation you need to pray the Lord of the harvest to send the needed workers into his harvest" (Matthew 9:37-38). At the proper time, God will grant that prayer. In the meantime God will work with those who are willing to serve him to teach lessons that will prepare them for what lies ahead.

Some people believe that motivation depends on a dynamic preacher, a dynamic music program, high-tech equipment, a beautiful building, or some combination of these factors. A dynamic preacher may help if the preaching and leadership are right, but I have personally experienced a church where the minister practically read his sermons in a monotone voice, even reading his prayers in a similar manner, yet the church grew, was strong, and was motivating enough to affect not only its own neighborhood but the whole region. And too often a dynamic speaker winds up leading in entirely wrong ways. A dynamic music program can help, but again I have experienced churches with mediocre music programs that provided enough motivation to see awesome growth both spiritually and numerically. And it is ridiculous to believe that a building or high-tech equipment would be spiritually motivating, though these things can help convey and even amplify the motivating factors when they are already present. After all, the early church grew rapidly with no buildings and no technology and very little trained leadership, and many churches today both in this country and in other parts of the world experience serious growth with very limited facilities. As far as the building is concerned, there are many cases where a beautiful building actually becomes a limiting factor on a church's numerical growth.

Wrong Ideas about "Church"

Before we get any deeper into this subject, let's consider what we're actually talking about—what "church" really is and what wrong ideas we tend to accept as right. One of the things that we need to understand clearly is what a church is and is not. The biblical word for a church means "an intentional gathering of people" or "a group of people sharing a common purpose." Literally, it means "an assembly," though it came to apply to a group of people who would assemble for a particular purpose whether they were actually assembled or not at the time of reference. In other words, this word may apply to a group that is physically together or it may apply to a group that is together in the sense of a shared purpose. This word is used in the Bible for both secular and religious gatherings. For example, in Acts 19:40 this word refers to a gathering of pagans to oppose Paul's ministry. But this word always refers to a group of people—never a building.

Church as a Building

In the Bible, the word "church" could not mean a building—no such meaning applied to this word and no one would have mistakenly understood it as referring to a building. And there is no record in the Bible of a building specifically dedicated to church meetings. In the Bible we read of churches meeting in people's homes and in rented facilities, but not in a building belonging to the church. So if we stay with the Bible, from a Christian perspective a church would be a group of Christians either gathered together as Christians or at least sharing purposes directly related to the fact that they are Christians. If two or three Christians gather in a restaurant or a home or a park or anywhere else as Christians, that meeting is a church meeting and the people are a church.

Using the word "church" to refer to a building is a misuse of the word—a misuse with motivational effects that are not good. We Christians are the church. When we speak of a building as "the church" we tend to distance ourselves from the purposes of the church. Thinking of the church as a building, we tend to think of the people paid to work in that building as the people responsible for doing what the church is supposed to do. The more we think of and speak of ourselves as the church, the more we are motivated to live daily in a manner consistent with being the church. We are the church. What we do, the church does. We are the body of Christ. As far as the world is concerned, what we do, Christ does.

This may seem like a small point, but just such small points can get us into big trouble. As was pointed out earlier, Satan can use such a small thing over time like a breeze blowing us gently but surely far off course. Remember, Christ died for the church—he did not die for a building (see Ephesians 5:25). We need to be constantly aware that we are that church—that the building is just a tool the church owns and uses in this world. The building is sacred and holy only because of the way the people who are the church use the building—dedicating it to God's uses. As soon as the congregation no longer uses the building for such purposes, it ceases to be sacred or holy. In itself, no building can be sacred or holy—in this world only people can have and impart those qualities.

But speaking of the building as "the church" is a hard habit to break. While it is not something we should make an issue that could cause division among the people who are the church, it is something we need to work on. We can learn to speak of the building as "the church building" or "the church house" or some other term. We can even invent a word for the building. But this is something we would do well to work on in order to strengthen motivation.

We are the church. We need to think of ourselves as the church. We need to think of every action we do in this world as an action of the church, bringing either credit or discredit to who we are as the church. Whether we are meeting with other Christians or not at any specific time, we are always an integral part of the God's church. If we are Christians, we are never outside of or away from the church, because we are the church.

A Building as "God's House"

Worse yet, we sometimes speak of the church building as "God's house." This has various negative motivational issues, and it just is not true. Let's start with the point that it is not true, because that will also capture at least one of the most important motivational issues.

First, someone will probably argue that the building is indeed God's house, as is every other building in the world. That argument is true, but it is not a valid argument for calling the building God's house. If we call every building in the world "God's house," then the argument works. If we only call the church's building "God's house," we imply that it is God's house in some special way that is different from all other buildings, and that is neither true nor appropriate. Legally, if you check the deed of ownership you will not find God named as owner.

Next, just as we are the church, according to the Bible we are also God's house. Under Old Testament Law, there were two buildings that were called "God's house." The first of these was the Tabernacle originally built by Moses and the Israelites at Mount Sinai. This was an ornate but portable structure that could be moved as the Israelites moved through their wilderness wanderings. During those travels, God was present at this tent in a special way, and even after those wanderings his presence was very real in association with the Ark of the Covenant that was housed in that portable building.

After the Israelites chose to have kings to lead them, their third king (Solomon) built a far more ornate temple of stone with the finest ornamentation available in that day. The Ark of the Covenant was moved into that building. It is worth noting that when King Solomon built this temple, in his prayer of dedication for the temple he called this building a house he had built for God, but he said, "Will God really dwell on earth with men? The heavens, even the highest heavens, cannot contain you—so how much less this temple I have built!" (2Chronicles 6:18).

God does not live in buildings. And from the day of Pentecost when the church first started, while there are some references to the old temple in Jerusalem as a place, every reference in the Bible to God's house, God's temple, or any similar terminology is always clearly to the people of the church. As Christians, we are God's house—God lives in us. As Solomon said, no building could ever be God's house. Thinking of ourselves as the dwelling place of Almighty God is motivational in a very positive sense. This is a message we need to hear frequently. Where we go, God goes, because he lives in us. Consider the following passages:

> Don't you understand that you are the temple of God and that the Spirit of God lives in you? If anyone defiles the temple of God, God will destroy him. For the temple of God is holy, and you are that temple (1Corinthians 3:16).
>
> We are God's fellow workers; you are God's field—God's building (1Corinthians 3:9).
>
> Don't you understand that your body is the temple of the Holy Spirit who is in you, whom you have from God himself, and you are not your own? (1Corinthians 6:19).
>
> What does the temple of God have to do with idols? And you are the temple of the Living God. As God has said, "I will dwell in and walk among them. I will be their God, and they shall be my people" (2Corinthians 6:16).

> You are no longer strangers and foreigners. You are now fellow citizens with the saints and members of the household of God, having been built on the foundation of the apostles and prophets, Jesus Christ Himself being the chief cornerstone. In him the whole building is joined together, growing into a holy temple for the Lord. Indeed, you are being built together as a home for God in the Spirit (Ephesians 2:19-22).

> I'm writing this so that you may know how you ought to conduct yourself in the house of God, which is the church of the living God, the pillar and ground of the truth (1Timothy 3:15).

> You too, as living stones, are being built up as a spiritual house (1Peter 2:5).

We are God's house. Thinking of ourselves as God's dwelling place is a positive motivation for living for God; thinking of a building as God's house is a negative motivation. This idea that a church building is God's house leads to a double standard problem that I call "Mothers' Day Syndrome." On Mothers' Day I go to Mother's house and while I am there I abide by Mother's rules, but as soon as I leave Mother's house I revert to my own rules. Similarly, many who think of a building as "God's house" have the attitude that they must behave one way in "God's house," but that this standard no longer applies as soon as they leave "God's house." We dress one way to go to this building, and another way the rest of the time. We talk one way when we are in this building, and another way the rest of the time. We are polite and kind in this building (sometimes), but far too often we are cruel or at least indifferent the rest of the time.

This attitude is Satan's victory, getting people to think it is appropriate to live for self except when in a certain building. And as a child, I recall people telling me that I should not run in "God's house" or make loud noises in "God's house," giving me the impression that God does not like children to have fun in his house. These things are negative motivational factors, and they all go against the biblical teaching that we are God's house. Not that children should be allowed to run undisciplined in the church building or to disturb serious times of prayer and worship, but that we should not give the false impression that it is God's rules that limit their activities. The truth is that God created children to run and play and make loud noises. It is entirely appropriate to tell a child to play quietly when people are trying to focus on prayer or worship or study of God's word. It is entirely appropriate to tell a child to respect and not damage the property of others including the church's building. But it is wrong to teach a child that he or she should not have fun in the building because it is "God's house."

Taking a side road for a moment, let's consider how we dress when we gather as the church. Some churches have specific dress codes. Some have cultural standards that serve as if they were dress codes. And some churches pride themselves in having no standards or codes. Legalistic standards are wrong—Christianity is never about legalism. But too often those who are supposed to be Christian dress in ways that discredit their Christianity and their Lord. So what should the standard be? For Christians, the standard is the same regardless of whether they are going to a church meeting or not—dress in a way that will not dishonor God or the testimony of the church. A person who dresses to show off his or her body or his or her belongings (clothing, jewelry, etc.) is dishonoring God by trying to gain glory for self. It is fine to welcome outsiders who may not understand this and who therefore dress in worldly ways, but if a Christian routinely dresses to selfishly steal the glory from God, the leaders of the church need to provide guidance in that area. As with every other part of our lives, our apparel should honor God.

And as mentioned above, if we simply look at the deed for the property we will find that, at least from a legal perspective, a church's building belongs to the church or to the trustees of the church or to the denomination or to some individual or group of people—never to God.

The Purpose of the Church Meeting

In many cases the main function of the church meeting is seen as a sermon to win souls to Christ, though in most cases few if any of the people present in the church meetings feel any need to be converted. Biblically speaking, in the entire New Testament there is only one case mentioned where a sermon focused on conversion was preached on Sunday, and that was not in a normal church meeting. That one case is the day of Pentecost recorded in the book of Acts chapter 2 when the first Christian sermon was preached and the first converts became the church.[21] Preaching is not the Bible's definition of the purpose of the church meeting.

The real biblical purpose of the church meeting is a cross between a training session and a pep rally. As was mentioned for other reasons above, in 1Corinthians 12 through 14 Paul addressed a situation where some Christians in Corinth were showing off their ability to speak in languages they had never learned—apparently languages no one in the church recognized. From what Paul wrote it seems the people involved claimed to be speaking in supernatural angelic languages (a difficult claim to refute) and claimed that this was the most important of God's gifts to Christians. Paul never questioned that God can and does empower individuals to speak in languages they had not learned when it is useful to him, but he insisted that this was appropriate in a church meeting only under certain very specific and limited conditions. In dealing with this problem of pride and arrogance over God's gifts, Paul briefly described a typical church service for that time and in that context he specified the real over-riding purpose of a church meeting: "Let everything you do be done to build each other up" (1Corinthians 14:26). In other words, a church meeting is to be a cross between a training session and a pep rally. To build each other up means education, training, encouragement, support, friendship, fellowship, and caring love. That is the purpose of the meeting.

If we look at the church meeting from God's perspective, this makes a lot of sense. After all, the non-Christians, at least for the most part, are not in the church meetings—they are out there elsewhere. So God's plan is, let's get the Christians together in church to train each other, encourage each other, help each other, and pray for each other. The more the Christians are built up, encouraged, energized, motivated, and trained; the better job each Christian can do in witnessing for Jesus and in living a Christian life, and the better each Christian will feel about being a Christian. When that happens, we can all go out to do the work where it needs to be done, which is in the worldly community in which we as the church live! If we hope to win the world, we need training, we need encouragement, we need the support of each other, and we need to sense the power of God's Holy Spirit mov-

21 There is a reference in Acts 20 that records an account of Paul visiting the church in Troas. In the King James Bible this passage is translated to say that Paul "preached" to the church. However, the word used in Acts 20:7 is the word from which we get the English term "dialogue," while the word for preaching throughout the New Testament means to announce news. Hardly any other translation has this error.

ing among us—and that will be our experience every time we go to church if each one of us takes that purpose seriously.

In any sport, those who would succeed must train, but they also need the encouragement of each other and of those around them. In the world of athletics, every coach has two important jobs. The obvious job is to train his athletes for competition, but just as important is the job of inspiring his athletes to do their best. Though Christianity is not a sport, that kind of training and encouragement is the purpose of the church meeting. As the author of Hebrews put it, "Let's think about each other's needs in order to stir up Christian love and good works, not neglecting the church meetings (as some have been doing), but exhorting each other with increasing zeal as you see the day of judgment approaching" (Hebrews 10:24-25). Notice, the purpose of the church meeting is concern for each other's needs, stirring up Christian love and good works, and exhorting each other. In other words, the church meeting is to be a cross between a training session and a pep rally. Any church meeting that is not fulfilling both of those purposes is off track.

If Christians really use the church meeting times as times for training and encouragement (building up), there is no limit to what could be accomplished for the Lord—and God knew this when he established the concept of church meetings. Consider Jesus' final orders to his disciples: "Wherever you go, make disciples of all the nations, baptizing them in the name of the Father and the Son and the Holy Spirit, teaching them to observe everything just as I have commanded you" (Matthew 28:19-20). The only command in these orders that is actually in the form of a command is the command to "make disciples." (While some translations read as if there is a command to "go," the word often translated as "go" is a participle that should be translated "going," "as you go," or "wherever you go.") However, having given the command to make disciples, Jesus emphasized that once people become disciples we as more mature Christians are to teach them. While "baptizing" and "teaching" are participles, they are unlike the participle "going" in that these participles are grammatically tied to the command to "make disciples" as necessary parts of the process of making disciples. So according to Jesus, our job as Christians is to lead others to discipleship and then to train them. Baptism is the break point between the task of leading them to discipleship and the task of training them as Christians.

And this is not the preacher's job—it is the job of every Christian. We are the church. If the church is to fulfill its purposes, we must fulfill those purposes. We are the body of Christ. If Christ is to minister to this world, we are his hands and his feet and his mouth. If Christ is to bring the good news that is the gospel to this world, we must do it. God has entrusted these tasks to us, and the church meetings are where we are to learn from each other, train each other, and encourage each other.

If we do our job well, we'll soon realize that we should expect neither conversion nor the associated act of baptism to normally take place in a church meeting. We as Christians can and should go out with the real plan of salvation: "Jesus is Lord, and he commands us to practice Christian love day by day." If we do this job as God expects us to, we'll quickly realize that converts should be baptized by the person or persons who convince them to turn their lives over to Jesus, whether the person doing the baptizing is a minister or a new convert, male or female, young or old. Any Christian can find a couple of witnesses (they don't even have to be Christians) and some water (preferably but not necessarily warm) and get on with it. If the Christian physically cannot administer the baptism, any willing volunteer may serve in that role.

If we want the congregation to witness the baptism (which would be a good thing), we can either play a video recording or re-enact the baptism at the next church meeting. This is motivational. This allows individual Christians to see the fruits of their labors and rejoice in the harvest. But to do this, Christians need training and encouragement, and that is the role of the church meeting. A limited number of churches are already doing things like these with great success. We just need a lot more churches getting serious about discipleship and edification.

Please understand, I do believe in the value of professional ministers. They are the ones who should provide trained guidance for what the church should be doing. But we have missed the mark in trying to have our professional ministers be the professional Christians. It's long past time that God's saints were empowered to be the church God intended them to be—a witness to the world and a powerful encouragement to each other. Let the minister's glory be not in how many he has converted but in how many of the people of his flock are doing the converting. In fact, the minister is the one person in a church who should be least likely to be actively converting others both because of his responsibilities in training others to do this job and because of his status as a "paid witness."

Finding a Ministry

The things addressed above are focused on conversion, and that is important, but for Christians to find the motivation God intended they need to be involved in a caring ministry of some sort—a ministry that is really accomplishing something for the Lord. Too often our churches focus on getting a person to a single point of conversion rather than to a lifetime of ministry for the Lord, in which case the "conversion" may be nothing more than show.

I heard the story of a woman who was seeing her pastor, a highly trained counselor, on a weekly basis to try to deal with her depression. After several sessions with no sign of progress, just before the time of one scheduled session the minister received word that he needed to visit a member in the hospital immediately. As the woman arrived for her appointment, the minister asked her to accompany him on his hospital rounds this time. They spent the next hour calling on and bringing cheer to several people in the hospital. The minister noticed as he and the woman were leaving the hospital that she seemed happier than usual. When he asked her about this, she replied that she felt really good after visiting with these people who were so in need of someone to care. The minister said, "Well, I think we've found the cure for your depression." To this the woman responded, "You don't mean you want me to do that again, do you?"

Even when we experience how exhilarating and motivating it can be to minister to others, at first we resist the obvious conclusion that this is an important part of what God designed us to do. We want to focus on ourselves and on our own problems, and that's the heart and soul of sin and a sure path to depression. But when we focus on the problems of others, we can see our own problems in a much more realistic perspective that tends to combat depression.

We never learn as much about Christianity as we do when we are ministering to the needs of others. While ministering within the church's facilities by teaching or singing or cleaning or whatever else we do is certainly important, every member needs to have some sort of ministry that demonstrates God's love outside the walls of any church building. The individual ministry may be working as part of an organized church ministry, or it may be a ministry the member feels called to perform apart from organized church activities. One person may take on a ministry of calling on the elderly and shut-ins. Another may take on a ministry helping in a community project as a representative of the church. A member who cannot get out of bed may have a ministry of prayer, a ministry of writing cards to others, a ministry of calling members when there are special needs, or any of an unlimited number of opportunities. If a Christian is ready to minister, God's Holy Spirit can always find a way to use that person's ministry.

I knew one woman who constantly insisted that she had no talent and no training. Yet when she started getting involved, she suddenly blossomed both in her own ministries and in leading others into ministry. God alone knows what each person can be when he [God] is allowed to be in control.

There is no shortage of opportunities for ministry because there is no shortage of need in this world. To experience the gospel, we need to be the body of Christ caring for the needs of a lost and dying world—we need to roll up our sleeves and get busy demonstrating God's love in this world. This is Christian love in action, and we need to be intentional about it. And when we are, we will experience motivation only God can provide by the presence of his Holy Spirit within us. There is no joy greater than the Holy Spirit within us cheering us on!

Christian Education and Training

We will address some of the problems with how we do Christian education and training in the church shortly. At this point it is only necessary to point out that we as Christians need to take advantage of whatever training is available to grow as Christians. I believe that the most significant need of Christians today is training in Christian living as taught in the Bible including the things covered in this book—the very basics of what Christianity was meant to be. With this much understanding, a Christian can safely evaluate the material presented in various other books, Internet courses, training offered by churches or by individuals, etc. Assuming that we have ended the rebellion, there is no excuse for failure to find training of some sort.

Fellowship

Christianity is all about relationships—relationships based on Christian love. The first and most important relationship is our relationship with God, but of nearly equal importance are our relationships with each other. After all, as Christians, God lives in us, and in our relationships with each other we find a stronger relationship with God. Remember, ending the rebellion involves Christian love—caring about the needs of others. This applies first of all to our fellow Christians who are part of our section of the church.

In the New Testament description of Christianity, fellowship is something much stronger than what we normally think of. Fellowship was a bonding that involved sharing both emotionally and physically with others. The fellowship of the early church meant that Christians shared what they had with those in need. Of course this goes back to Christian love as unselfish, caring, generous, and active.

One of the strongest expressions of Christian fellowship is found in Paul's letter to the church in Corinth. In this letter Paul wrote, "By partaking of the blessed cup which we bless in the communion service, isn't it a fellowship in the blood of Christ? The bread we break in the communion service, isn't it a fellowship in the body of Christ? For though there are many of us, we are one bread—one body; for we all partake of that one bread" (1Corinthians 10:16-17). To put it a little more bluntly for our times, Paul was telling the Christians in Corinth that when we share in the communion service we become flesh and blood kin to each other, because we are all sharing in the flesh and blood of Jesus Christ.

In fact, in the Bible the word for "communion" is the same as the word for "fellowship," and the point is a common bond. The very first description of the church in the Bible says, "And these first Christians continued steadfastly in the apostles' doctrine, fellowship, breaking of bread, and prayer. Then awe came over every soul, and many wonders and signs were done through the apostles. Now all who believed were together and shared all things in common" (Acts 2:42-44). Notice how in this passage the word "fellowship" is followed immediately by the words "breaking of bread" which included a communion service. Notice also how Luke describes this fellowship as including sharing "all things in common."

This was not communism as some have claimed, because communism forces sharing by means of a police state. Based on what Luke recorded later in Acts 5, the church made no claim on anyone's possessions. Enforced communal living was known at that time and practiced at least in a community described in the Dead Sea Scrolls, but that is not what the church practiced. The church shared because Christians cared about each other and shared from their available resources to help those in need.

In writing to the churches of Galatia, Paul said, "As we have any opportunity, let's do good to everyone—especially to those who are of the household of faith" (Galatians 6:10). We are always to do good to anyone in need, but our first concern is to be for our fellow Christians. This is our fellowship—our sharing in common. There is a rock song that could easily be adapted to Christians fulfilling their role properly: "We Are Family!" Every time we lift the bread and the cup of communion, we need to understand that we are saying, "I am flesh and blood the brother or sister of every person who shares in this ceremony, regardless of where they are or what their circumstances are. We are family! We are one!" As Paul wrote while in prison,

> As a prisoner for the sake of the Lord, I urge you to walk in a manner worthy of your calling with all humility and gentleness, with longsuffering patience, bearing with one another in love, endeavoring to keep the unity of the Spirit in the bond of peace as one body and one Spirit, just as you were called in the one hope of your calling—one Lord, one faith, one baptism, one God and Father of all who is above all and through all and in every one of you (Ephesians 4:1-6).

This bond of fellowship is one of the most motivational parts of being a Christian, and you cannot experience it unless you are in some way part of a church family. And if your church family does not practice this kind of fellowship, the church cannot be healthy. When we gossip about each other and criticize each other with hurtful words and when we ignore each other's needs and try to build up our own selves rather than each other, the church cannot be what God intends. But too often we get this entirely wrong.

The Need for Church

Many today have become discouraged with church (which is understandable given the way we practice church) and with what they refer to as organized religion. Many have decided that they don't need a church to worship God. And I must admit that if all I knew of church were what I have experienced in some churches, I would not want to be part of that kind of church. But if a person is truly a child of God, he or she should experience a longing for real church, a longing to be part of a fellowship of God's family of love. As Christians, either we need the help of other Christians in our spiritual growth or we need to be helping other Christians in their spiritual growth or more likely, both.

While the attitudes of those who claim to worship God without a church affiliation are certainly understandable, the results are tragic. But only when we who are the church behave as the church will we see this trend change. I am firmly convinced that those who claim not to need a church really feel a deep desire for a church that practices what a church should practice—but that is not what they find. No wonder so many in the world are turned off by organized religion when organized religion so often gets Christianity so wrong. Yes, it's Satan who blows us gently but firmly off course, but it's we ourselves who do not pay attention—it's we ourselves who do not make the needed course corrections when we could have.

During the Vietnam War, I was serving as a youth minister. I recall hearing a news story about the cost of the war. I can't recall now whether the cost per enemy soldier killed was about $50,000 or about $500,000, but it was high. Shortly after hearing that report, we had a report from a missionary working in Vietnam. His report included financial information, and at that point the cost per Vietnamese person converted to Christianity was about $50. A few months later I learned that a sister church in a nearby town had erected a bell tower next to their building at a cost of about $50,000. So that sister church spent enough money to convert about 1,000 pagans to Christianity in order to have a bell tower! No wonder people reject "organized religion" when it is so obviously focused on worldly pleasures rather than spiritual needs.

I have heard that Mahatma Gandhi, the man who was most influential in freeing India from colonial rule, once told some Christians "I like your Christ, I do not like your Christians. Your Christians are so unlike your Christ." Too many people have the same reaction to the Christianity we too often practice. There is no way to know what might have been different if Mahatma Gandhi had experienced real Christianity.

Christian Explosion

So the church meetings are meant to be a cross between a training session and a pep rally. And in the training sessions there needs to be a plan to take people from some starting point and bring them to some defined point of greater spiritual maturity. In order to fulfill the purposes of the church, we need to realize that we are the church and we need to speak of ourselves as the church and as the very house of God. We need to try to stop calling a building either "the church" or worse yet "God's house," because no building can be either one. When we decide to really be the church, we will find that there is a role available in the church for every Christian either as a teacher and leader or as a learner and follower or, as is often the case, as both teacher and learner in different areas. Christianity is about ministering to people's needs, us ministering to others and other Christians ministering to us. When we learn to live church in this way, church will be motivating and people will be drawn to our Lord and to our church meetings. It is far past time that we learned to be the church God intended us to be.

If Christians will live as the church and as the very house of God, if Christians will shine the light of God's love and grace to others wherever they go, if Christians learn to show love to enemies and really care about the needs of others, if Christians learn to encourage and inspire each other instead of picking at and criticizing each other, then Christianity would experience explosive growth. The weakness of the church is not God's fault, it is ours. But we need to wake the sleeping giant that is the church—and the path to that task is real discipleship.

CHAPTER TWELVE: DISCIPLESHIP— THE ULTIMATE GOAL

Whoever refuses to carry his own cross and follow me cannot be my disciple – Luke 14:27

When Jesus began calling his disciples, he did so with one simple phrase: "Follow me." That's what a disciple is—one who follows his leader. And for the Christian, Jesus is that leader. As far as the Bible is concerned, there is no such thing as a Christian who is not a disciple. Remember the passage in Hebrews we've seen before: "And without faith it is impossible to please God, because anyone who comes to him must believe that he exists and that he rewards those who sincerely seek him" (Hebrews 11:6) Discipleship is all about diligently seeking God, and as a disciple of the Lord, we must make following the Lord the primary goal of life. It is certainly OK for a Christian to have other goals in life, but all of these other goals must be secondary to the goal of discipleship.

Discipleship Training

Beyond accepting Jesus as the Lord of one's daily life by practicing Christian love for God and for others, the only other thing a Christian needs to understand is the next subject we will address—the need for discipleship training (which is a life-long task with no end). It does no good at all to just get people converted and baptized. Too many times in the past we have simply converted a dry sinner into a wet sinner. This goes back once again to Jesus being Lord—once we accept him, we need to learn how to live for him. While the answer of Christian love is simple, the details of application require a lifetime of learning and growing.

Once Christians find that they can easily communicate God's real plan of salvation and that they can actually bring new Christians into the kingdom without having to go to a minister or anyone else, we will have enabled an explosion of conversions. And if we include a good discipleship program, there's no telling how powerfully we will see God's Holy Spirit in action.[22] Unfortunately, most of the church study materials published today are practically useless for serious discipleship training, though there are some very good exceptions. Generally the exceptions are a little more expensive (though not always), but it's far past time that we got serious about discipleship training. As we mentioned earlier, Jesus' final Great Commission to his disciples contains only one command (though English translations generally get this wrong), and that command is to "disciple the nations." Following this command Jesus used two participles to expand the command: "baptizing" and "teaching." (The Great Commission, as Jesus actually said it, is found in Matthew 28:19-20 and is best translated as "So wherever you go, make disciples of all the nations, baptizing them in the name of the Father and the Son and the Holy Spirit, teaching them to observe everything just as I have commanded you[23]." Or as it is recorded in Mark 16:15-16, "As you go throughout the whole world, announce this good news to the whole creation. Whoever believes [focuses his or her life on God] and is baptized will be saved, but whoever doesn't believe [focus his or her life on God] will be condemned.")

Discipleship training should be an integral part of the church meetings—in fact it should be one of the primary goals of the church meetings—but it can and should go on in people's homes and anywhere else people get together. It should go on via email and other Internet services—the simple message of how to live out a life of Christian love for the Lord.

---

22 There are examples of this in several large churches today that have implemented these two lessons about discipleship.

23 An interesting side note along the lines of what we are dealing with here is that if we actually translate the word "baptizing" and if we clarify the use of the word "name" we get a translation of the Great Commission that reads more like this: "So wherever you go, make disciples of all the nations, immersing them into the essential nature of the Father and the Son and the Holy Spirit, teaching them to observe everything just as I have commanded you." Note the double meaning for "immersing": immersing in water, and immersing into the essential nature of God. The first meaning is to symbolize the second meaning—and the second meaning is the essence of discipleship.

Discipleship and Witnessing

Beyond even these things, we have allowed one of the most powerful weapons in our armory to be shelved, and that weapon is witnessing. We have shifted more and more toward having a professional Christian speak for us once a week while we simply keep silent. A professional can provide important help in leadership, but he or she can never have the influence found in a personal testimony from someone who is not paid to bear witness and who is not polished in bearing witness. (We need the professionals, and it is appropriate for the professionals to be the primary voice in the church assemblies, but if we limit the witness to professionals we lose a powerful tool for reaching the lost.) Individuals need to be encouraged to tell what God is doing in their lives. That is what it means to be a real witness. And in the church meetings is a good place to practice witnessing, but the goal needs to be carrying our witness out into the world—the "as you go" of the Great Commission. Just before returning to heaven, Jesus told his disciples that their job would be to act as witnesses (see Acts 1:8). The job of a witness is to tell what he or she has personally experienced. That is what convinces a jury in a trial, and that is what convinces people in daily life.

Professional church leaders are the ones trained to prepare messages for the church that will provide the planned guidance every church needs. Professional church leaders are the ones trained to see the specific spiritual needs of the congregation and to provide the instruction necessary to meet those needs. It is entirely appropriate for professionals to be the primary voice of the church meetings, but not to the exclusion of the untrained or how will the untrained ever become trained? Sometimes the extensive training of professionals tends to minimize dependence on and response to the leading of God's Holy Spirit, and when that happens we all lose.

Granted, when we open the door for non-professionals to speak, we will have some people speak up who will say things that are not true and who will say things we may wish they had not said, but God and the church's professional leaders can work through that. We cannot cut off people's access to false teaching—it is useless to even try. Just consider the deluge of emails that purport to bear witness to things that could not be true! It would be better to hear what people have to say and thereby learn more about the spiritual needs of the congregation.

In addition, we will probably have people say things that do not exactly match the doctrine of the professional Christians in a congregation. (I have certainly heard many trained professional ministers say things that were definitely wrong.) If someone says something in a church meeting that could mislead others, the officers and professionals can apply whatever correction is needed. But more often than not, the errors of non-professional Christians are no worse than the errors of the professionals, and God can work through both if they are truly seeking to live for him.

If we want to restrict the Sunday morning program to professional leaders, why not use a Sunday evening meeting or whatever other time the church meets to encourage testimonies. (If your church does not meet except on Sunday morning, perhaps the leaders need to rethink a practice that shuts out anyone who has to work Sunday mornings.) Why not use at least part of whatever alternative services are available as a time of witnessing by the non-professionals. And small groups (Sunday school, Bible study, fellowship groups, etc.) should be a natural place for testimonies to flow if only a little encouragement is provided.

If your church does not have small group meetings where members can give their testimony more comfortably, getting these started should be a high priority. Christians need fellowship. The Bible strongly teaches the value of such fellowship.

> We should keep bearing witness to our hope without doubting, for he who gave us the promises is faithful. And let's really care about each other's needs in order to stir up Christian love and good works, not neglecting the church meetings (as some have been doing), but exhorting each other, with increasing zeal as you see the day of judgment approaching (Hebrews 10:23-25).

Notice the emphasis on witnessing and on encouraging each other. That is Christian fellowship, and it includes each person bearing witness to his or her experiences in Christian living.

Once we learn how to encourage personal witnessing, we may find it worthwhile to allow a few minutes of testimony in the Sunday morning services. Remember what Jesus said to his disciples: "You shall receive power when the Holy Spirit has come on you, and you shall be my witnesses in Jerusalem, in all Judea and Samaria, and even to the farthest end of the earth" (Acts 1:8). I am convinced that we need to let God's Holy Spirit loose among our people.

What are we afraid of? Do we not trust God's Holy Spirit to work through his people? It's far past time for Christians to trust God to work among us. We will never reach the world through professionals. First, there are not enough of them and there never will be. Second, much of the world does not trust the professionals. It's past time to empower God's saints.

As a final helpful hint, many Sunday school teachers and small group leaders do not know how to get group participation. The secret is the sixty second rule. If the leader of a group will simply stop talking and count slowly (and silently) to sixty, members of the group will start to participate—especially if the leader has just given a good discussion question or asked for group input. Very few people can feel comfortable in a group setting if everyone is silent for sixty seconds. In fact, the silence is normally broken in less than thirty seconds.

Before he ascended to heaven, Jesus told his disciples,

> I have been given all authority in heaven and on earth. So wherever you go, make disciples of all the nations, baptizing them in the name of the Father and the Son and the Holy Spirit, teaching them to observe everything just as I have commanded you. And know this: I am always with you, even to the end of this age (Matthew 28:18-20).

As mentioned earlier, if there is an area where the church falls flat on its collective face, it is the teaching ministry that actually turns converts into disciples, training Christians to live as Christians. It is no wonder the church is losing ground. Let's take a brief look at what we are doing and see how we ourselves would evaluate this.

Sunday School

Let's use the Sunday school program as our primary example because this is the primary teaching tool for most churches today. So let's look at how this program works.

We'll start with an overview of the most common approach for the material used in Sunday school programs. The concept is to have all age groups study the same material at the same time so that members of a family can discuss the lesson after church. (Never mind that this discussion never takes place or that this approach assumes that the adults would not know enough to intelligently discuss what the children had studied if they had not just studied the same thing.) In order to teach people about all parts of the Bible, the normal pattern is to go through the Bible in a seven-year program. Generally each three-month period focuses on a key area—sometimes from the Old Testament and sometimes from the New Testament—with no clear rationale for the pattern followed. And the lessons are designed so that a person coming into the class as a visitor or first-timer will not be at a loss to understand. That means each lesson must be fully self-contained—not requiring any knowledge of what came before or what is to come afterward. Every seven years, the cycle repeats with slight variations.

With this approach, there is no concept of a goal or destination. There is no need or reason to identify point A as where we are and point B as the goal of our studies. There is no reasonable way to track progress, because the lessons are not about progress. And there is no way to know when the program has achieved one or more of its goals, because it has no goals.

Can you imagine a teacher in any secular school approaching his or her task with no goal in mind? Can you imagine texts of lessons that are intentionally unrelated to each other so that there is no way to build on what has already been learned (if anything) and therefore no way to ever move beyond the most basic levels? Yet in far too many cases this is exactly what we are doing! How can we possibly excuse ourselves before God? (Thankfully, many churches do have adult classes that do try to accomplish something—but even the best is generally far from what we should be doing.) With such an approach, it's no wonder that most Christians do not attend Sunday school.

Worse yet, a teacher can never become expert in what he or she is teaching. If a very conscientious person tries to teach and diligently prepares each lesson for an entire year, do you think that what this teacher has learned and developed in that year can then be used to build on for the next year so that the teacher is a better teacher? No. In fact, it will be seven years before that teacher will use any of the same materials, and by then he or she will have forgotten what was learned the last time through that material—that is if this teacher has not already quit in frustration. And even when the lessons get back to the same general area, the details change!

This is even worse among children. One year the small children are starting out studying Old Testament prophets, the next year they may be starting out learning about Moses, and the next year about Jesus or Paul. The teacher can never become expert at what he or she is teaching, and each year the children take a different path for their formative years of study through the Bible. How would you react if the secular schools followed a similar pattern for your children or grandchildren? I believe most people would insist on a program that would educate and train—and we should do the same!

Think of this from a motivational perspective. The teacher has no goal and no way to measure what if anything the students have learned. Typically the students tend to show the same level of understanding (or lack of understanding) week after week and year after year. So the volunteer teacher may start out spending a fair amount of time studying for each lesson, but soon he or she learns that there is no benefit—the students gain almost nothing. Many classes turn into a session where the teacher practically reads the lesson to the students, often reading it for the first time during class.

Similarly, the students are not expected to grow in understanding. There is never any effort to determine whether the lessons are actually communicating anything to the students in such a way that the students retain key points of the lessons. There is generally no effort to have the students put the lessons into practice. Soon the students realize that nothing but attendance is really expected of them—so that is all they deliver—and many even stop attending.

I recall when I was asked to teach a class of third-grade students for Sunday school. The church had an attendance of over 500, and the church's Sunday school director was a professional teacher in the public school system. When I first agreed to take on this task, I went to the director and asked, "What are the children expected to have learned by the end of each year?" I'll never forget the stunned look on the director's face—that question had never been raised before and no one had even considered it.

Ideally, children's Sunday school programs should be designed to take a child from the earliest level and bring him or her to a strong, active faith by the time he or she finishes high school. Of course, along the way and especially in the early teen years, the lessons need to address how Christians are to deal with various social pressures and how these lessons need to be put into practice. But there is no reason that a high school senior should not know as much about Christianity as most ministers know now and be able to share that with others. (This does not mean studying the history of theology or philosophy or social services, etc. It means a high school senior should know enough about the Bible and Christianity to be able to meet the challenges of the secular world as a Christian, whether in college or in some job situation.) And there is no reason that most high school students should not be involved in some form of ministry. Learning for the sake of knowledge is not God's plan. If we do not put what we learn into practice, we have failed.

Adult classes generally form a strong social bond, and that is good. Trying to push adults into different classes based on what the class is teaching would work against that social bond of fellowship that is such an important part of Christianity. But classes can still be designed for measurable growth. In some cases, it may be good to have a teacher who is expert in some specific area to move between classes, sharing his or her expertise. In other cases special classes may be offered, allowing adult members from various classes to temporarily attend a class of special interest. Most of the time an adult class may pursue whatever area of spiritual growth the members see fit to work on as a group. The point is, keeping a class of friends together should never interfere with having planned spiritual growth. The two are not exclusive, and local leaders need to find ways to maintain the fellowship while providing the growth.

But whatever is being studied, there should be class surveys to determine whether the lessons are being learned and there should be life application opportunities where the things learned are put into practice. Education without application is a complete waste. Remember, faith is focusing your life on living for God. If our Christian education is not applied to our lives, we might as well stay with the educational pattern we have today (or shut it down all together as some churches are doing).

All classes should include measurable goals and some means of actually measuring whether the students are reaching the goals. And the goals we measure need to be about spiritual growth, not about attendance and money. Does this require something like tests? Yes, but not tests for a grade—rather surveys to determine what has been accomplished and where help is needed. Surveys should be taken with no names on the answer sheets, serving as a tool to help the teacher improve his or her teaching based on what the class did or did not grasp. As many have pointed out, we emphasize what we measure. If what we measure is attendance and offering, then our congregation will know that our main interests are attendance and offering. If we measure spiritual growth, our congregation will understand that such growth is important.

Granted, many larger churches are developing their own class materials that do not follow the traditional pattern and there are other options from some publishing companies, but serious planning for education and training is extremely rare in any church or group of churches. And Satan loves this. At best our efforts are tactical rather than strategic. Roman Catholicism has done so well because of leaders who understand the need for diligent training of the members.

Just learning some Bible facts is not the answer. Christians need to know key Bible facts, but even more than this they need to learn what it means to live for God in the practical setting of the world they live in. Also, as mentioned earlier, by the time a child reaches the end of high school, if he or she has been involved in church training of some sort, that child should be capable of handling the challenges of non-Christians in the business world and unbelieving college professors. Remember, part of the job of a college professor is to teach students to challenge the concepts with which they have grown up. This is not a bad thing, but Christian children need to be ready.

In any training program, we need to remember that training people to live for God is far more important than training them to know a lot of details about the Bible. Knowing the Bible well enough to be able to use it intelligently is always good and important, but many of the most evil people this world has ever known have been very familiar with the Bible. Christians need to teach and practice ministry with enough biblical knowledge to keep the ministry truly Christian. That is the point of discipleship.

Fellowship

The small groups of Sunday school and other small group church meetings also provide another important factor for churches that we have already mentioned briefly—the factor of fellowship. In the New Testament, the word for fellowship implied a very strong bond of oneness. Since our adult Sunday school classes tend to be more social than educational, this might not seem like a serious need, but in too many cases students come to class, sit through a long lecture-type lesson (or worse yet, a lesson simply read aloud), and then leave with no real opportunity for fellowship or education. At least in classes for adults and older youth, it is important to allow a time for class chatter as well as prayer requests. But beyond that, it is good for classes to meet at regular intervals outside the classroom in people's homes wherever possible. This is especially important in larger churches where the Sunday school or other small group needs to take on the role of a small church within a larger church. Fellowship without education is a disaster, but so is education without fellowship.

Remedial Training

Now, what about visitors? What about new members who have not been through the program? In fact, this is another of the very important areas we have dealt with very poorly. Every church needs a program for new members to set their feet on the right path. It would be great if such a program were available on CDs or DVDs for self-study. My suggestion would be at least a 3-month program, and possibly a year-long program. And children coming into the Sunday school program will need remedial help. A church that is serious about Christian education and training will provide ways for newcomers to catch up.

With today's technology, new members who come in with little or no knowledge of what the Bible is and what Christianity is all about could be provided with multimedia materials to help with catch-up. But if we create Sunday school programs and other small group programs that really train disciples, I am convinced attendance will increase dramatically. In most cases people do not drop out because the program is too difficult, they drop out because the program is boring.

For visitors there are two options. For some visitors, simply placing them into a class will be fine. Let them see real Christian education and training at work. In my experience many people long for that very experience. For others, perhaps a video class just for one-time visitors to introduce what this church is doing would be good. Each church needs to consider how it can best meet the needs of its community, but what most churches are doing is not the right answer for any of them. At least once a year almost any church should offer a class in basic Christianity with all new members urged to attend.

Other Discipleship Opportunities

If we are serious about discipleship, we will not stop with the Sunday school program, or even Sunday morning and evening and a midweek service. When I was in college, I drove for a school bus company to help pay my way through school. One of the buses I drove was specifically for the Jewish community in that area. I would pick up the Jewish children from school and deliver them to a synagogue for religious training. Then after an hour I would return and drive the students to their homes. These children received an hour of instruction by the synagogue every evening. There is no reason Christians could not do that. At the time of this writing it is actually legal for churches to take students out of school for one class session a day and provide off-campus religious education and training for that session. We cannot use the facilities of the public schools (buses, classrooms, materials, etc.), but we can use the time.

I know that any church will initially cringe at this idea unless it is a true mega-church. Where will we find the instructors? Where will we find the materials? How will we afford a program like this? The answer is team work. There is no reason that churches in a community should not work together to teach the basics they all agree on. At the same time, churches could provide children with help learning to do the secular schoolwork—thereby teaching the children that the church does care about their problems. If we could reserve doctrine and disputed points for Sunday activities, focusing rather on what the Bible is, what the Bible says, and things we can agree on about how Christians should live, how much stronger our Christian education and training programs could be!

John recorded an incident that occurred after Jesus' resurrection and shortly before his ascension. Not knowing what else to do, the disciples had gone back to fishing. Using nets cast from their boat, they had fished all night with very little to show for it. In the early morning the disciples saw Jesus on the shore but did not realize who he was. Jesus told them to cast their net on the opposite side of the boat, and the net was filled. At that they realized that it was Jesus on the shore. They brought the fish to the shore and prepared a breakfast of fish and bread. John records what happened next as follows:

> So when they had eaten breakfast, Jesus said to Simon Peter, "Simon, son of John, do you truly care about me more than you care about this fishing?"
>
> Peter said to Him, "Yes, Lord; you know how much I like you."
>
> Jesus told him, "Feed my lambs."

> Shortly after that Jesus said to Peter again, "Simon, son of John, do you truly care about me?"
>
> Peter replied, "Yes, Lord; you know how much I like you."
>
> Jesus told him, "Tend to my sheep."
>
> Finally Jesus said to Peter a third time, "Simon, son of John, do you even really like me?"
>
> Peter was grieved because this third time Jesus asked, "Do you even really like me?" and he said to Jesus, "Lord, you know all things. You know how much I like you."
>
> Jesus told him, "Feed My sheep." (John 21:15-17).

There are very few things that Jesus specially emphasized during his earthly ministry by repeating the same basic concept two or three or even four times in a row. This is one of those cases. The charge to Peter is equally to anyone who seeks to serve the Lord—the charge to feed and care for the flock. For a church, the spiritual feeding is done in Christian education and training—and we are not doing this well at all. On judgment day I tremble to think what Jesus will say about our failure to feed his flock.

In light of the attacks of the world and of Satan, Paul wrote,

> Therefore you need to stand firm with the belt of truth around your waist, wearing the bullet-proof vest of righteousness, and having your training in the gospel of peace to make your feet feel like running. Beyond all this, hold firmly to the shield of faith that can extinguish Satan's flame-thrower. Also wear the helmet of salvation, and always carry the sword of the Spirit (which is the word of God) (Ephesians 6:14-17).

But we send our high school graduates into the world with little if any of this armor, and almost no training in how to use their armor. Beyond this, what armor they do have is thin and flimsy. It's no wonder we lose the majority of them to the world and never get them back.

Bottom line, it's long past time for us to take Christian education and training seriously. Let's establish goals for learning. Let's empower people to use what they learn. Let's establish ways to find out if the students are learning the lessons we think we are teaching. Let's have a strategic plan for what we need to accomplish and how we will use the resources developed. Let's take Christianity seriously! That's when Christianity becomes truly motivational.

Sermons

Note: What follows in this section is primarily for professional ministers, church officers who advise ministers, those who train professional ministers, and anyone else involved in sermon preparation or training in how to do sermons. If this is not your area, you may want to skip this section.

At this point I want to consider lecture sermons. Most people know that lecture is about the poorest educational tool. And if you think the sermon is about evangelism, not education, think again. That makes no sense at all. Who are we trying to evangelize—the Christians? With few if any exceptions, that's who is present for most sermons. But just listen to the sermons you will hear. With almost no exceptions (and the rare exceptions are even worse than this), the normal sermon in an evangelical church is educational up until the last one or two minutes, at which point the speaker may shift into evangelism mode.

So if the sermon is to be educational, make it educational. Three of the most important questions a minister needs to be able to answer are 1) "In spiritual growth, where are we now?" 2) "Where does God want us to be?" and 3) "How are we going to get there?" Each sermon should be planned to take the congregation one step closer to the goal. And the goal is not knowledge—the only appropriate goal is Christian living—discipleship.

Some of the simplest things can help. Pick important key phrases in the sermon—something you would really like the congregation to remember—and then have the congregation say this phrase together at least two or three times during the sermon. Repeat the key phrase or phrases after the sermon. Make that key phrase or those key phrases the first phrase or phrases of the sermon. Then bring those phrases up again in subsequent weeks and have the congregation join in saying them again and again until these key phrases become ingrained. There are unlimited candidates, but some you may want to use early and often include "Jesus is Lord," "the rebellion must end," "faith is focusing your life on God," "repentance is shifting your life focus from yourself to God," "God is love," "Love God with all your heart, soul, mind, and strength," "Christian love is unselfish, generous, caring, forgiving, and active," "love and care for your neighbor the same way you love and care for yourself," "in the church service, everything is to be focused on building each other up," "if you forgive those who hurt you, your Father in heaven will forgive you," "Grow up to be spiritually mature like your heavenly Father," "God lives in us every day," and on and on. There is absolutely no limit to the phrases that are worth learning this way. Consider the impact of Martin Luther King Junior's phrase, "I have a dream."

One way to make sermons extra powerful is to keep them very short and focused on a single target. The longer a sermon is and the more areas it deals with, the less likely anyone will be to remember the content. I once preached a sermon that consisted of a sermon title seven words long and a sermon body of only one word. Almost 40 years later a couple who had been present for that sermon approached me and commented on that sermon. The first time I preached a sermon that was only 15 minutes long, a rancher who lived with his wife out in the desert and who had never gone beyond high school came up to me a month later to discuss that sermon point by point—and to the best of my knowledge he had never done anything like that before.

Shorter sermons are harder to prepare, but they have an impact that lasts. Look at the Gettysburg Address compared to other political speeches. After all, there is only so much a listener can retain in one session.

Visuals can help. Just putting the key words for a sermon on a banner or a video screen or a large poster can help. Cartoon graphics or simple illustrations can help. You might get youth to make posters with key words or illustrations to put up around the church building, in which case the youth involved get an additional learning activity.

Conclusion

The conclusion is simple: Jesus is Lord, and it's far past time that we as his people acted as if we believe that. It is far past time that we took the truths of Christianity seriously and demonstrated true Christianity before the world around us. It is far past time that we made it clear that all people, whether Christian or not, are sinners justly condemned by God for rebellion and treason—the only difference being that Christians have ended the intent of rebellion and are forgiven. It is far past time that we taught saving faith as obedient faith. It is far past time that we taught a perspective of heaven that is truly motivating. It is far past time that we practiced forgiveness the way God has demonstrated for us. It is far past time we got serious about church meetings as real training sessions and as real pep rallies. It is far past time that we got serious about discipleship. And it is far past time that we learned to present God as he really is instead of all the wrong concepts we tend to present.

This is not everything, it is only a beginning. These are not all the areas where Satan has blown us off course and where our errors have hurt our Lord's work. There is still much to learn and much to do, but the ideas in this book provide an important beginning.

APPENDIX A: HEAVEN AND SIN

I believe Christians are in general agreement on the point that sin will not be present in heaven. If that were not true, heaven would not be heaven. I fully agree with that point. However, I believe that many Christians have misunderstood the *possibility* of sin in heaven as taught in the Bible. Let's start at the top.

God's Choice to Do Wrong

I believe that all Christians would agree that God is good, just, righteous, faithful, and true. This is certainly the teaching of the Bible. But if God is incapable of doing wrong, then he has no moral credit for doing right. God may be "good" from our perspective because he is and does what we like, but if he has no choice in the matter, he is actually amoral.

To illustrate this, let's think of an automobile. We may refer to an automobile as a "good car" or a "bad car," but when we do so we do not mean that in a moral sense. The car is amoral; it cannot choose whether to do right or to do wrong. If we describe a car as a "good car," what we really mean is that the people who designed it made good choices in the design and the people who made the parts made good choices in the manufacturing process and the people who assembled the car made good choices in how they assembled it. The moral quality of good goes to those who had moral choices, not to the car.

If God is like a car with no moral choices, then he is not really good because he cannot choose to be bad. If God is really good, he must be good because he chooses to be good.

To understand this from a biblical perspective, Jesus came into this world as God incarnate. The Bible teaches that Jesus was tempted in every way that other humans are tempted. He was tempted by money, by power, by pride, by gluttony, by sex, by apathy, and by every other area of sin, but he chose not to sin. If Jesus was God incarnate (and he was), then God was tempted. If God could not do wrong, then the temptations were not real or effective.

So the message of the Bible that God is good and righteous and faithful and true must mean that God never has done wrong and never will do wrong—but it must also mean that God could do wrong if he chose to do so. That is the only way that God can be morally good.

Once we accept that truth, we're ready to look at our own condition in heaven. But let's start from a different reference point this time.

God's Creation of a World for People

Let's consider God's creation of people. If it is impossible for people to sin in heaven, then why did God create a world where sin is possible and put humans into that world if their final destination was to be heaven anyhow? Why did he put the potential for sin right where those original people would have to confront it day after day? And why did he allow Satan to come into that world and tempt his beloved creation? If God could have placed people into a paradise where sin is impossible, why did he intentionally put them into an environment where sin is possible? And why would he do this knowing that most people would wind up in hell and that those who were saved would need Calvary?? If God chose to put people in a world where sin is possible, knowing before he did so that these people would sin and that most would wind up in hell, when he could have put them into a heaven of eternal bliss where sin is not possible, then God would not be good—he would be a terrible monster.

This World as a Vaccination for Sin

However, if sin is possible in heaven, then it would make sense that God would want to find a safe way to condition humans before they get there so that he could be certain that they would never want to sin once they reached heaven. He would need a vaccination. And if we consider what the Bible teaches, that's just what this world should be.

Let's start at the beginning again. When the humans God had created rebelled against him, God had three choices: 1) he could destroy all humans and thereby wipe out all sin; 2) he could replace the humans with a version incapable of sin; or 3) he could allow sin to run its course and let the humans see how terrible sin really is, working a plan to rescue those who learned the lesson.

Remember, God warned those first humans that their sin would bring all kinds of pain and suffering and even death into this world. The message of the Bible is that all of the pains, all of the sufferings, all of the deaths, all of the physical, spiritual, psychological, and mental illnesses in the world have resulted from sin.

And it's not that this suffering is proportional to a person's sins or as if the suffering somehow pays for sin. Suffering is the natural result of sin, and it is not distributed fairly. An innocent baby who has never rebelled against God—who could not comprehend the concept of rebelling against God—comes into the world with pain. That pain is the result of this world's sin environment.

A person's sin may cause the sinner to suffer, but it is far more certain that it will cause others to suffer. A sociopathic murderer may feel no suffering at all for his murders, but the families of the murder victims who had nothing to do with the murder certainly do suffer. But more than this, the very environment of sin permeates this world so that all are affected—even animals that have no ability to sin.

Again, sin is not fair. Sin does not distribute its suffering in any righteous way. The Bible teaches that Satan is the prince of this world, and he has no desire to be righteous or fair.

But why does God let this situation continue? The answer to that question should be obvious—God wants us to learn just how bad sin really is. He wants us to learn to hate sin. He wants us to see that no existence with sin can ever be a paradise—that sin would destroy the most wonderful paradise.

Repentance

This is where repentance comes in. Repentance means to change one's mind, and in the context of Christianity initial repentance is a major change—changing the focus of your life from yourself and the things of this world to God and the things of his kingdom. See Luke 14:25-35 for Jesus' description of the things that would prevent a person from being his disciple. In order to be his disciple, Jesus emphatically says that a person must be willing to give up family and possessions and even life itself in order to follow him. Or recall Jesus' words in the Sermon on the Mount:

> Not everyone who calls me "Lord, Lord" will get into the kingdom of heaven—only the one who does the will of my Father in heaven. On the Day of Judgment a lot of people will say to me, "Lord, Lord, haven't we preached in your name, cast out demons in your name, and even done miracles in your name?" Then I will plainly tell them, "Get away from me! you who live by uncontrolled desires, I never even knew you" (Matthew 7:21-23).

This is the key to understanding why God would put humans in a world where sin is possible. This is the key to understanding why God would plant the tree of knowledge of good and evil in the midst of the garden. This is the key to understanding why from Genesis to the Revelation the whole Bible is so focused on our need to accept God's authority over our daily lives.

As a parent, I can recall how I wanted my children to experience something hot enough to burn them in an environment where I could rescue them before they were burned badly. I wanted them to learn the meaning of the word "hot." I wanted them to fear "hot." I could not bring myself to actually cause the burning pain, but I wanted to be close when they chose to do something that would provide this experience. If they could have gone through life without ever experiencing anything that could burn them badly, I would not have cared. But knowing that they would have to deal with hot things, I wanted them to learn the lesson early and well.

God can forgive our sin. He can forgive any kind of sin and any amount of sin except final rejection of his authority. But in order to take us to heaven, he must know that we will not bring our rebellion with us, lest we destroy heaven. God will heal the blinding effects of sin that make it impossible to avoid sin in this life. He will take away the power of Satan and his angels to tempt us and deceive us. He will open our eyes to recognize sin for what it is. But he will not take away our free will. So he can safely take us to heaven only if we by our free will choose him as the Lord of our lives.

The Big Error

Here is the error of those who teach that a person can accept Jesus as savior without accepting him as Lord. That is impossible. This is also the error of those who do not emphasize our need to accept Jesus as Lord. A sinner's prayer that does not include acceptance of Jesus as Lord is just words. It is saying "Lord, Lord" without surrendering to him as our real Lord. Nothing in the Bible even suggests that God will save those who call on him for salvation if they are not willing to accept him as Lord. We cannot be part of the kingdom if we have not accepted the authority of the King.

Many church leaders have taught that Christians experience two levels of salvation. In the first level they experience what these leaders call "justification" by which a person accepts Jesus as savior without accepting him as Lord. In the second level they experience what these leaders call "sanctification" at which point the person does accept Jesus as Lord. In this teaching, only the first level is required for salvation. The Bible never indicates such a two-level process. In the Bible, justification and sanctification go together. In the Bible, Christians are called saints, and that word means "sanctified ones." If a person is not sanctified (set aside for serving God), he or she is not a Christian.

It all comes back to the potential to sin in heaven. Once we learn what is in sewage, we would never voluntarily wade through it. Once we learn what sin is, we will never voluntarily wade into it again, and God guarantees that he will not let any power drag us back into it. That is an important part of what makes heaven a paradise, the knowledge that we have indeed overcome the power of sin by the grace of God, and that sin is no longer a threat to us.

Satan in Heaven

Did Satan rebel in heaven? There are a few passages in the Bible that are sometimes used to support the idea that Satan was an angel who rebelled and was thrown out of heaven. None of these passages is a clear declaration that this actually happened, but perhaps the one in Philippians 2:5-11 (where Paul speaks of Jesus' willingness to humble himself as if comparing that perhaps with Satan's rebellion) is the strongest, especially when taken with the other passages. If Satan did rebel in heaven, then sin must be possible in heaven; but the passages about this are not clear enough to make this the deciding factor.

Conclusion

For me the deciding factor is that if God is good and loving and if he does not desire to have anyone perish, then the only explanation for creating humans in a world where sin was certain enough that God had already planned for Calvary would be to vaccinate the humans against the possibility of sinning once they reach heaven. No other explanation works.

Author's Note

About Bible Quotations

All Bible quotations are my own translations unless otherwise noted. To be honest, this is not easy for me, but it allows me to translate with a focus on the author's ideas rather than strictly on his words and to clarify some mistaken understandings as discussed elsewhere in this book. I am not an expert either in Hebrew or in Greek, so I have carefully consulted the experts wherever I had a question. My expertise is more in an understanding of how God's message works together and therefore what ideas the authors were seeking to communicate—and my effort has been to clarify those ideas to form the framework in which they fit from God's perspective. What I found is that the framework was always there and not that hard to find, but that human mistakes and a tendency to look at God's ways from a human perspective have all too often concealed the awesome beauty and wonder of what God is doing. I hope you as a reader will find the same beauty and wonder that I have found, and that it won't take you the 60+ years it took me to see this.